移动应用对英语词汇学习与记忆的效果研究

EXPLORING THE EFFECTS OF USING A MOBILE APPLICATION ON ENGLISH VOCABULARY LEARNING AND RETENTION

马星星 著

图书在版编目(CIP)数据

移动应用对英语词汇学习与记忆的效果研究 / 马星星著.
—长春：东北师范大学出版社，2022.2
ISBN 978-7-5681-8880-7

Ⅰ.①移… Ⅱ.①马… Ⅲ.①互联网络－应用－英语－教学研究－高等学校 Ⅳ.①H319.34-39

中国版本图书馆 CIP 数据核字(2022)第 037474 号

□责任编辑：于天娇　　□封面设计：王培花
□责任校对：朱丽平　　□责任印制：许　冰

东北师范大学出版社出版发行
长春净月经济开发区金宝街118号(邮政编码：130117)
销售热线：0431-84568025
网址：http://www.nenup.com
电子函件：sdcbs@mail.jl.cn
东北师范大学出版社激光照排中心制版
河南省环发印务有限公司印装
2022年2月第1版　2022年2月第1次印刷
幅面尺寸：185 mm×260 mm　印张：14　字数：314千

定价：38.00元

如发现印装质量问题，影响阅读，可直接与承印厂联系调换

CONTENTS

001 **Chapter 1 Introduction**
002 1.1 Background of the Study
002 1.1.1 The Importance of Vocabulary in Language Learning
003 1.1.2 Vocabulary Retention
005 1.1.3 Vocabulary Teaching and Learning in the Chinese Context
006 1.1.4 Current Situation of the Research Site
007 1.1.5 MALL and Mobile-assisted Vocabulary Learning
010 1.2 Statement of the Problems
011 1.3 Purposes of the Study
012 1.4 Research Questions
013 1.5 Significance of the Study
013 1.6 Scope of the Study
014 1.7 Limitations of the Study
014 1.8 Definitions of Key Terms
016 1.9 Summary

017 **Chapter 2 Literature Review**
018 2.1 Theoretical Framework
019 2.1.1 Ten Design Principles for MALL
022 2.1.2 Dual Coding Theory
023 2.1.3 The Cognitive Theory of Multimedia Learning
026 2.1.4 The Memory-based Strategic Framework for Vocabulary Learning
028 2.2 Vocabulary Knowledge
028 2.2.1 Two Dimensions of Vocabulary Knowledge

034	2.2.2 Research on the Relationship between Vocabulary Knowledge and Language Skills as well as Language Proficiency
038	2.3 EFL Vocabulary Teaching and Learning in Chinese Universities
039	2.4 Vocabulary Learning Incidentally and Intentionally
039	2.4.1 Incidental Vocabulary Learning
040	2.4.2 Intentional Vocabulary Learning
041	2.5 Vocabulary Retention
045	2.6 Mobile-assisted Language Learning
047	2.6.1 Research on Mobile-assisted Language Learning
051	2.6.2 Students' Perceptions of Mobile-assisted Language Learning
053	2.6.3 Research on EFL Vocabulary Learning and Retention via MALL
062	2.7 Summary

063	**Chapter 3 Research Methodology**
064	3.1 Research Design
066	3.2 The Population and Samples
067	3.3 Research Instruments
067	3.3.1 The Target Words
069	3.3.2 The Mobile App
078	3.3.3 Vocabulary Size Test
080	3.3.4 Vocabulary Knowledge Scale
081	3.3.5 The Questionnaire on Students' Perceptions
083	3.3.6 Interview
085	3.3.7 Diary
085	3.4 Procedure of the Experiment
087	3.5 Data Collection
087	3.5.1 Vocabulary Size Test
088	3.5.2 Vocabulary Knowledge Scale Test
088	3.5.3 The Questionnaire on Perceptions
088	3.5.4 The Semi-structured Interview
089	3.5.5 The Diary

089   3.6 Data Analysis
090   3.6.1 Analyzing the Data of VST
090   3.6.2 Analyzing the Data of VKS
091   3.6.3 Analyzing the Data of the Questionnaires
091   3.6.4 Analyzing the Data of the Semi-structured Interviews
092   3.6.5 Analyzing the Data of the Diaries
092   3.7 Implications from Pilot Study and Adjustments for Main Study
094   3.8 Summary

095 Chapter 4 Results and Discussion

096   4.1 Results of the Vocabulary Size Test
097   4.2 The Effects of Using the App on Students' Vocabulary Learning
098   4.2.1 Results of an Independent-samples T-test of the Pre-tests for Two Groups
098   4.2.2 Results of the Post-test and a Paired-samples T-test for EG
099   4.2.3 Results of the Post-test and a Paired-samples T-test for CG
100   4.2.4 Results of an Independent-samples T-test of the Post-tests for Two Groups
101   4.3 Discussion about the Effects of the App on Vocabulary Learning
103   4.4 The Effects of Using the App on Students' Vocabulary Retention
104   4.4.1 Results of the Delayed Post-test and a Paired-samples T-test for EG
105   4.4.2 Results of the Delayed Post-test and a Paired-samples T-test for CG
105   4.4.3 Results of an Independent-samples T-test for the Delayed Post-test
106   4.5 Discussion of the Effects of the App on Vocabulary Retention
108   4.6 The Students' Perceptions of the App
108   4.6.1 Results of the Questionnaire
111   4.6.2 Results of the Semi-structured Interview
114   4.6.3 Results of the Students' Diaries from EG

119 4.7 Discussion on the Students' Perceptions of the App
124 4.8 Results of the Diaries from CG and Discussion
128 4.9 Summary of the Results and Discussion

131 **Chapter 5 Conclusion, Implications and Recommendations**
132 5.1 Conclusion of the Study
137 5.2 Pedagogical Implications from the Present Study
138 5.3 Recommendations for Further Research
140 5.4 Summary of the Chapter

141 **REFERENCES**

181 **APPENDICES**
182 APPENDIX A
183 APPENDIX B
184 APPENDIX C
185 APPENDIX D
185 APPENDIX E
187 APPENDIX F
188 APPENDIX G
189 APPENDIX H (English Version)
192 APPENDIX H (Chinese Version)
194 APPENDIX I
195 APPENDIX J (English Version)
196 APPENDIX J (Chinese Version)
196 APPENDIX K
197 APPENDIX L
205 APPENDIX M
208 APPENDIX N
208 APPENDIX O
211 APPENDIX P
216 APPENDIX Q

Chapter 1

Introduction

An introduction to the book is presented in this chapter. Firstly, the background of the present study is introduced. Then, a statement of the problem, purposes of the study, research questions, significance of the study, the scope of the study, limitations of the study, and the definitions of the key terms are given, respectively. Lastly, this chapter concludes with a summary.

1.1 Background of the Study

1.1.1 The Importance of Vocabulary in Language Learning

Vocabulary is essential for language learning because language learners cannot understand others or express their ideas without vocabulary. Wilkins (1972:111—112) pointed out: "Without grammar very little can be conveyed, without vocabulary nothing can be conveyed." This viewpoint reflects the great importance of vocabulary in language communication. Based on McCarthy (1990), without vocabulary to express various kinds of ideas and meanings, communications with a second language cannot be fulfilled in a meaningful way even if learners have mastered L2 grammar and pronunciations well.

Besides, Laufer and Hulstijn (1998) claimed that learners should learn a lot of second language vocabulary before learning a second language, and vocabulary learning should continue throughout the entire process of second language learning. Similarly, Gass (1999) maintained that to learn a foreign language is to learn its vocabulary. Therefore, it is not difficult to find that learning vocabulary is central for any language learning.

Research findings have shown that improvement in vocabulary is likely to enhance learners' performances in listening (Afshari & Tavakoli, 2017; Wang & Wu, 2011), reading (Li, 2003; Liu, 2006; Qian, 1999, 2002; Staehr, 2008, 2009; Shen, 2011, 2013; Song, 2014; Zhang & Qiu, 2006), speaking (Liu, 2016; Shi, 2012), writing (Hou, 2016; Milton, Wade & Hopkins, 2010; Wu, 2010; Zhang, 2012), and language proficiency (Huang, 2003; Liu, 2016). Thus, vocabulary can make a significant contribution to the test scores of the four skills and language proficiency. Afshari and Tavakoli (2017) revealed that test-takers' vocabulary knowledge could explain 57% of TOEFL (Test of English as a Foreign Language) listening scores. Another study by Wang (2010) revealed that students' vocabulary knowledge had a strong correlation with their reading scores in the TEM-4 (Test for English Majors Band 4) of China, with the correlation coefficient being 0.853. Similarly, Shi (2012) found that there also existed a significantly positive correlation between test-takers' vocabulary knowledge and their speaking scores of IELTS (International English Language Testing System), with the correlation coefficient being 0.863. Moreover, Hou (2016) highlighted that vocabulary knowledge could account for 81.3% of writing scores in writing tests. Furthermore, according to Liu (2016), 56% of the total score in the CET-4 (College English Test Band 4) of China could be predicted from students' vocabulary knowledge. The studies above indicate that the more vocabulary the students know, the better the performances they can achieve in the four language skills as well as in language proficiency. Thus, given the importance of vocabulary in language learning and tests, improving learners' vocabulary is essential.

1.1.2 Vocabulary Retention

Retention refers to the ability to keep something continuously in mind. Vocabulary retention is defined by Maryam and Ahmad (2017) as the ability to remember or retain vocabulary in one's mind. Vocabulary retention, vocabulary memory, and vocabulary maintenance are interchangeable in the present study.

On the one hand, the primary purpose of learners' learning vocabulary is for keeping the learnt words in their minds. On the other hand, it has been pointed out that what has been learnt is rapidly forgotten in terms of the forgetting curve (Wozniak, 1999). As cited by Wozniak (1999), Ebbinghaus (1885) found that information loss is exponential with time going on. Additionally, the forgetting curve illustrates that memory decay starts immediately and then slows down over the next six days. After Ebbinghaus' (1885) study, much research on information retention and rapid forgetting was conducted (Bahrick, 1992; Conway, Cohen & Stanhope, 1992; Farjami & Aidinlou, 2013; Thalheimer, 2010). Bahrick (1992) highlighted the fact that, in the first six days, learners' brains would lose 20% of what they just learnt exceptionally rapidly. Conway et al. (1992) got an almost the same conclusion to that of Bahrick (1992). However, Thalheimer (2010) believed that forgetting information varies significantly relying upon the teaching approaches that were used for the beginning, the times of review, and the information processing level initially. It was also found that those students employing the least effective ways would lose 21.7% of the learned information (Thalheimer, 2010). Thus, the studies above show that teaching methods might affect information retention negatively.

For vocabulary retention, Farjami and Aidinlou (2013) stated that a very challenging obstacle for foreign language learners was the necessity of mastering lots of words and that they forgot the acquired vocabulary very quickly. It was also revealed that it is really difficult to maintain many EFL (English as a Foreign Language) vocabulary items for a long term (Orozco, 2019). To find ways of preventing learners from forgetting words and helping them retain the words in long-term memory, the following studies have been conducted: Icht and Mama, 2019; Immordino-Yang and Damasio, 2007; Karousou and Nerantzaki, 2020; Koester, 2015; MacLeod et al., 2010; McBride and Dosher, 2002; Ozubko and MacLeod, 2010; Senkfor et al., 2008; Wammes et al., 2016. Additionally, various ways to improve vocabulary retention have been identified, which are rehearsal

(Atkinson & Shiffrin, 1968; Rundus, 1971), elaboration (Anderson & Reder, 1979; Rinne et al., 2011), enactment (Mohr et al., 1989; Senkfor et al., 2008), oral production (Icht & Mama, 2019; Karousou & Nerantzaki, 2020; MacLeod et al., 2010; Ozubko & MacLeod, 2010), emotional arousal (Cahill & McGaugh, 1995; Immordino-Yang & Damasio, 2007), and pictorial representation (Koester, 2015; McBride & Dosher, 2002; Wammes et al., 2016).

1.1.3 Vocabulary Teaching and Learning in the Chinese Context

In China, students spend much time and effort on learning wordlists throughout their English studies. Zhang (2008) found that reciting wordlists was ranked the most frequent vocabulary learning strategy to retain vocabulary among Chinese university students, which is also consistent with Schmitt's (1997) research. The most frequent vocabulary learning strategy may have been greatly influenced by the traditional teaching methods used in the Chinese EFL classroom. Wang (2014) demonstrated that wordlist-based teaching was the most typical teaching method from Grade 3 of elementary school to higher education, leading to the habit of reciting wordlists among Chinese students.

There are some advantages of traditional wordlist-based teaching and learning. It was claimed that wordlist-based teaching could directly require learners to memorize the spelling, pronunciation, and words' meanings at a time (Carter, 1987; Clipperton, 1994; Nation, 1993). Also, Meara (1995) stated that wordlists played a key role at the first stage of learning a language. Furthermore, Zeng (2007) argued that reciting wordlists was an efficient method and of great importance in language learning: for one thing, there is a possibility that learners can master large amounts of words in a short time by using a wordlist; for another, wordlists meet learners' psychological needs for mastering many words.

However, there are also some disadvantages concerning wordlist-based teaching and learning. Gairns and Redman (1986) proved that using wordlists hindered vocabulary processing and thus they resulted in students losing a base for long-term retention. Later,

Mondria et al. (1991) proposed that learners should refuse to use wordlists to memorize vocabulary, because they can confuse students and make them forget some items. Meanwhile, Gui (1991) pointed out that using wordlists for vocabulary learning and retention was in vain, for it treated the target words as if they had an equivalent meaning in Chinese which was not helpful in students' forming a semantic network. However, Oxford and Scarcella (1994) experimented and found that wordlists were helpful in vocabulary tests, but resulted in the vocabulary being forgotten too quickly. Another study conducted by Ye (2016) showed that the traditional method of wordlist-based teaching in Chinese universities failed to help students retain new words or to have a significant influence on the efficiency of vocabulary learning.

1.1.4 Current Situation of the Research Site

The research site in the current study is located in Anshun University (ASU). It belongs to Anshun city in the Guizhou province of China, where 35 ethnic minority groups live in the same community. In ASU, there are 16 institutes and an affiliated senior high school. In detail, 57 majors are offered, 29 of which are in pedagogic specialities. In the 2019 academic year, 9,308 full-time undergraduate students were enrolled in the university.

All non-English majors are compulsory for taking the College English course in the first two years of a four-year program. College English course is compulsory for non-English majors to attend. The number of teaching hours in College English 1 (CE1) is two hours a week for fourteen successive weeks within the first semester. Also, the objective of CE1 is facilitating students' reading, listening, translating, speaking, and writing skills. However, little attention is paid to vocabulary. Besides, according to a classroom survey by a researcher in 2018, 80% of the students complained that they had no choice but to learn words by reciting wordlists in the textbooks on their own.

Moreover, the pilot study in September of the 2018 academic year at ASU revealed that the average number of vocabulary items among non-English students was 2,300 words. The vocabulary size was far from the requirement of 4,500 words for passing CET-4, which is the prerequisite for university non-English majors to obtain a bachelor's degree and then to find a job (Jiang, 2016). Unsurprisingly, the pass rate of CET-4 has stayed low, ranging from 4.11% to 5.8% in the past five years (2014—2018). This indicates the low vocabulary level among the university students at ASU. Therefore, the need to improve students' vocabulary knowledge has become an urgent issue which needs solving by the English teachers at ASU.

Lastly, *College English Curriculum Requirements* issued by the Ministry of Education (2007) in China emphasized changing from teacher-centered to student-centered patterns with the use of modern technology. These changes are likely to break the barriers or the constraints of time and place to some extent which might improve the efficiency of English learning and facilitate more individualized learning.

To sum up, in the Chinese context, wordlist-based teaching and learning are widespread, and there are disadvantages as well as advantages. Combined with the current situation at ASU and the proposed changes in teaching methodology, it is needed urgently for continuing research into EFL vocabulary learning to broaden the theoretical understanding of vocabulary acquisition and in practice to explore new ways to improve the vocabulary learning and retention of Chinese EFL learners. Nowadays, with the rapid development of technology, one possible way to improve vocabulary learning is through MALL (Mobile-assisted Language Learning).

1.1.5 MALL and Mobile-assisted Vocabulary Learning

The term "MALL" has many definitions. MALL is referred to as any kind of learning that happens when one is movable, or learning that happens when he/she makes use of the chances provided by mobile technologies (O'Malley et al., 2003). In addition, Chinnery (2006) referred to MALL as language learning that is supported or enhanced by using a handheld mobile device. Subsequently, Kukulska-Hulme and Shield (2008) pointed out that MALL distinguishes from CALL (Computer-Assisted Language Learning) in using portable facilities that create innovative learning types, putting an emphasis on the accessible spontaneity and interaction among various contexts. Based on the definitions above, in the present study, MALL is defined as the process of language learning, which is assisted or enhanced by mobile devices, mobile technologies, or learners' mobility.

The features of mobile devices that can result in educational benefits may explain the effectiveness of MALL on language learning: being portable, being interactive socially, being connective, and being individual (Klopfer, Squire & Jenkins, 2002). In particular, portability means that mobile devices are easy to carry or to move. That is, one can carry his/her phone all the time in the pocket, and an iPad in ones' backpack, even in a handbag. Social interactivity means that mobile devices allow learners to communicate with other users or learners, offering them a chance to interact with each other. Connectivity indicates that mobile devices can be connected to the Internet because most of them have a wireless function. Connectivity makes learners able to obtain access to online learning materials anytime and anywhere. Lastly, individuality means that learners can study individually by using a mobile device.

1.1.5.1 Mobile-assisted Vocabulary Learning

Research on MALL has indicated the effectiveness of using mobile devices in vocabulary learning. Mobile devices help increase learners' vocabulary achievements for their convenience (Basal et al., 2016), enjoyment (Bensalem, 2018), and flexibility (Jafari & Chalak, 2016). In addition, Osaki, Ochiai, Iso, and Aizawa (2003) examined how three ways of learning modes: a paper dictionary, an electronic dictionary, and without any dictionary affected secondary vocabulary acquisition. Results from delayed vocabulary tests suggested that learners with electronic dictionaries got higher scores than the counterparts with paper dictionaries and those who did not use dictionaries.

From a similar perspective, Lu (2008) inspected the effectiveness of SMS (short message service) on vocabulary lessons when they appear on the screen of mobile phones. Thirty high school students in Taiwan were involved in the program, and they were randomly distributed in the SMS group and a traditional paper group. Pre-test, post-test, and delayed tests were carried out in the experiment. Moreover, the results showed that both groups made some improvements. Nevertheless, "the students recognized more vocabulary during the post-test after reading the regular and brief SMS lessons than they did after reading the relatively more detailed print material" (Lu, 2008: 515).

More recently, Basoglu and Akdemir (2010) compared MALL with traditional approaches to vocabulary learning in an attempt to examine which method worked better for learners. In their study, a mobile phone-based flashcard application (also app hereafter) was used by an experimental group for learning vocabulary while a printed flashcard was employed as a vocabulary learning tool by a control group. As a result, the flashcard app was more powerful in supporting vocabulary improvement than the printed flashcard. The findings also revealed that students found the flashcard app-based learning vocabulary helpful and entertaining.

Although the research found that students could learn vocabulary effectively or achieve more vocabulary via MALL, less encouraging and even negative results about the effectiveness of mobile devices on vocabulary learning do exist. Stockwell (2007) disclosed that using mobile phones to learn vocabulary was not so good as employing desktop computers. By comparing the effectiveness of the two techniques on vocabulary learning, few differences on learners' performances were seen. Moreover, Stockwell (2010) found that learners were not willing to use mobile phones for learning vocabulary, which was contrary to previous research. His explanation of the results might be high cost of accessing the Internet, the small-sized keypad of a mobile device, and the display screen. Also, Okunbor and Retta (2008) carried out an experiment for a year to examine if using mobile phones could improve learners' learning. The results were that many students perceived mobile phones as ineffective in learning.

The effectiveness of MALL on vocabulary learning has been examined by some studies (e.g. Basal et al., 2016; Başoğlu & Akdemir, 2010; Bensalem, 2018; Jafari & Chalak, 2016; Lu, 2008; Osaki et al., 2003), while negative results concerning the role of MALL were identified in the research of other studies (Stockwell, 2007, 2010; Okunbor & Retta, 2008). Thus, further research is needed to be carried out to investigate the impacts of MALL on vocabulary learning.

To summarize, with regard to the importance of vocabulary, vocabulary retention, vocabulary teaching and learning in the Chinese context, and also the current situation of Anshun University, a detailed study of the use of a mobile application as a tool for EFL vocabulary learning as well as retention among Chinese university students is urgently needed to test its effectiveness.

1.1.5.2 Perceptions of MALL

The learners' perceptions of learning can be an indicator of their level of language acquisition. According to Yu (2019), the learners' perceptions of technology had a direct impact on their language learning. Additionally, Muhanna and Abu-Al-Sha'r (2009) explored how university students perceived a learning environment with cell phones by selecting twenty graduates and thirty undergraduates of Jordan as samples. They found that those who preferred learning by using cell phones were the undergraduates, while graduate students did not. Barbour et al. (2014) probed into students' perceptions of mobile learning in one virtual school, and found that they were not fond of mobile learning. However, Bensalem (2018) investigated EFL learners' perceptions of learning vocabulary through WhatsApp, and revealed that they held positive perceptions of learning words via WhatsApp. Also, Gonulal (2019) revealed that English language learners' experiences of employing Instagram to learn a language were mainly good. In terms of the studies above, it can be stated that EFL learners' perceptions of MALL are various.

Furthermore, little research has been done on L2 vocabulary learning through mobile applications (Afzali et al., 2017; Burston, 2013).

1.2 Statement of the Problems

The English vocabulary of Chinese university students is currently at a low level. According to Zhang (2008), the vocabulary level of non-English major students was investigated, and the results showed that their vocabulary size was 2,703 words. Similarly, Wu (2011) revealed that the percentage of the number of students whose vocabulary size was no more less than 3,000 words accounted for 68% of university EFL counterparts. By looking more closely at the vocabulary size of non-English majors from two aspects, Wang (2010) found that their average receptive vocabulary size was about 3,000 words, and their average controlled-productive size was 1,142 words. Compared with the requirement of 4,500 words for passing CET-4 in China or the requirement of an 8,000—9,000 word-family to be competent in different English skills as proposed by Nation (2006) and Schmitt (2010), the vocabulary level can be considered as at a low level among Chinese university students. Their low vocabulary level can be attributed to the following reasons.

One reason may have something to do with the disadvantages of wordlist-based teaching and learning, for example, easily making learners confused and forgetful (Mondria et al., 1991), useless in students' forming a semantic network (Gui, 1991), fast memory loss of vocabulary (Oxford & Scarcella, 1994), and low efficiency in memorizing words (Ye, 2016).

The other reason may be due to limited classroom time for Chinese university students to learn vocabulary. Non-English major students only attend an English course for two hours per week for four semesters, and no course is offered for vocabulary learning (Ministry of Education, 2007). Nevertheless, vocabulary knowledge is considered as a continuum or incremental in nature, which cannot be achieved through a limited time (Henriksen, 1999; Schmitt, 1998, 2000). Also, it has been pointed out that EFL vocabulary learning and retention are time-consuming tasks in EFL settings (Chumcharoensuk, 2013; Ko & Goranson, 2014; Somnuek, 2011; Zeng, 2012). Therefore, limited in-class time will not be sufficient to enable EFL learners to achieve wide vocabulary knowledge.

Providing students with contextualized vocabulary learning and making use of their fragmented time together may be a possible way to improve their vocabulary learning and retention. To achieve this goal, MALL could be a useful tool (see "Advantages of MALL" in Section 2.6).

1.3 Purposes of the Study

Therefore, in order to fill in the gaps above and follow the changes of times, the first aim of the present study was to develop a mobile application, especially for vocabulary learning and retention among Chinese university students. The next aim was to test its effects on their vocabulary learning and retention. Additionally, their perceptions of the mobile application were explored, because little research has focused on using technology in English learning among university students in China (Yu, 2019) and various perceptions of MALL emerged (Barbour et al., 2014; Bensalem, 2018; Gonulal, 2019; Muhanna & Abu-Al-Sha'r, 2009).

One purpose for the present study was for using a theory-based mobile app as a means for Chinese university students to learn vocabulary, which can be employed outside the classroom with the hope of improving their EFL vocabulary learning and retention. The other is to examine whether the mobile app can positively affect EFL learners' vocabulary learning and retention in a Chinese EFL setting. The purposes of this study are listed as follows:

(1) To investigate what effects a theory-based mobile app has on EFL students' vocabulary learning achievement. [1]

(2) To examine what effects a theory-based mobile app has on EFL students' vocabulary retention. [2]

(3) To explore EFL students' perceptions of using a theory-based mobile app to learn EFL vocabulary.

1.4 Research Questions

According to the purposes above of this study, three research questions were proposed:

(1) What are the effects of using a theory-based mobile app on EFL students' vocabulary learning achievement?

(2) What are the effects of employing a theory-based mobile app on EFL students' vocabulary retention?

(3) What are the EFL learners' perceptions of vocabulary learning via a theory-based mobile app?

---

1 The operational definition of vocabulary learning achievement means the scores that the students achieve in the Knowledge Scale of Target Words for the post-test.

2 The operational definition of vocabulary retention means the scores that the students achieve in the Knowledge Scale of Target Words for the delayed post-test.

1.5 Significance of the Study

Firstly, this study fills in the research gap with a mobile app specially designed for vocabulary learning and adds to research on mobile app-assisted EFL vocabulary learning in the Chinese EFL setting as little empirical research has been carried out so far based on the researcher's literature review.

Secondly, the mobile app is based on the design principles of MALL, vocabulary learning, and memory theories, especially for vocabulary learning (see details in Section 2.1), so the findings of the study will help mobile app developers assist in vocabulary learning in EFL settings.

Thirdly, the results from learners' perceptions of mobile-assisted vocabulary learning in this study offer guidelines to the writers of vocabulary learning materials as well as mobile app developers.

Fourthly, the present study, with its focus on CET-4 vocabulary learning and retention via a mobile app, is especially helpful in the Chinese EFL setting where all non-English majors have hopes of passing the national CET-4 before graduation.

Finally, this study may enrich the understanding of using a mobile app in the Chinese EFL context for both pedagogical and methodological reasons. For vocabulary pedagogy, English teachers can require students to learn words via mobile apps with careful monitoring. As for the methodological reason, students can not only study words in classrooms or from textbooks, but also use mobile apps to learn vocabulary for offsetting the weaknesses of traditional vocabulary learning.

1.6 Scope of the Study

(1) The context of this study was the EFL setting of China. The present study was carried out at a local university in the southwest of China, where the English proficiency of

the university students is relatively low based on their English scores of National College Entrance Exams (see Table 3.1). For this study, 114 freshmen out of 850 non-English major newcomers in the 2019 academic year were chosen as participants.

(2) The focus of this study was to examine the effects of using a mobile app on EFL learners' vocabulary learning and retention. The mobile app used in this study was developed by a computer engineer for which the vocabulary learning activities were designed by the researcher.

1.7 Limitations of the Study

A number of participants in this study were selected from a limited population of undergraduates at a local university in China. Therefore, the participants may not be representative of students who enroll in other universities, because they may have different vocabulary proficiency, learning environments, and needs.

Furthermore, the participants in the study were selected based on availability and convenience. This kind of sampling procedure probably restrains the generalizability concerning the results of the study.

Lastly, the subjects were from first-year non-English majors. So the university counterparts among various majors and at different levels were excluded, then the scope of the findings' generalizability is limited.

Because of these limitations, it should be cautious to treat those findings from this study in making generalizations concerning university students' vocabulary learning via a mobile app in the Chinese EFL setting.

1.8 Definitions of Key Terms

(1) Mobile-assisted Language Learning (MALL) or M-learning or MobiLearn

(Chinnery, 2006) refers to any kind of learning language via mobile facilities, such as smartphones, MP4/MP3 players, tablets, or electronic dictionaries (Kukulska-Hulme & Shield, 2008).

(2) A mobile device is referred to as any device being automatic, small-sized (Trifanova et al., 2004). In the present study, mobile devices refer to smart mobile phones (smartphones).

(3) A mobile app is a computer program developed for operating on a portable device such as smartphones or tablets. The term "app" is a short name of "software application". Technology columnist David (2009) argued that nowadays smartphones can be called "app phones" to differ from less-sophisticated ones.

(4) EFL stands for English as a foreign language in the study, which refers to the English language learned by non-native speakers as a foreign language at the environment in which English is not used as his/her mother language.

(5) EFL learners refers to the people learning English as a foreign language in the EFL context. In this study, EFL learners refers to any one who learns or uses English non-natively in China.

(6) Non-English majors refer to students whose majors are not the English language at university, and who learn English mainly for graduation and good jobs.

(7) Vocabulary is defined as a collection of words in a language that consists of word forms (spelling and sounds) and word meanings used in various contexts in order to convey different meanings (Gutlohn, 2006; Hubbard, 1983; Jackson & Amvela, 2000). In this study, vocabulary refers to the vocabulary in College English Test Band 4 (CET-4) of China, which university students have to master in order to pass it.

(8) Vocabulary learning is the process of acquiring vocabulary knowledge, which commonly includes vocabulary size and depth (Qian, 1999, 2002; Wesche & Paribakht, 1996). Vocabulary size means a learner's vocabulary size (Nation, 2001) or the amount of words about which one knows something related to their meanings (Stahr, 2009). Vocabulary depth means how well he/she knows vocabulary, or one learner's knowledge level concerning every aspect of vocabulary (Qian, 1999; Read, 1993).

(9) Vocabulary retention refers to the ability to remember or retain vocabulary in

mind (Maryam & Ahmad, 2017) or the ability to provide the meaning of a new word after a given period of time (Ramezanali, 2017). In the study, vocabulary retention means how many words the students can retain after four weeks.

(10) Vocabulary Size Test (VST) is an instrument to assess the total vocabulary size for ESL/EFL learners. It was constructed by Nation and Beglar (2007).

(11) Vocabulary Knowledge Scale (VKS) is a measurement that gauges a broad range of word knowledge types: being aware of a word's form, knowing a word's form-meaning link, and using a word to make sentences. It was developed by Paribakht and Wesche (1993).

(12) CET-4 is the abbreviation of College English Test Band 4, which is a nation-wide standardized English level test for Chinese non-English majors, which has been held twice a year since 1987.

(13) TEM-4 refers to Test for English Majors Band 4, which is a nation-wide standardized English test for English majors of China, which has been held once a year since 1991.

1.9 Summary

This chapter firstly states the current background of the study, followed by problems' statement, the research purposes and questions, the significance, the scope, the limitations, and the key terms' definitions. In the upcoming chapter, a review of the literature concerning theories and related research about vocabulary learning as well as studies about MALL are presented.

Chapter 2

Literature Review

This chapter begins with an introduction to the theoretical framework for the present study. Next, several central constructs to the present study, including vocabulary, vocabulary knowledge, vocabulary retention, and related research are reviewed. Later, Mobile-assisted Language Learning (MALL) is introduced, and the studies on MALL are presented. Then, a review of the research on EFL vocabulary learning and retention through MALL is given. Moreover, the gaps in the previous studies on mobile-assisted EFL vocabulary learning and retention are pointed out, and the present study is proposed. Finally, this chapter ends with a summary.

2.1 Theoretical Framework

The design of the mobile app and the presentation of the vocabulary contents in the present study are based on four theories, which are derived from ten design principles for MALL (Stockwell & Hubbard, 2013), dual coding theory (Paivio, 2007, 1986, 1971), the cognitive theory of multimedia learning (Mayer, 2005, 1997), and the memory-based strategic framework for vocabulary learning (Ma, 2014). Then, they are introduced respectively, and the implications for the present study are also presented.

2.1.1 Ten Design Principles for MALL

Stockwell and Hubbard (2013) proposed ten principles for the design and implementation of mobile devices as well as tasks using mobile functionalities in language learning environments based on theories from MALL, ML (Mobile Learning), and CALL (Computer-assisted Language Learning). They examined the studies from MALL, exploring the issues that emerged from this body of research through a framework distinguishing physical, pedagogical, and psychosocial dimensions. Recognizing not only the contributions, but also the limitations of existing MALL literature, they then identified the findings from the closely allied fields of ML and CALL that could inform both research and practice in MALL. Drawing from MALL, ML, and CALL, they put forward ten general principles to guide teachers and learners on how to integrate mobile devices and tasks into language learning environments effectively.

Principle 1: Mobile apps, tasks, and activities should distinguish both the affordances and limitations of the mobile device, and the affordances and constraints of the environment in which the device will be used in the light of the learning target (Herrington et al., 2009; Reinders & Hubbard, 2013).

Principle 2: Limit multi-tasking and environmental distractions. According to Ophir et al. (2009), most people are not good at multi-tasking, and it may increase stress levels, error rates, and lower productivity. Furthermore, it is likely to interfere with both deliberate and incidental language learning.

Principle 3: Push, but respect boundaries. Stockwell (2013) found that the push mechanism has the potential to remind learners to take action, but at the same time, learners should know when and how frequently they may receive these reminders (Kennedy & Levy, 2008). These reminder messages have the potential to shift learners' attention to the learning task.

Principle 4: Strive to maintain equity. In a formal or an informal language learning setting, essential issues should be considered that include whether the learner owns a mobile device, what device the learner has in terms of functionality and compatibility, how consistent its connectivity is, and what the expense is for employing the devices to carry out tasks in language learning.

Principle 5: Acknowledge and plan for accommodating language learners' differences. According to Chun (2001) and Heift (2002), learning styles and learners' differences in a public or a private place should be taken into account in mobile learning.

Principle 6: Be aware of language learners' existing uses and cultures of use with their devices. Liu (2013) and Stockwell (2010) found that students may consider their mobile devices as being for personal and social use rather than as educational tools. So the more consistent a task or app is with its purpose, the more likely learners will accept it.

Principle 7: Keep mobile language learning activities and tasks short and succinct when possible. According to mobile learning frameworks put forward by Elias (2011) and Herrington et al. (2009), long activities or tasks should be divided into short, coherent ones.

Principle 8: Let the language learning task fit the technology and environment, and let the technology and environment meet the task. If there is an assumption that learners will use a mobile phone at short intervals during the day (e. g. 10 minutes between classes) in settings where it may be challenging to incorporate sound, then tasks should be designed for fitting that environment. If there is another assumption that learners would do a task that requires reading substantial texts or videos from the screen, then appropriate technology (e. g. smartphones with bigger screens) and a quiet environment would be needed.

Principle 9: Some, possibly most, learners will need guidance and training on how to use mobile devices for language learning effectively. Hubbard (2013) claimed that it is necessary to make learners aware of the impact of task learning and the environment in which they use mobile devices, and then to train them to use mobile devices for doing a task as efficiently as possible.

Principle 10: Recognize and accommodate multiple stakeholders. For example, in the workplace, the impact of the potential ubiquity of mobile learning on co-workers, bosses, and productivity should be taken into account.

Applications in the present study: Table 2.1 below illustrates how each principle is used.

Table 2.1 The ten design principles and their applications in the present study

Principles	Adoption in the present study
1. Mobile apps, tasks, and activities should distinguish both the affordances and limitations of the mobile device, and the affordances and constraints of the environment in which the device will be used in the light of the learning target	Students can download and install the mobile app for the first time through smartphones to learn and review vocabulary on their own
2. Limit multi-tasking and environmental distractions	The tasks of one-word learning consist of a learning section and a retrieval section (see Section 3.3.2)
3. Push, but respect boundaries	Students would receive a message on smartphones that their diaries are due, which helps them carry out the learning schedule
4. Strive to maintain equity	Every student in the experiment group owns a smartphone with similar capacities, such as approximately a 5-inch screen, an Android operating system, and a wireless network function
5. Acknowledge and plan for accommodating language learners' differences	Students have very similar learning and living environments, as they are classmates and live in the dormitories of university in the 2019 academic year
6. Be aware of language learners' existing uses and cultures of use with their devices	The subjects are all Chinese, and they mainly use QQ and WeChat for communication, so the cultures for using their smartphones are similar
7. Keep mobile language learning activities and tasks short and succinct when possible	Students are required to learn ten words via the app at a time which will not surpass their working memory capacity (Miller, 1956). Besides, the vocabulary in the app is presented in multimedia and is simple to follow

(续表)

Principles	Adoption in the present study
8. Let the language learning task fit the technology and environment, and let the technology and environment meet the task	The tasks are for students to read short texts with big fonts from the screen and they can watch the images or listen to audios of the words with a loudspeaker/earphones
9. Some, possibly most, learners will need guidance and training on how to use mobile devices for language learning effectively	Instructions on how to use the app to learn and review vocabulary should be provided in detail to the students in the first class
10. Recognize and accommodate multiple stakeholders	The students with the mobile apps are required to learn or review words on their own, so the impacts on mobile apps' usage from their classmates, teachers, or other people can be ignored

2.1.2 Dual Coding Theory

Definition: DCT (Dual Coding Theory) proposed by Paivio (2007, 1986, 1971) attempts to give equal weight to verbal and non-verbal/visual systems, and to explain the powerful effects of mental imagery on the memory.

Verbal and Non-verbal Systems: The verbal system stores and processes linguistic information/units (such as text and sound), and the non-verbal/visual system stores and processes visual information/units (such as pictures, animations, and videos). Also, these verbal and non-verbal/visual systems interact, and the activation of both systems results in better recall (Al-Seghayer, 2001; Paivio, 2007).

According to Paivio (1986), and Clark and Paivio (1991), three different processing levels (i.e. representational, referential, and associative processing) take place within or between verbal and non-verbal/visual systems. Representational processing refers to the activation of the verbal and visual representation by a stimulus as words or sounds can activate verbal representation and pictures visual representation. Referential processing refers to the activation of one system by the other. That is, words in the verbal system can activate images in the non-verbal/visual system and vice versa. Associative processing refers to the activation of additional information in representational or referential systems. At this level, the associative connections between words or sounds in the verbal system and images in the visual system are activated.

Accordingly, words associated with images are acquired more quickly and retained more effectively than those which are presented alone (Clark & Paivio, 1991). Ramezanali (2017: 141) stated that "use of pictures and illustrations associated with unknown words are effective instructional devices that are superior to words alone for memory tasks and will help L2 learners remember the words sooner and retain them longer". Lin (2009:24) claimed that the dual association of verbal and visual modes are also valid for recall, because "when one memory trace is lost, the other remains and is accessible". Exposing learners to multiple ways of presentation, such as printed text, sound, pictures, and video/animations, can produce a language learning environment with a significant effect on vocabulary learning (Al-Seghayer, 2016, 2001).

Application for the Current Research: The target words in the mobile app are presented in both visual and audio ways for activating the learners' two systems to facilitate their learning and retention.

2.1.3 The Cognitive Theory of Multimedia Learning

Definition: The Cognitive Theory of Multimedia Learning (CTML) is about how people learn from multimedia presentations (Mayer, 2005, 1997). It is based on three assumptions, which are dual channels, limited capacity, and active processing.

The assumption of dual channels suggests that humans have two separate information processing channels (auditory/verbal and visual/pictorial). The auditory/verbal channel receives information (such as spoken words, narration, or sounds) through the ears and the visual/pictorial channel receives information (such as pictures, videos, or on-screen texts) through the eyes.

The second assumption of limited capacity signifies that there is a limit on the amount of information that learners can process in one of the above two channels at one time. This may be the reason why learners can only hold a few words in the auditory/verbal channel of their working memory at one time when presented with narration, and the same is also true of the visual/pictorial channel (Mayer, 2005).

Lastly, for building a connection between verbal and visual representations and integrating them into the learners' existing knowledge, some cognitive activities should be processed in long-term memory and brought back into the working memory. This cognitive process accounts for the third assumption of active processing. In detail, the assumption of active processing includes:

"(1) Selecting relevant words for processing in the verbal working memory; (2) Selecting relevant images for processing in the visual working memory; (3) Organizing selected words into a verbal model; (4) Organizing selected images into a pictorial model; (5) And integrating the verbal and pictorial representations with relevant prior knowledge activated from the long-term memory." (Mayer, 2005: 54)

Figure 2.1 below shows the processes of learning L2 vocabulary in a multimedia-based setting.

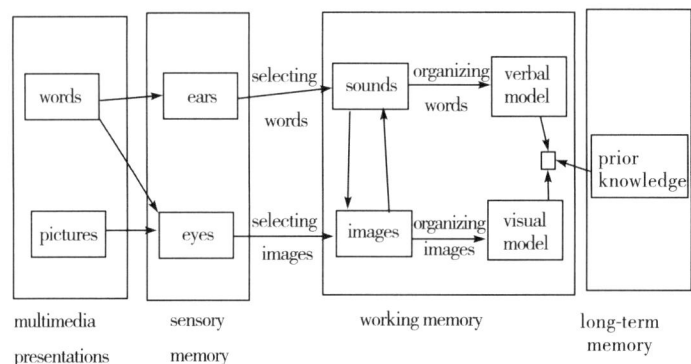

Figure 2.1 Cognitive theory of multimedia learning (Mayer, 2005: 52)

Figure 2.1 shows that words and pictures, as the two multimedia presentation modes, come to the sensory memory through the ears and eyes from outside. Words are kept in the auditory sensory memory and pictures in the visual sensory memory temporarily. Later, learners can select materials by giving their attention to the appropriate words and pictures. When the relevant materials are selected, structural relations are built between the elements in the working memory. Then, the information is transferred to the working memory, where materials are temporarily held and manipulated.

As illustrated in Figure 2.1, working memory consists of two dimensions: the left side represents "the raw material" such as "verbal words and visual images", and the right side "the knowledge constructed in the working memory" such as "verbal models and visual models and the links between them" (Mayer, 2005: 53). On the right hand side of Figure 2.1, the last box shows long-term memory, which can hold large amounts of information over long periods. However, according to Mayer (2005), for the materials to stay in the long-term memory, they should be actively moving back and forth from long-term memory to working memory, as shown in Figure 2.1 above. In this way, knowledge in the long-term memory can be activated and brought into the working memory if there exists a connection between new materials and the learners' prior knowledge (Mayer, 2005).

Two Principles of Multimedia Learning: One principle is the multimedia principle (Fletcher & Tobias, 2005; Mayer, 2005), and the other is the temporal contiguity principle (Mayer & Fiorella, 2014). According to Fletcher and Tobias (2005), and Mayer (2005), the multimedia principle suggests that learners can learn more effectively if they are presented with words and pictures rather than words alone. Also, Butcher (2014) claimed that the multimedia principle is not limited to words and pictures but refers to a broader term encompassing different forms of visual and verbal representations when presented together. According to Sweller (2005), it was assumed that L2 learners could learn the target words better and more effectively when offered in dual modes rather than a single mode, for using both words and pictures allows the brain to process more information in the working memory, and can be recalled from the long-term memory when required.

The temporal contiguity principle refers to learners learning more deeply from learning media when the text, audio, pictures, and video/animation are presented simultaneously rather than successively or sequentially (Mayer & Fiorella, 2014). Moreover, learners must have corresponding words and images in the working memory at the same time to make connections between them, which means that simultaneous presentation is likely to result in better learning than successive and separate presentations (Mayer, 2008; Rusanganwa, 2015).

Application: In the present study, text, audio words, as well as Chinese definitions and pictures are used as the verbal and visual components to present the target words for the learners. In addition, both the verbal and visual elements concerning the target words are displayed simultaneously in the mobile app.

2.1.4 The Memory-based Strategic Framework for Vocabulary Learning

Definition: The memory-based strategic framework for vocabulary learning was proposed by Ma (2014) based on the findings of memory in psychology and L2 vocabulary acquisition. The framework is illustrated in Figure 2.2 below.

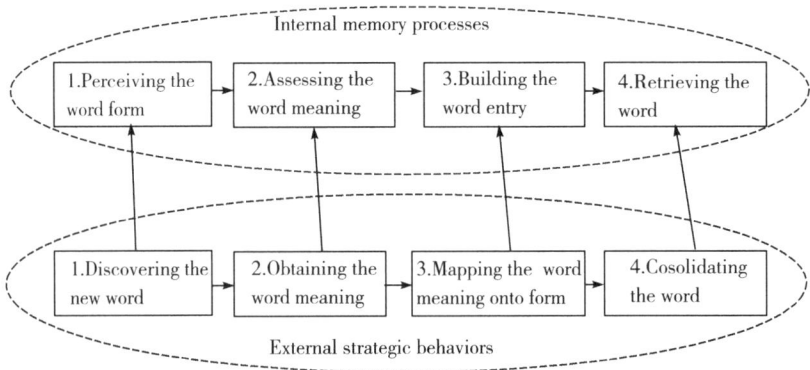

Figure 2.2 The memory-based strategic framework for vocabulary learning (Ma, 2014: 43)

Four-stage Vocabulary Learning Process: For each stage, a cognitive process takes place invisibly in the internal memory system, and a corresponding external, strategic behavior takes place as well. Firstly, the new word in a visual or auditory form needs to be noticed by the brain. Secondly, the meaning of the new word needs to be accessed, which could be achieved by looking it up in a dictionary or utilizing other sources. Thirdly, the original word needs to be established as a new L2 lexical entry in the brain by connecting the meaning (L1 definition) with the new form via repetition or imagery. Finally, each time the newly learned word is retrieved for receptive or productive use, the memory trace for the word will be strengthened.

Application in the Present Study: In the first stage, the target word in the mobile app is presented in both visual and audio modes simultaneously to attract students' notice. In the second stage, students can find the meaning of the target word by looking at the Chinese definition and the example sentence. In the third stage, to help students map the meaning of the new word onto its form, two multiple-choice exercises, the first "selecting the right meaning for a given word" and the second "selecting the right word for a given meaning" are provided for students to complete. In the fourth stage, to consolidate the words in students' minds, spelling exercises for students to write down the corresponding English words based on Chinese meanings are provided to help them retrieve the words they have learned from memory.

Feedback is provided in form of pop-ups when students finish any kind of exercise in the present study. It includes both positive and negative feedback which can improve learning effectiveness as the practice-takers can correct errors and make correct responses (Pashler, 2005; Roediger & Butler, 2011). In Figure 2.3 below, when students do the first multiple-choice exercise for the word "involve", on touching the third column (right answer), they would see positive feedback with a tick ("√"). However, on touching one of the other columns, they would receive negative feedback with a cross ("×") and then they are automatically linked to the learning section of "involve".

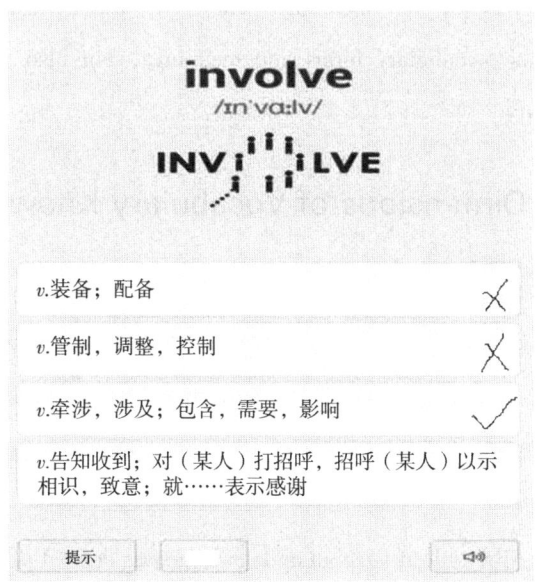

Figure 2.3 The picture of the word "involve" in the first
multiple-choice with feedback

2.2 Vocabulary Knowledge

Firstly, a definition of vocabulary is presented in this section. Then, two components comprising vocabulary knowledge are provided. Next, studies over the correlation between vocabulary knowledge and different language skills, as well as language proficiency, are reviewed.

Hubbard (1983) defined vocabulary as a dominant carrier of meaning. More specifically, Jackson and Amvela (2000) regarded that vocabulary is a collection with words or a package of subsets of words employed for particular contexts or in a certain textbook. From another perspective, Diamond and Gutlohn (2006) argued that vocabulary is the knowledge of words' forms and their meanings, and can be applied receptively or productively for various meaning making.

Based on the above definitions, vocabulary can be seen as a collection of words in a language that consists of word forms (spelling and sounds) and word meanings used in various contexts to convey different meanings. Therefore, when learners learn vocabulary, they not only learn the vocabulary forms and meanings, but also learn the appropriate usage of the vocabulary.

2.2.1 Two Dimensions of Vocabulary Knowledge

Although researchers regarded vocabulary knowledge as comprising multidimensional aspects (Chapelle,1998; Henriksen,1999; Nation,2006; Qian,2002; Richards,1976), vocabulary knowledge should include two primary dimensions: size/breadth and quality/depth, which are accepted commonly (Qian, 1999, 2002; Read, 1993; Wesche & Paribakht, 1996).

Vocabulary Size: Breadth of vocabulary knowledge was defined as the size of a learner's vocabulary (Nation, 2001) or the number of words of which the learner has at least some knowledge of the meanings (Qian, 2002; Stæhr, 2009). Meara (1996) believed that vocabulary size is a basic dimension to judge a learner's vocabulary knowledge, and claimed that students with larger vocabularies are more likely to be proficient in English than those with little vocabulary size. As for L2 learners, researchers have revealed their insights about the number of word families L2 learners typically need to acquire to function in diverse contexts (Ko, 2012; Laufer, 2003; Nation, 2006). A word family includes a base word, its grammatical inflections, and its closely related derivatives (Nation, 2001).

For L2 learners, Nation(2006) estimated that 6,000~7,000 word families got from Wellington Corpus of Spoken English is needed to function in a speaking context, and 8,000~9,000 word families (based on the British National Corpus) is needed to function in a written context. These estimates are based on the criterion that they would account for 98 percent of vocabulary coverage (Adolphs & Schmitt, 2003), and that is the percentage of known words in all contexts.

It was demonstrated that it is necessary for L2 learners to master 5,000~10,000 word families to infer new words right during university-level passage reading (Coady, 1997; Huckin & Coady, 1999; Ko, 2012; Nation, 2006). Therefore, it is not difficult to understand that this enormous figure demonstrates a significant challenge faced by L2 learners. In other words, they have to learn thousands of words in the target language.

Measurements for Vocabulary Size: At present, two widely accepted and validated measurements for gauging learners' vocabulary size are the Vocabulary Levels Test (VLT) (Nation, 1990; Schmitt et al., 2001) and the Vocabulary Size Test (VST) (Nation & Beglar, 2007).

Vocabulary Levels Test (VLT): It contains 5 tests with 4 different word-frequency levels tests and an Academic Word List developed by Nation (1990). According to Nation, the VLT measures "whether the learner knows enough of the vocabulary at a given word level for instruction to move on to the next frequency level" (2001: 373). Among the first four levels, the 2,000 and 3,000-word levels are representatives of high-frequency words. The 10,000-word level covers low-frequency words. The 5,000-word level is the dividing line between the high-frequency and the low-frequency level. The Academic Word List is the one that university students often encounter in their textbooks.

Format of VLT: Six clusters comprise each level, and each cluster is composed of 6 words on the left as well as 3 short definitions on the right. Among the six words, the test-takers are required to choose three counterparts, which correspond to the three definitions. One example below is taken from VLT (Nation, 1990) to illustrate the above descriptions.

Instructions: You can select the word from the left side matching with meanings of the right side. Fill in the number in the appropriate square frame. An example is taken as follows.

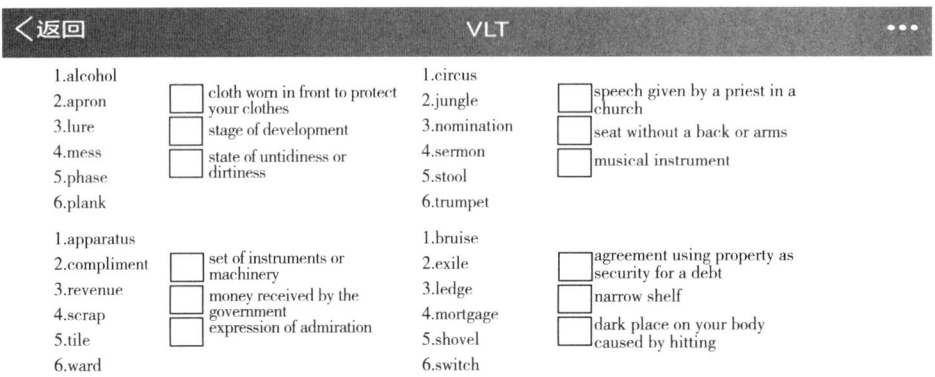

Figure 2.4 A picture of 5,000-level items in VLT (Nation, 1990)

VLT has been proved to be a useful diagnostic tool for the vocabulary levels of migrant or international students in an English-speaking country. Moreover, VLT is a very reliable instrument in measuring the vocabulary size of a language learner (Zhang, 2012) and has been used as a measurement of vocabulary size in many studies (e.g. Afshari & Tavakoli, 2017; Guo, 2017; Liu, 2016; Staehr, 2009; Wang, 2010; Zhang, 2011; Zhang, 2012; Zha, 2015).

Vocabulary Size Test (VST): Nation and Beglar (2007) designed the VST as a tool for measuring vocabulary size of ESL/EFL learners. It consists of one hundred and forty items with ten items forming each of fourteen 1,000-word levels selected from British National Corpus.

Format of VST: The test has a four-item multiple-choice format. A sample item below is taken from the fifth 1,000-word level of VST (Nation & Beglar, 2007).

Instructions: In each item, you should choose the right meaning of capitalized word from a, b, c, d by clicking the small circle. Here is an example, as displayed in Figure 2.5 below.

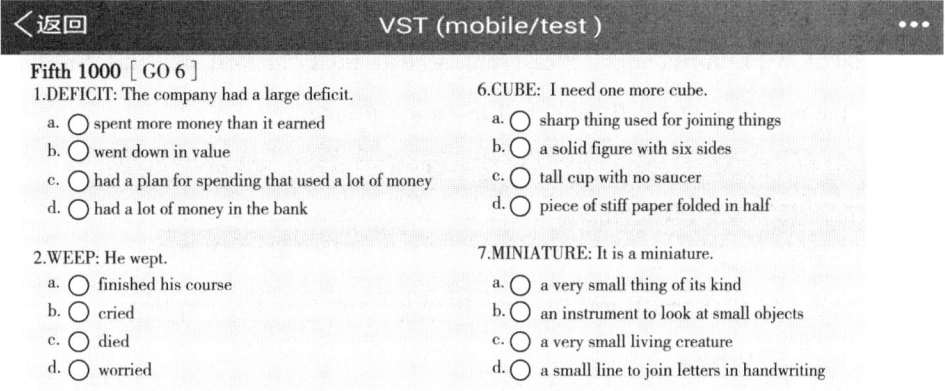

Figure 2.5 The picture of 5,000-word level in VST (Nation & Beglar, 2007)

Each tested word is situated in one simple sentence context. Because every word item in the test stands for a 100-word family and ten ones form a 1,000-word frequency level, a learner's total vocabulary size can be attained with his/her scores of the test multiplying by 100.

To sum up, it can be seen that the above breadth or size tests can provide the necessary measurements for vocabulary size of learners, but the way of assessing how well a student masters a word is not given. To find out the extent of a learner knowing a word, a method is illustrated below.

Vocabulary Depth: It means a student's knowledge level of different aspects about a word, or the extent of his/her mastering one word (Qian, 1999; Read, 1993). For measuring vocabulary depth, two reliable and popular tests are the Word Associates Test (WAT) (Read, 1998, 1993) and the Vocabulary Knowledge Scale(VKS) (Paribakht & Wesche, 1997).

Word Associates Test (WAT): It is a measurement for assessing vocabulary depth through word associations, and was developed by Read (1993) and revised by Read (1998) later. Word associations mean different collocational and semantic correlations that one word exhibits with other words. It can be used as an examination for testing the extent of your knowing the meanings of the adjectives employed frequently in English. The test contains forty items. One item comprises an adjective followed by 8 words, 4 of which are relevant to target word's collocation and meaning, but the other 4 are not. Test-takers are required to pick out 4 words closely correlated to target word, so the number of right choices is 4.

Format of WAT Instructions: Please choose four words in total from the two boxes which are the meanings and collocations of the word in bold.

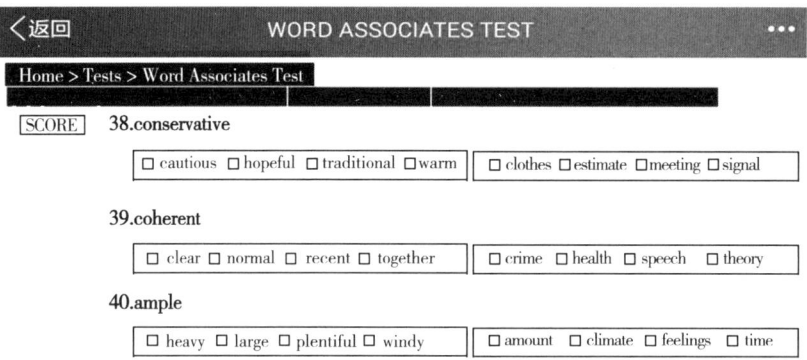

Figure 2.6 The picture of the last three items in WAT (Read, 1998)

In the left hand box above, there are synonyms (one to three) of the target word (ample), and in the right hand box, one to three words are collocations of the target word (ample). So in this sample, the correct choices from the left hand box are large and plentiful, and the correct ones from the right hand box are amount and time. However, exceptions exist. For example, there may be one, two, or three correct choices in the left hand box and three, two, or one correct choice in the right hand box, respectively, because there are four correct choices in total. The test-takers received one score with one correct word. The maximum scores are 160 for 40 items. It probably takes test-takers 35 minutes to finish all items.

WAT is regarded reliable with a high coefficient up to 0.93 (Read, 1998), and researchers like Qian (1999, 2002) and Nassaji (2004) have also stated that the coefficient of WAT reliability is more than 0.9. Therefore, it has been adopted in vocabulary studies to measure vocabulary depth (Afshari & Tavakoli, 2017; Greidanus & Nienhuis, 2001; Guo, 2017; Liu, 2016; Staehr, 2009; Shi, 2012; Wang, 2010).

Vocabulary Knowledge Scale (VKS): It is an instrument for gauging how well a learner knows a given word through using a Five-point Elicitation Scale which ranges from "no recognition" to "the usage of the word in a sentence context". VKS was developed by Paribakht and Wesche (1993) and refined by Paribakht and Wesche (1997) later.

Format of VKS: An example of the instructions for the Vocabulary Knowledge Scale is shown.

Instructions: Choose the most suitable one (I — V) going with the bold word to fill in the bracket, and do as told if you choose one from III to V.

I. I don't remember having seen the word before.

II. I have seen this word before, but I don't know what it means.

III. I have seen this word before, and I think it means _____. (L1 meaning or L2 synonym)

IV. I know this word. It means _____. (L1 meaning or L2 synonym)

V. I can use this word in a sentence: _____. (make a sentence)(If you do this section, please also do Section IV.)

One example is shown how to do it.

E.G.   drive (V)   I can drive the car. 驾驶

Figure 2.7 The picture of one item in VKS (Paribakht & Wesche, 1997)

These categories are coded by the VKS Scoring Scale as in Figure 2.8 below, in which possible points range from 1 to 5. As illustrated in Figure 2.8, the selection of category I would result in 1 point and the selection of category II 2 points. For categories III—V, various points can be awarded based on the quality of the answers provided.

Categories Possible Scores	Meaning of Scores
I ⟶ 1	Word is not familiar at all.
II ⟶ 2	Word is familiar but its meaning is unknown.
III ⟶ 3	A correct synonym or translation is given.
IV ⟶ 4	Word is used with semantic appropriateness in a sentence.
V ⟶ 5	Word is used with semantic appropriateness and grammatical accuracy in a sentence.

Figure 2.8 VKS Scoring Scale (Paribakht & Wesche, 1997: 181)

The VKS reliability was as high as 0.89 (Wesche & Paribakht, 1997). The values for the reliability coefficients range from 0 to 1.0, and the value "0" means there is no reliability, and "1.0" means perfect reliability. The closer the values of the reliability coefficients are to 1.0, the more reliable the test is. So the VKS is very reliable. Next, the VKS has been proven useful in gauging the stages of vocabulary learning and retention (Paribakht, 2005; Wesche & Paribakht, 2009). Furthermore, it estimates the learning stages in the growth of vocabulary knowledge, which means realizing a word's form, explicitly knowing a word's meaning-form link, and using a word appropriately in a sentence context.

In the present study, VST (Nation & Beglar, 2007) was chosen to measure the students' vocabulary size. VST was designed for measuring the total vocabulary size of ESL/EFL learners. While Nation (2001) claims that VLT weighs if one learner knows enough words at a given word-frequency level for determining the teaching of next frequency level or not. Before the treatment in the study, the researcher aimed to examine whether any difference on vocabulary size existed between the two groups of EFL students and whether they were qualified for the treatment or not. So it was determined that VST was more suitable for the present study.

VKS (Paribakkht & Wesche, 1993, 1997) was selected in the present study. VKS measures the vocabulary learning stages from being aware of a word form to using the word in a sentence context. These stages are very similar to the steps of learning the target words in the mobile app of the present study. Nevertheless, WAT (Read, 1993) was developed for evaluating 2 aspects of one word: collocation and meaning, which could not fulfill the aim of learning target words via the app of this study. Therefore, it was decided to use VKS for the study for it can better gauge learners' learning and retention of target words.

2.2.2 Research on the Relationship between Vocabulary Knowledge and Language Skills as well as Language Proficiency

2.2.2.1 Relationship between Vocabulary Knowledge and Listening

A moderately to strongly positive relationship between them was revealed by the studies, with the strong correlation coefficient being 0.65 to 0.7 (Staehr, 2009), from the moderate to the strong coefficient being 0.46 to 0.52 (Zhang, 2011), from the moderate to the strong coefficient being 0.353 to 0.51 (Zhang, 2012), and with the strong correlation coefficient being 0.833 to 0.852 (Afshari & Tavakoli, 2017). They indicated that the more vocabulary knowledge students have, the better the scores they obtain in the listening sections of different tests. Table 2.2 below shows the studies concerning the participants, instruments, and correlation coefficients.

Table 2.2 **The research on the relationship between vocabulary and listening**

Studies	Participants	Instruments		Correlation coefficients	
		Listening tests	Vocabulary tests	Vocabulary size	Vocabulary depth
Staehr, 2009	115 Danish freshmen	Cambridge test	VLT, WAT	0.7	0.65
Zhang, 2011	237 Chinese sophomores	TEM-4	VLT, PLT	0.52	0.46
Zhang, 2012	126 Chinese college students	CET-4	VLT, WAT	0.51	0.353
Afshari & Tavakoli, 2017	32 Iranian students	TOEFL	VLT, WAT	0.852	0.833

Notes: PLT for Productive Levels Test (Laufer & Nation, 1999); the correlation coefficient ranges from -1 to 1, the greater the coefficient, the closer the correlation.

2.2.2.2 Relationship between Vocabulary Knowledge and Speaking

Vocabulary knowledge has a positively moderate or strong correlation with speaking based on these studies: Guo (2017); Milton et al. (2010); Shi (2012); and Zhang (2015). This signifies that learners' speaking performances improve with increasing vocabulary knowledge. Table 2.3 below illustrates the studies by the participants, instruments, and correlation coefficients.

Table 2.3 **The research on the relationship between vocabulary and speaking**

Studies	Participants	Instruments		Correlation coefficients	
		Speaking tests	Vocabulary tests	Vocabulary size	Vocabulary depth
Milton et al., 2010	30 EFL learners	IELTS	Self-developed test	0.71	0.35

(续表)

Studies	Participants	Instruments		Correlation coefficients	
		Speaking tests	Vocabulary tests	Vocabulary size	Vocabulary depth
Shi, 2012	32 EFL learners	IELTS	VLT, WAT	0.816	0.843
Zhang, 2015	179 sophomores	TEM-4	VLT, PLT	0.44	0.39
Guo, 2017	39 freshmen	Self-developed test	VLT, WAT	0.726	0.730

Notes: PLT for Productive Levels Test (Laufer & Nation, 1999); the correlation coefficient ranges from -1 to 1, the greater the coefficient, the closer the correlation.

2.2.2.3 Relationship between Vocabulary Knowledge and Reading

It was proved that reading has a close correlation with vocabulary knowledge from the findings of the research (Hou, 2016; Li, 2012; Song, 2014; Wang, 2010). These results mean that students' reading would be much improved with increasing vocabulary knowledge. Table 2.4 below illustrates the studies by participants, instruments, and correlation coefficients.

Table 2.4 **The research on the relationship between vocabulary and reading**

Studies	Participants	Instruments		Correlation coefficients	
		Reading tests	Vocabulary tests	Vocabulary size	Vocabulary depth
Wang, 2010	146 sophomores	TEM-4	VLT, WAT	0.853	0.691
Li, 2012	115 freshmen	CET-4	VLT, WAT	0.495	0.284
Song, 2014	69 freshmen	PRETCO	VLT, PLT	0.73	0.63
Hou, 2016	188 sophomores	TOEFL	VLT, PLT	0.775	0.765

Notes: PRETCO for Practical English Test for Colleges; the correlation coefficient ranges from -1 to 1, the greater the coefficient, the closer the correlation.

2.2.2.4 Relationship between Vocabulary Knowledge and Writing Skills

It was found that vocabulary knowledge positively affected writing performances based on the following studies: Chen (2011); He (2012); Hou (2016); and Milton et al.

(2010). They highlighted that the more vocabulary knowledge the students had, the better their writing performances became. Table 2.5 below shows the studies with regard to the participants, instruments, and correlation coefficients.

Table 2.5 **The research on the relationship between vocabulary and writing**

Studies	Participants	Instruments		Correlation coefficients	
		writing tests	Vocabulary tests	Vocabulary size	Vocabulary depth
Milton et al., 2010	30 EFL learners	IELTS	Self-developed test	0.766	0.44
Chen, 2011	69 high school students	CEE	VLT, WAT	0.553	0.572
He, 2012	70 sophomores	TEM-4	PLT, WAT	0.495	0.284
Hou, 2016	188 sophomores	TOEFL	VLT, PLT	0.69	0.799

Notes: CEE for College Entrance Exams; the correlation coefficient ranges from -1 to 1, the greater the coefficient, the closer the correlation.

2.2.2.5 Relationship between Vocabulary Knowledge and Language Proficiency

It was claimed by researchers that vocabulary knowledge played a greatly facilitating role in enhancing language proficiency (Huang, 2003; Liu, 2016; Milton et al., 2010; Zhen, 2007). They stated that students' language proficiency was greatly increased when they acquired more vocabulary. Table 2.6 below demonstrates the research in terms of the participants, instruments, and correlation coefficients.

Table 2.6 **The research on the relationship between vocabulary and proficiency**

Studies	Participants	Instruments		Correlation coefficients	
		Proficiency tests	Vocabulary tests	Vocabulary size	Vocabulary depth
Huang, 2003	90 sophomores	CET-4	VKS	N/A	0.872
Zhen, 2007	50 juniors	TEM-4	VLT, VKS	0.357	0.453
Milton et al., 2010	30 EFL learners	IELTS	Self-developed test	0.68	0.55
Liu, 2016	127 sophomores	CET-4	VLT, WAT	0.729	0.619

Notes: The correlation coefficient ranges from −1 to 1, the greater the coefficient, the closer the correlation.

In brief, vocabulary knowledge has a strong correlation with the four skills and language proficiency based on the research above. This means that the more vocabulary students have, the more likely it is that they will perform better in the four skills and among various language proficiency tests. Also, the results above indicate that improving vocabulary is indispensable to develop good performances in language skills as well as language proficiency.

2.3 EFL Vocabulary Teaching and Learning in Chinese Universities

EFL vocabulary has been given little attention in Chinese universities. It was found that many university English teachers care little about vocabulary and believe that vocabulary learning should be done independently by students before or after the English class (Liu, 2018; Yang, 2013; Yang, 2018). He et al. (2017) explained that English teachers of Chinese universities have to distribute time to teach listening, speaking, reading, and writing skills within a limited 3-hour period per week. Consequently, little time or attention from English teachers is given to vocabulary.

Next, even if some teachers come to realize the importance of vocabulary, they mainly use traditional wordlists to teach students vocabulary in the university EFL classroom. Wang (2014) discovered that word list-based teaching was the most typical EFL vocabulary teaching method from grade three of elementary school to university. Similarly, English teachers mainly rely on the wordlists in English textbooks to teach vocabulary by directly translating without any context being given and then learners read after the teacher (Liu, 2015). This typical word list-based teaching may greatly influence students' methods of learning vocabulary. Such an influence has been confirmed in a survey by Zhang (2008), who found that reciting wordlists was ranked the most frequent vocabulary learning strategy among Chinese university students.

Under such teaching conditions, it is not surprising to find that vocabulary levels are low among Chinese college students. Wang (2010) revealed that the average size concerning receptive as well as productive vocabulary among Chinese non-English major sophomores was 3,174 words and 1,142 words, respectively. Later, Cai (2012) conducted a large-scale survey of vocabulary size covering 36 universities in 21 provinces of China with 6,625 first-year students. The results illustrated that the number of mean vocabulary size from university learners was 2,899 words. Furthermore, Tang and Yin (2015) demonstrated that the students' average size for receptive vocabulary and productive one was 3,945 and 3,045, respectively, among 76 non-English major freshmen. The vocabulary size of Chinese university students can be recognized as insufficient if it is compared with the requirement of 4,500 words for passing CET-4 in China (Yang, 2018) or the necessity of 8,000~9,000 word families in different English skills (Nation, 2006; Schmitt, 2010).

2.4 Vocabulary Learning Incidentally and Intentionally

Nation (2001) generally categorized vocabulary learning into two categories: learning vocabulary incidentally and learning vocabulary intentionally. Incidental vocabulary learning refers to the process of learning vocabulary unconsciously without attending to an individual word (Paribakht & Wesche, 1999). While intentional vocabulary learning is for learners to learn words consciously and on purpose, such as reciting a list of words from textbooks or vocabulary books (Barcroft, 2009).

2.4.1 Incidental Vocabulary Learning

Many studies examining differences between 2 approaches of learning vocabulary were reviewed by Krashen (1989), who found that learning vocabulary incidentally would make learners achieve more words than intentional vocabulary learning did since words in natural texts are encountered in a variety of contexts, which helps readers acquire their full semantic and syntactic properties. This claim is also supported by the following researchers: Coady and Huckin (1997); Gass (1999); and Nagy and Herman (1987).

However, the disadvantages of incidental vocabulary learning in EFL settings cannot be ignored. To learn new words in the contexts, such as reading context, the prerequisite is that a learner's vocabulary coverage of a text needs to be at least 95% ~ 98% for adequately comprehending the text (Hirsh & Nation, 1992; Hu & Nation, 2000; Laufer, 1989; Liu & Nation, 1985; Nation, 2001). This means that 3,000 word families at the minimum is needed for learners to understand the text independently (Coady, 1997; Laufer, 1989). Nevertheless, Nation (2006) argued an even higher threshold of 8,000 ~ 9,000 word families. Therefore, it is unlikely for learners with small vocabulary size to learn new words through contexts. Besides, Krashen (1987) found that learners must have already mastered a substantial core vocabulary for the settings to become the kind of "comprehensible input" that can facilitate incidental L2 vocabulary learning. Furthermore, the researchers (Hulstijn, 1992; Mondria & Wit-de Boer, 1991; Nation, 1982) pointed out that contextual information in the texts was puzzling sometimes which made EFL/L2 learners difficult to infer the correct meanings of strange words. Also, incidental L2 vocabulary learning emploied in texts yielded little favorable vocabulary gains (Elgort & Warren, 2014; Zahar, Cobb & Spada, 2001).

2.4.2 Intentional Vocabulary Learning

Intentional vocabulary learning is practical and necessary, especially in foreign language learning. Laufer (2003) revealed that learners could memorize L2 words' meanings better by being involved in word-focused tasks than with texts. Besides, Rosalia (2012) showed that the process of incidental vocabulary learning was slower, and the words to be learned were unpredictable in what time, or to what degree. Nevertheless, the process of intentional vocabulary learning is direct and fast, which could improve vocabulary learning. Besides, Nation (2013) argued that foreign language learners could not master a second language as they learn their mother tongues because of time shortage, millions of vocabulary items, and lacking of native language environment. Moreover, intentional vocabulary learning can fully activate students' attention. During the process of intentional vocabulary learning, attention can be activated by various ways, such as a word list learning, learners' discussion of words' meanings, words' elaboration, or words' spelling (Nation, 2013). Moreover, the positive influences of attention on learning vocabulary were mentioned by the studies (Boers et al., 2006; Laufer & Shmueli, 1997; Ramachandran & Rahim, 2004). Finally, the proponents of intentional vocabulary learning claimed that learners can keep a lot from what words they pay attention to in their minds (Laufer, 2003; Nation, 2007, 2013).

Therefore, intentional vocabulary learning is selected as the way of learning vocabulary for the study. Given the curriculum arrangement in the 2019 academic year, the college English course for the non-English major freshmen in the target university lasts for two hours a week, and no class time is specially arranged for students' vocabulary learning. Besides, the students also pay little attention to vocabulary outside the classroom (Zhang, 2008). As a result, they only pick up a few words by luck in the classroom. Next, the students stay in China all the time, not at the original states where native English language is used, and probably have no friends to practice English outside the classroom. This situation is further verified by Wei (2018), who found that Chinese EFL students do not equip with the advantages as first language speakers hold: learning words, phrases, their usages, and grammars by exposing themselves to the input almost anytime or anywhere. Thus, it is almost unlikely for EFL learners to acquire much vocabulary incidentally outside the classroom. Moreover, the vocabulary size of non-English major newcomers in the target university is around 2,000 words, which makes it almost impossible to implement incidental English vocabulary learning (Coady, 1997; Laufer, 1989; Nation, 2006). Under these circumstances, the intentional vocabulary learning is applied in the present study.

2.5 Vocabulary Retention

Vocabulary retention is defined by Maryam and Ahmad (2017) as the ability to remember or retain vocabulary in the memory. It has been shown that there is a close relationship between human memory and the mental ability to remember or retain information (Ellis, 1997; Stevick, 1996). Additionally, Ramezanali (2017) stated that memory is the mental capacity to retain, store, and retrieve past events, impressions, and facts.

Three Types of Memory: Zhang (2004) stated that memory would be separated into 3 types: sensory memory, short-term memory, and long-term memory, relying on its lasting time. Sensory memory is the shortest-lived memory that lasts for milliseconds to a few seconds (Zhang, 2004: 1). When the information lasts from several seconds to a few minutes, the memory is then called short-term memory (Zhang, 2004: 1). Short-term memory is responsible for allocating a limited amount of attention and temporarily holding information available for processing with limited capacity (Gathercole & Baddeley, 1993; Preston et al., 2010). In contrast, long-term memory lasts forever (Zhang, 2004). Sweller and Chandler (1994) indicated that there is no limitations for information storage capacity in the long-term memory.

Three Phases of Memory: Ramezanali (2017) claimed that there are three main phases in information processing and retrieval of memory: ① encoding or registration, which entails receiving, processing, and the combining of received information; ② storage of information, which encompasses creating a permanent information recording; ③ recalling or retrieving, which includes getting back the maintained information in response to some cues for use in a process or activity.

Spacing Effect: According to Kang (2016), the first study and subsequent review being spaced over time often results in learning better than the massive repetitions (the total time length being equal for both situations). This phenomenon is called the spacing effect or distributed practice effect. Also, the spacing effect in improving learning memory is better than massed repetitions. It has been demonstrated in the studies (Bird, 2010; Carpenter et al., 2012; Cepeda et al., 2006; Namaziandost et al., 2019; Rogers, 2015, 2017; Rohrer, 2015; Serrano & Huang, 2018).

Concerning vocabulary retention, Kachroo (1962) found that learners could retain new words by repeating the words seven times or more. Next, it was claimed that vocabulary retention required at least six or seven repetitions (Crothers & Suppes, 1967). Furthermore, it was recommended that learners needed to meet one word for five to sixteen times for acquiring it thoroughly, and frequent re-encountering of the word was crucial for their keeping the word in long-term memory (Nation, 1990, 2001). Furthermore, Oxford (1990) and Schmitt (2008) revealed that learners should re-encounter a word seven times for retention by intervals of fifteen minutes, an hour, two hours, one day, four days, a week, and 2 weeks after the first time learning. According to Daloglu et al. (2009), vocabulary can be stored in long-term retention when learners encounter the strange vocabulary for three times at least. Serrano and Huang (2018) found that reading the passage one time a week for five successive weeks (spaced practice) led to a longer retention of target words than reading it once every day for five successive days (intensive practice).

Ebbinghaus (1885) examined the information forgetting rate with time passing by, as shown in Figure 2.9 below. It depicts the rate at which information is forgotten over time, if there is no attempt to retain it, and demonstrates that information could be stored for a long term with little loss after four weeks. Later, the findings were confirmed concerning rapid forgetting and information retention in much research (e.g. Bahrick, 1992; Conway et al., 1992; Farjami & Aidinlou, 2013; Thalheimer, 2010). One effective way to prevent forgetting and improve retention is to review the information learned, which was proposed by the following researchers: Averell and Heathcote (2011); Dongale et al. (2018); Hu et al. (2013); Murre and Dros (2015); Namaziandost et al. (2019); Serrano and Huang (2018).

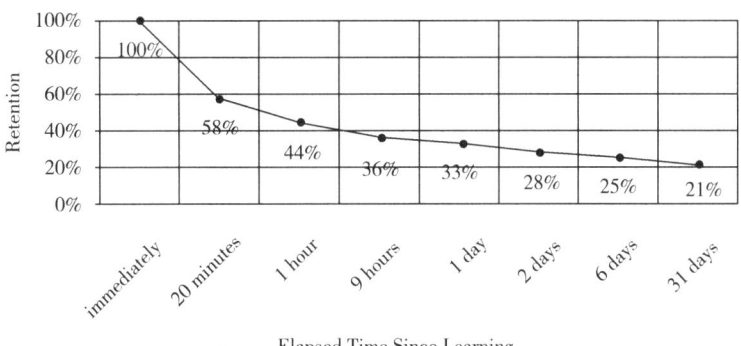

Figure 2.9 Ebbinghaus Forgetting Curve (Ebbinghaus, 1885)

Combined with the memory theory above and the curriculum schedule for the freshmen in the academic year 2019, the students reviewed the target words four times in one week at intervals of 9 hours, 1 day, 2 days and 6 days after their first-time encounter was arranged for the present study. Although repetitive vocabulary learning at intervals of 15 minutes, 1 hour, 2 hours seems to be reasonable based on Ebbinghaus Forgetting Curve (1885), it is almost impossible for the freshmen to review the vocabulary at the intervals above, for they have a 3 ~ 6 hours' course to attend each day for five successive days per week. Therefore, spaced review of vocabulary at intervals of 9 hours, 1 day, 2 days, and 6 days after their first-time learning was considered appropriate and practical for the freshmen in the present study. Secondly, to measure vocabulary retention, a delayed-post-test was done out 4 weeks after the post-test in the study. The reason for the 4-week interval between the 2 tests above was that the information kept in the human memory is lost little and can be stored stably in long-term retention (Ebbinghaus, 1885).

Techniques for Improving Vocabulary Retention: For enhancing vocabulary retention in long-term memory, several techniques are provided, which aim at the three types and phases of memory (Ramezanali, 2017; Zhang, 2004) above.

Firstly, to arouse learners' attention of the target word and encoding it in their minds, imagery and verbal representations of the word are presented. Also, recall can be enhanced by showing the word with dual channels of visual and verbal forms rather than showing it in a single channel, which would find support from dual coding theory (Clark & Paivio, 1991) and from the cognitive theory of multimedia learning (Mayer, 2014).

Next, according to Groot (2000), the contexts, even the sentence context, can better facilitate learning and retention of the word than without any context.

Finally, retrieval practice, also known as the practice effect, measures not only the student's knowledge but also his/her strengths (Karpicke & Roediger, 2008). Whenever information is retrieved or recalled from memory once, then the knowledge is strengthened, as knowledge recalling practice can enhance one's ability of getting it back in the future (Karpicke & Roediger, 2008; Karpicke & Zaromb, 2010). According to Brown et al. (2014), repeated retrieval makes memories more durable and creates knowledge that can be retrieved more efficiently in multiple settings. Additionally, Carey (2015) stated that when knowledge was retrieved successfully, neural paths to the information were strengthened, and additional paths formed. As a result, the recall of the information is faster and easier in the future. Many studies have revealed that information that was practiced through retrieval was better retained than those that were not (e.g. Barcroft, 2006; Carrier & Pashler, 1992; Reimer, 2019; Rickard & Pan, 2018; Roediger & Butler, 2011).

2.6 Mobile-assisted Language Learning

According to Church and Oliver (2011), the term "mobile" is associated with "on-the-move". Based on Brown et al. (2014), the term "mobile" includes several aspects that refer to devices for communication, to the ones for delivering learning or training, and to the movement from the fixed learning to portable learning.

Mobile Learning (M-Learning) is a widely accepted term for using mobile technologies to assist learning. Rajan and Kumar (2014) defined M-Learning as the acquisition of knowledge and skill through using mobile technology anytime, anywhere that result in alteration of behavior. The cardinal aspect of M-Learning, which separates it from any previous form of learning is that learning is no longer confined by location and time (MacCallum, 2009). Learning anywhere and anytime is made possible by the portability of mobile devices as well as mobile technologies (Chen & Hsu, 2008; Peters, 2007; Soleimani et al., 2014). Some studies (e.g. Geddes, 2004; Hockly, 2013; Kukulska-Hulme & Shield, 2008; Sandberg et al., 2011) have found that M-Learning can assist learners to learn different subjects at the time and place they prefer, also allowing for both informal and formal learning.

According to Kukulska-Hulme and Shield (2008), the sub-area of M-Learning, where mobile technologies are used exclusively for assisting language learning, is defined as Mobile-assisted Language Learning (MALL). The term MALL describes an approach to language learning that is assisted or enhanced through the use of a handheld mobile device (Valarmathi, 2011: 2). Viberg and Grönlund (2012) claimed that MALL refers to using mobile technologies as supplements for making language learning better. Later, MALL was redefined by Kukulska-Hulme (2013) as the use of mobile technologies in language learning, especially in situations where device portability offers specific advantages. Chen (2013) defined MALL as a formal or an informal learning of foreign languages with the aid from mobile devices.

In the present study, MALL is regarded as one process of learning languages with the help from mobile devices, mobile technologies, or learners' mobility.

Kukulska-Hulme (2009) claimed that the differing advantages of MALL from learning language by a traditional way are the portability and the mobility, creating countless learning chances. This viewpoint was supported by Jee (2011), who stated that portability and easy access to the Internet through mobile devices enable learners to be exposed to second or foreign language resources anytime and anywhere, which would facilitate language learning.

Firstly, MALL can provide a variety of multimedia, such as texts, pictures, sounds, animations and videos by easy access to the Internet, allowing for creating authentic, meaningful vocabulary learning environments, which not only stimulate learners' motivation and interest but also help them understand words easily, resulting in good vocabulary learning and retention (Al-Seghayer, 2016; Gonulal, 2019; Govindasamy et al., 2019; Mayer, 1997; Ramezanali, 2017; Wang, 2015).

Secondly, the time and space flexibility of using mobile devices enables students to choose convenient time for vocabulary learning anywhere since their amount of classroom time is limited. Therefore, learners who can use MALL have an opportunity to learn and retain their vocabulary knowledge whenever and wherever they want (Cheung, 2012; Kiliçkaya, 2007).

Furthermore, the immediate feedback offered by MALL can facilitate vocabulary learning with the increase of cognitive involvement load (Hulstijn & Laufer, 2001), by helping learners store the correct meanings as well as forms of words in their minds (Henderson, 2019; Soria et al., 2020; Sprenger, 2018). The cognitive involvement load hypothesis (Hulstijn & Laufer, 2001) indicates that how well a word is learnt depends upon cognitive processing degree needed for a task. Hence, the more cognitive involvement the students have in MALL, the better the performance they can achieve in vocabulary learning.

In addition, it has been found that mobile devices have positive effects on L2 vocabulary acquisition, such as improving vocabulary learning with flashcards of mobile phones (Basoglu & Akdmir, 2010), learning more English idioms via Short Message Service of mobile phones (Hayat, Jalilifar & Mashhadi, 2013), and enhancing students' engagement in vocabulary learning through smartphones (Wu, 2015).

Another advantage is that mobile devices can deliver information ubiquitously through mobile technologies (Younus, 2014). Many studies find that mobile devices are quite convenient for students' usage no matter inside or outside the classroom and they facilitate remote participation in language learning (e. g. Godwin-Jones, 2008; Huang et al., 2012; Kukulska-Hulme, 2006; Miangah & Nezarat, 2012).

Last advantage of MALL is the potential of learning language personally, spontaneously, and informally based on many studies (e. g. Jaris & Krashen, 2014; Olmsted & Terry, 2014; Stockwell & Hubbard, 2013; Viberg & Grönlund, 2012). In the next section, the research on MALL is reviewed.

2.6.1 Research on Mobile-assisted Language Learning

The research on MALL is reviewed by means of different impacts of MALL on listening (Azar & Nasiri, 2014; Kim, 2013; Zhang, 2014), reading (Hazaea & Alzubi, 2016; Leila & Mehry, 2016), speaking (Ana & Anna, 2015; Hadi & Emzir, 2016; Saran et al., 2009; Sun et al., 2017), and writing (Al-Wasy & Mahdi, 2016; Chen et al., 2017; Ebadi & Rahimi, 2017).

2.6.1.1 Effects of MALL on Listening

To demonstrate the effects of MALL on EFL listening skills, Kim (2013) conducted an empirical study among Korean non-English major students. Twenty students from the experiment group listened to authentic listening materials twice a week through a smartphone app of an English radio broadcast out of class for ten weeks while those in the control group were not. On week 14, all participants took the post-test of TOEIC like in the pretest. What was found was that the experiment group students obtained higher marks on the listening section than those peers of the control group did. Besides, it was concluded that it could be effective for improving EFL learners' listening by apps of smartphones outside the classroom.

Azar and Nasiri (2014) examined the effects of MALL on listening skills in an Iranian EFL setting. Thirty-five EFL college students formed an experiment group, and thirty-five counterparts formed a control group at random. The experiment lasted for a period of 16 sessions in one term, and the single difference between them above was that the experiment group used audiobooks to assist their English listening learning outside classroom, but another group did not. As a result, in the post-test, the experiment group got higher mean than another group, and impacts of audiobooks on the mobile phone on listening comprehension were shown to be statistically significant.

Zhang (2016) explored if employing mobile technology could facilitate EFL students' listening ability. 120 Chinese university students were divided randomly into two groups: one experiment group (60 students) practicing extensive listening through mobile phone apps after class and the other control group (60 students) practicing listening via the traditional method of listening to a CD-ROM after class. After a ten-week experiment, all participants took a listening comprehension in a post-test. As a result, on the listening comprehension post-test, the app group outperformed the control group greatly.

In short, the mobile apps or audiobooks of mobile phones can be more effective than traditional methods in improving EFL learners' listening skills outside the classroom. Therefore, mobile technologies can be useful instruments in fully using students' after-class time to enhance their listening.

2.6.1.2 Effects of MALL on Reading

Hazaea and Alzubi (2016) explored what effects on EFL learners' reading through mobile technologies among Saudi Arabian college EFL students. An EFL reading class of 30 college students was encouraged to use their mobile phones to help them with reading inside and outside the classroom. During the treatment of fourteen weeks, the classroom observations, self-reflection journals, and semi-structured interviews were used to collect data. It was highlighted that the students' reading practices improved considerably after using their mobile phones. And it was proposed that in a Saudi Arabian EFL context, shifting from the traditional reading way to a stress-free reading way in MALL environment could be conducted gradually.

Leila and Mehry (2016) conducted a study for probing the impact of MALL on learners' reading comprehension by randomly assigning twenty students to each group: one control group and one experiment group in an Iranian EFL context. During the twenty-session experiment, the control group did reading practice by a pencil and a paper, but the experiment group did the same by mobile phones. It was found that MALL had significantly positive influences on learners' reading comprehension of the experiment group.

These studies found that MALL could enhance learners' reading comprehension more effectively than a traditional way of paper and pencil whether it was conducted inside or outside the EFL classroom (Hazaea & Alzubi, 2016; Leila & Mehry, 2016).

2.6.1.3 Effects of MALL on Speaking

Saran et al. (2009) investigated the potentials and effectiveness of using mobile phones on EFL learners' pronunciation using a mixed method. Twenty-four university EFL learners at elementary level were selected as participants and then separated into three groups with a different mode: handouts, web pages, and mobile phones. For four weeks, the students attended classes regularly with one mode (mobile phones/web pages/ handouts) to improve their pronunciation. It was showed that the mobile phone group increased by 11.94% and the other two groups increased by 6.81% for pronunciation performances. Furthermore, the interviewees responded that they holding mobile phones preferred to save and review information for pronunciation practice later than their peers in the other two groups. The researchers proposed that using mobile phones could increase learners' motivations in learning and reviewing English materials.

Ana and Anna (2015) explored the effects of MALL on EFL students' accuracy and fluency in oral production with a mobile app named VISP (Videos for Speaking) among Spanish college EFL students. 16 Spanish college EFL learners with an intermediate English proficiency were chosen to learn how to use the mobile app for practicing their speaking whenever it was convenient. As a result, the accuracy and fluency of all the students were improved after using the mobile app VISP. Also, they all declared that the mobile app VISP made them realize the significance of accuracy in using vocabulary (100%), of considering the audience (100%) as well as their language learning (100%), and 90% of students believed that the mobile app helped them realize the close relationship between the way of communication and the way of perceiving things (90%).

Hadi and Emzir (2016) carried out an action research to investigate how to improve English speaking proficiency via the MALL among Indonesian EFL college students. Thirty second-year English major students in an Indonesian university participated in the research in three cycles in which they were required to use smartphones to practice speaking and find help. The result was that an improvement in speaking could be seen from the increased scores in the preliminary stage, the first cycle, the second cycle, and the third cycle, respectively. In addition, MALL increased the students' involvement in speaking, which was characterized by the responses they gave to teachers, the questions they asked, and finding answers via their smartphones independently.

Sun et al. (2017) probed into the impact of MALL on English speaking among young Chinese EFL learners. One first-grade EFL class in an elementary school was named as the experiment group and the other one as the control group. The experiment group used Social Networking Sites (SNS) on mobile phones to practice English speaking, while the control group did not. In the speaking post-test, achievements concerning English fluency with the experiment group were more substantial. The reason for this may be found from one specific strength of SNS for mobile learning could situate learners to speak with low or zero stress.

In brief, MALL can positively facilitate EFL learners' pronunciation or speaking by increasing their motivation and review (Saran et al., 2009), by improving their awareness towards the importance of vocabulary accuracy, their audience and the method of communication (Ana & Anna, 2015), by forcing them to become more involved in asking questions (Hadi & Emzir, 2016), and by enabling them to speak more in low-stress and situated contexts (Sun et al., 2017).

2.6.1.4 Effects of MALL on Writing

Al-Wasy and Mahdi (2016) explored the influences of mobile phones' usage on writing in a Saudi Arabian EFL context. During the four-week treatment, the students had one session of two hours every week. In the session, one of the four areas in the mobile app White Smoke: grammatical errors editing, spelling errors editing, punctuation errors editing, and capitalization errors editing, was taught. After the treatment, in the fifth week, the subjects had to compose a paragraph and then edited their paragraphs by using the traditional method of self-editing. In the sixth week, they wrote down a paragraph and edited their paragraphs by using the mobile app. Every participant had to submit two drafts (first and last) of his paragraph using the traditional method and the mobile app. According to the analysis, the student's ability in self-editing improved two aspects: grammar and punctuation after using the mobile app. This study encouraged EFL teachers to engage students in as many self-editing activities as possible employing MALL.

Ebadi and Rahimi (2017) examined the impact of using MALL on learners' writing performance among Iranian college EFL students. 60 students comprised a control group and another 60 peers comprised an experiment group. The experiment group received the writing instructions via a mobile phone app as a writing enhancement, but the control group was instructed with a traditional way. An independent-samples t-test detected a huge difference in writing performance between the two groups. Thus, mobile-assisted writing instructions can positively affect students' writing and result in better performance in writing and spelling. The reasons may be due to factors such as increased motivation in using the mobile app, the interesting and appropriate design of the mobile app, and the more time that students spent on their cell-phones than their counterparts in the control group.

Chen et al. (2017) explored how using scaffolding influenced young English Language Learners' (ELLs) writing skills through an app (Penultimate) on iPad in the USA. Five ELLs (2 boys and 3 girls, aged 9 ~ 13) participated in the four weeks' writing project assisted by mobile technologies. During the narration writing, the participants composed one pre-essay with paper and pen. A week later, they finished the post writing tasks with a writing app: iPad 2 and Penultimate. After all tasks were finished, an informal interview was conducted for every participant to share his/her thoughts or feelings within fifteen minutes. The findings suggested that the English language learners' writing ability and learning motivation were much improved with the mobile technologies.

To sum up, MALL would enhance EFL students' writing abilities positively by increasing their engagement in writing (Al-Wasy & Mahdi, 2016) and arousing their motivation and interest in writing (Chen et al., 2017; Ebadi & Rahimi, 2017), whether they are young students or university students. Thus, the research reviewed above supports the use of MALL to improve EFL learning with regard to listening, reading, speaking, and writing skills.

2.6.2 Students' Perceptions of Mobile-assisted Language Learning

The definition of "perception" is "the ability to see, hear, or become aware of something through the senses" from the Oxford dictionary of American English (2014).

As for the perceptions of MALL, its main components include attitudes towards using, continued intention to use, perceived convenience, perceived ease of use, and perceived usefulness in terms of Chang et al. (2012) and Davis (1989).

Steel (2012) explored how using mobile apps affects EFL students' language learning. It was found that students perceived mobile apps as convenient, portable, and on-the-go learning. Also, students exhibited more content with low cost or free mobile apps.

Kim and Altmann (2013) examined the influences of employing mobile devices on learners' perceptions. 53 MA students for TESOL were surveyed, and it was disclosed that learning language through mobile devices offered them a new learning experience.

Faqe (2015) investigated how mobile apps influenced students learning English in a Japanese university. As a result, most students had positive perceptions of learning English with mobile apps, which found support from the studies (Dashti & Aldashti, 2015; Fujimoto, 2012; White & Mills, 2012).

Zhang (2016) explored Chinese students' perceptions of MALL with two instruments: an interview and a questionnaire. According to the responses from the questionnaire, 88% of the participants regarded mobile-assisted listening learning as quite convenient. 85% of participants considered that usage of mobile apps indeed stimulated them to learn English and to practice more. Also, they reported that using mobile apps increased their interest in English, changed their attitude towards learning, and developed their confidence. From the interview responses, the respondents showed that they were willing to make more efforts in listening via a mobile app, and MALL also enabled them to control their learning better.

However, different perceptions of MALL were identified. In order to find students' in-depth perceptions of mobile-assisted learning, Barbour et al. (2014) collected data through a survey and an interview with six students, and revealed that they dislike learning with mobile phones. In addition, Dukic, Chiu, and Lo (2015) examined how university learners in Hong Kong and Japan perceived smartphones as learning tools. They found that learners employed smartphones mainly as entertainment, socializing, communication, and quick searching for their information needs in daily life. Moreover, the students commented that it was useful and easy for them to employ smartphones to do simple tasks:

taking notes, assignments' discussion with peers, searching course materials and information. Nevertheless, they perceived that it was not suitable for using smartphones to do academic writing and reading with needing much attention.

Furthermore, the small size of the smartphone screen was considered as an obstacle for using a smartphone to learn a language. The research disclosed that the size of a smartphone screen was too small for learners to write and read academic papers concentratedly (Stockwell, 2010; Woodcock et al., 2012). Additionally, most students found that they used smartphones mostly on-the-go and outside the classroom, but it would not suitable for students' serious learning in the environment above (Faqe, 2015; Godwin-Jones, 2011; Steel, 2012). So they were more willing to do academic work with computers or by a paper-based method in a quiet environment (Stockwell, 2008).

2.6.3 Research on EFL Vocabulary Learning and Retention via MALL

The research on the effects of MALL on EFL vocabulary learning or retention is reviewed with regard to the effectiveness of SMS (Alemi et al., 2012; Cavus & Ibrahim, 2009; Kim, 2011; Motallebzadeh et al., 2011; Ornprapat & Wiwat, 2015; Tatabaei & Goojani, 2012; Zhang, 2011), mobile phones (Azabdaftati & Mozaheb, 2012; Başoğlu & Akdemir, 2010; Nikoopour et al., 2014), WhatsApp (Basal et al., 2016; Bensalem, 2018; Dehghan et al., 2017; Jafari & Chalak, 2016), and self-developed mobile apps (Agca & Özdemir, 2013; Makoe & Shandu, 2018; Ou-Yang & Wu, 2017; Wu, 2015).

2.6.3.1 Short Message Service (SMS)

Cavus and Ibrahim (2009) explored the potential of using SMS to learn English words in an EFL context in Turkey by selecting 45 college non-English major freshmen as subjects. During the nine-day treatment, forty-five students received and learned word pairs through SMS every half an hour daily between 9 a.m. and 5 p.m. The result of a paired-samples t-test demonstrated that students did better in the post-test than in the pretest ($p < 0.05$).

Motallebzadeh et al. (2011) explored the effect of using SMS of mobile phones on English collocations' learning of Iranian EFL learners with forty college EFL students as subjects. During the five-week treatment, the experiment group of twenty students received and learned seven collocations with descriptions and examples through SMS twice a week outside the classroom while the control group with the other twenty counterparts received and learned the same number of collocations using a paper-based method in the classroom. After an analysis of the post-test, it was found that the SMS group students significantly achieved more than their peers of the paper-based group, indicating that using SMS exhibited a facilitating impact on English collocations' learning.

Kim (2011) probed into the impact of employing SMS on English words' learning in a Korean EFL context by choosing sixty-two non-English major students as subjects. During the six-week treatment, the 21 students in the control group learned thirty English words only in class every week, while the 41 counterparts of two experiment groups got 2 text messages with the same number of target words through the SMS every week after class. Moreover, the difference between the first experiment group with 21 students and the second experiment group with 20 counterparts was related to interactivity. In detail, the first experiment group students only received and did not send any text messages back, while the second experiment group peers got and sent texts to answer quizzes. With one-way ANOVA, it was found that there was a statistically significant difference in vocabulary achievements between the three groups, and the two experiment groups showed considerably more improvement in their vocabulary learning than the control group. Additionally, the second experiment group with interactivity via SMS achieved significantly higher means than those in experiment group one without it. Furthermore, according to the students' responses to the survey, the benefits of using SMS were listed as follows: repetition, easiness, immediate accessibility, learning words effectively in their spare time and without effort. Its drawbacks were also discussed. For example, students said it was almost impossible to read text messages in busy hours. It caused problems because of receiving many text messages at the same time, and it limited the saving capacity of their mobile phones.

Zhang et al. (2011) examined the effectiveness of EFL vocabulary learning and retention via SMS of mobile phones among Chinese college EFL students with 78 non-English major sophomores as subjects. During the twenty-six-day period, the experiment group with 40 students learned five English words every day via SMS after class, while the

38 counterparts received 130 words on paper sheets at the beginning and learned them in a self-regulated way outside the classroom. From the post-test, it was found that learners of experiment group attained more words than their peers of control group. However, by means of an analysis of the delayed post-test, little difference was detected in vocabulary retention between the two groups. According to the students' self-reports in the experiment group, the advantages of vocabulary learning via SMS were that it made full use of fragmented time, and it was also convenient and motivating. The disadvantages were as follows. Firstly, the memory capacity of mobile phones was usually restrained for storing too many received words. Next, even worse, when messages were too many for the memory capacity, dysfunction would appear frequently. For example, phonetic symbols could not be operated on the phones. Thirdly, long messages were likely to be sent as separate shorter ones. When the number of words in a message exceeded the limitation, the system would divide the message into separate mini-messages. Furthermore, those mini-messages were received usually out of order, which confused and annoyed the students. Finally, reviewing the text messages could be troublesome, because it would consume students' much time to find previous messages, especially difficult for those receiving many different kinds of messages every day.

Alemi et al. (2012) conducted an investigation on the impact of SMS on learning vocabulary as well as its retention by choosing forty-five Iranian college non-English major newcomers as subjects. During the sixteen-week treatment, 28 students in the experiment group received and learned ten headwords with definitions (both in L1: Persian and L2: English) and example sentences via SMS every session in class for two sessions a week. In contrast, 17 students in the control group learned the same headwords by looking them up in a dictionary independently during the same period in class. The results showed that the mean ($M = 25.17$) of the post-test got by experiment group was higher than that ($M = 22.64$) from control group, but little difference between two groups was seen. However, the delayed post-test demonstrated a significant difference between them, suggesting that the SMS group retained better than the control group.

Tabatabaei and Goojani (2012) explored the impact of using SMS of mobile phones on vocabulary learning by selecting 60 Iranian senior high school students as subjects. During the six weeks of treatment, thirty students sent a message with target words to the teacher, and the teacher provided them with feedback through SMS. Next, the students also had to deliver one message with a sentence to three partners some time before they came to class. The other 30 counterparts finished the same assignments but on paper. From an analysis of the post-test, the experiment group obtained a significantly better result on the vocabulary than the control group.

Ornprapat and Wiwat (2015) examined the effects of using SMS of mobile phones to complete vocabulary exercises on vocabulary acquisition in the Thailand EFL context. Forty freshmen were assigned to the experiment group and 40 counterparts to the control group. During the six weeks of treatment, the control group wrote vocabulary exercises on paper, including 100 words in class, while the other group did those vocabulary exercises through SMS, then sent them to the teacher's mobile phone after class. From the analysis of the post-test, the vocabulary means of the SMS-based group were significantly higher than that of the paper-based group.

To sum up, the studies found that using SMS of mobile phones was helpful for learning EFL vocabulary inside or outside the classroom in different EFL contexts (Alemi et al., 2012; Cavus & Ibrahim, 2009; Kim, 2011; Motallebzadeh et al., 2011; Ornprapat & Wiwat, 2015; Tabatabaei & Goojani, 2012; Zhang et al., 2011). Next, most of the subjects in the studies are college EFL students from all majors. Only one study (Tabatabaei & Goojani, 2012) comprises senior high school students. Furthermore, what most studies focused on were only the effects of SMS on vocabulary learning. Only two studies not only investigated the impact of applying SMS to vocabulary learning but also to vocabulary retention in the long term (Alemi et al., 2012; Zhang et al., 2011). However, they obtained contrary results in the post-test and delayed post-test. Yet the drawbacks, such as the cost of SMS, limited memory capacity, and dysfunction, as mentioned in the studies of Azabdaftati and Mozaheb (2012) and Zhang et al. (2011) should not be overlooked when using SMS to assist vocabulary learning.

2.6.3.2 Mobile Phones as Platforms

Başoğlu and Akdemir (2010) compared the effects of learning vocabulary by way of paper flashcards and of mobile phones among Turkish college EFL students. During the six weeks period, the experiment group of 30 students learned about 1,000 words outside the classroom through the app, ECTACO Flashcards on the mobile phone, while the control group of another 30 counterparts learned the same number of words with paper flashcards after class. From an analysis of the post-test, mobile phones did better on enhancing EFL learners' vocabulary than paper flashcards.

Azabdaftati and Mozaheb (2012) explored what method to assist vocabulary learning more effectively: a mobile phone-based method or a flashcard-based method among Iranian university EFL students. During the seven weeks, forty English major freshmen in the experiment group learned about 1,200 new words through the app SRS (Spaced Repetition System) and SMS of the mobile phone while forty peers learned the same words by paper flashcards inside and outside the classroom. It was found that the students in the experiment group achieved more than the counterparts in the control group on the post-test, suggesting that mobile technologies (the app SRS and SMS) are more effective in assisting students' vocabulary learning than paper flashcards.

Nikoopour et al. (2014) explored the effects of vocabulary learning when mobile phone-based, computer-based, and paper-based flashcards served as tools among Iranian college English major students. During the ten weeks of treatment, 36 students learned seventy words from TOEFL & IELTS every week in paper-based flashcards inside the classroom, 36 counterparts learned the same words through online flashcards of the computer inside the classroom, while 37 peers learned the same words via mobile phone-based flashcards outside the classroom. Using the one-way ANOVA test on the post-test, the mobile phone-based group outperformed the computer-based group in the post-test on vocabulary acquisition. Compared with the computer-based group, students from the paper-based group achieved better results. However, there was no significant difference in the post-test between the mobile phone-based group and the paper-based group. It might have something to do with the inconvenience of not taking flashcards everywhere, while the mobile-based group students and the paper-based group ones benefitted a lot from the portability and ubiquity.

To summarize, mobile phones used as platforms for improving vocabulary teaching and learning have been approved inside/outside the classroom compared to the paper-based methods in the studies (Azabdaftati & Mozaheb, 2012; Başoğlu & Akdemir, 2010). Nevertheless, Nikoopour et al. (2014) found that the mobile phone-based method did not demonstrate any more benefits than the paper-based method in assisting vocabulary learning.

2.6.3.3 WhatsApp and Self-developed Mobile Apps

Basal et al. (2016) investigated the role of WhatsApp of mobile phones in learning vocabulary among Turkish EFL students by choosing 50 first-year college students as subjects. During the four weeks of treatment, the experiment group of twenty-five students received and learned ten idioms with meanings, example sentences and exercises through WhatsApp in the classroom every week, while the control group of another twenty-five counterparts received and learned the same idioms using a paper-based method in the classroom. From an analysis of the post-test, the experiment group obtained better results in vocabulary tests than the control group, which suggested that teaching idioms for EFL learners was effective by WhatsApp.

Jafari and Chalak (2016) explored how WhatsApp affected vocabulary learning by selecting 60 Iranian junior high school students as subjects. During four weeks, 30 students in the experiment group received vocabulary instructions through WhatsApp four days a week, while 30 counterparts in the control group were taught the same vocabulary inside the classroom by the traditional paper-based method. From an analysis of the post-test, it was found that the students with WhatsApp performed better on vocabulary acquisition than their counterparts in the control group and that there was not a substantial difference on their performances between females and males students.

Dehghan et al. (2017) studied how WhatsApp impacted vocabulary teaching in an Iranian EFL context by selecting 32 teenaged students as subjects. The experiment group of 16 students received instruction by means of a vocabulary list through WhatsApp on their smartphones, while the control group of another 16 counterparts received the same vocabulary list through traditional textbooks in the classroom. With an independent-samples t-test, it was found that few differences on vocabulary acquisition existed between two groups. According to the researchers, this might be attributable to several reasons. The first reason may be that students could not control their process of learning vocabulary because of WhatsApp nature with the flood of irrelevant or nonsensical messages, posts, links or chatting and listening to music, that easily distracted them from learning the vocabulary. The second reason could be related to the reputation of WhatsApp as an entertainment and communication app. According to Church and de Olivia (2013), social networks such as WhatsApp were assumed by many teachers and students as informal communication devices which were not suitable for formal learning in educational settings. Finally, the limited number of students and of words might impact the results' difference from two groups.

Bensalem (2018) explored the impact of WhatsApp of mobile phones on vocabulary learning in a Saudi Arabian EFL context with forty college students as subjects. During the six weeks, both groups were offered 120 words for six weeks to learn with 20 words per week. The experiment group of 21 students received word lists via WhatsApp, while the control group of 19 counterparts was given printed copies of the same word lists in class. From an analysis of the post-test, it was found that the WhatsApp group learned significantly more words than the control group.

Agca and Özdemir (2013) investigated how two-dimensional (2D) barcode technology affected vocabulary learning among Gazi college EFL students. During the two weeks of treatment, forty students were selected to learn 84 words independently in the classroom by scanning a 2D barcode on the pages of an English book with a smartphone that could display the words' definitions and images. Using a paired-samples t-test, the 2D barcode of mobile phones could greatly increase the students' vocabulary and facilitated their learning of new words.

Wu (2015) examined the effectiveness of a self-developed app on a smartphone on learning EFL words among EFL students of China universities by selecting 50 non-English major sophomores as subjects. During the one semester experiment, students of 2 groups were taught 852 words as they appeared in the different units, the glossary and the appendix of the students' textbooks during classes. The only difference was that the 25 students in the experiment group could review the words with the mobile app Word-Learning developed by the researcher, while the other 25 counterparts of control group could not access it. Later, it was demonstrated that learners of experiment group obtained higher scores in post-test than their control group peers.

Ou-Yang and Wu (2017) studied how employing a self-developed mobile app:

MyEVA influenced vocabulary learning among university EFL students in Taiwan. 55 English majors and 53 non-English majors were selected as participants to learn fifty words from a TOEIC vocabulary list with the mobile app (MyEVA) in two weeks. Using a t-test and one-way ANOVA, it was found that the mobile app significantly enhanced the vocabulary acquisition of both majors, and achievements of English majors were greater than those from non-English majors.

Makoe and Shandu (2018) designed a smartphone app (VocUp) for enhancing South African university EFL students' vocabulary learning in an open distance learning context. Firstly, they developed the app VocUp in terms of a design-based research methodology. Then, the app VocUp was tested among 29 first-year university students. According to 18 interviewees' responses, the results showed its benefits in vocabulary content, ease of use, being familiar with smartphone systems, and prompt feedback. Despite the benefits above, some difficulties were experienced, for example, problems with the phones, issues of the network connection, lacking knowledge of phone usage.

To summarize, WhatsApp is a social communication app. Language learners would often choose not to use or are very reluctant to use the target language via social communication apps for fear of not being understood by others (Alm, 2013; Chen, 2013). Furthermore, there are few studies (e.g. Agca & Özdemir, 2013; Makoe & Shandu, 2018; Ou-Yang & Wu, 2017; Wu, 2015) developing mobile apps for vocabulary learning, and what they focused on was only the impact of mobile apps on vocabulary learning, but not on vocabulary retention. Additionally, the mobile apps above lack of theoretical support concerning vocabulary learning and memory. Although there may be mobile apps for vocabulary learning in other countries, it is almost impossible for Chinese learners to connect to Google and get access to the apps due to the policy of the government for accessing to applications in overseas app stores. Therefore, in order to fill these gaps, a mobile app was developed based on four theories relevant to vocabulary learning as well as retention, and its effects were tested among Chinese EFL learners.

2.6.3.4 Conclusions on the Research about Mobile-assisted Language Learning

Most of the studies have proved that to teach and learn vocabulary can be better facilitated via mobile phones or mobile technologies compared to traditional methods of paper-based or textbook-based study inside/outside the classroom (Azabdaftati & Mozaheb, 2012; Başoğlu & Akdemir, 2010; Basal et al., 2016; Bensalem, 2018; Jafari & Chalak, 2016; Kim, 2011; Motallebzadeh et al., 2011; Ornprapat & Wiwat, 2015; Ou-Yang & Wu, 2017; Tabatabaei & Goojani, 2012; Wu, 2014). What's more, the studies which explored learners' attitudes towards mobile-assisted vocabulary learning show that they held positive views, and such words as "convenient, effective, available, entertaining" are often used to describe their attitudes (Azabdaftati & Mozaheb, 2012; Agca & Özdemir, 2013; Başoğlu & Akdemir, 2010; Bensalem, 2018; Cavus & Ibrahim, 2009; Motallebzadeh et al., 2011; Nikoopour et al., 2014; Ornprapat & Wiwat, 2015; Tabatabaei & Goojani, 2012).

Firstly, some research studies showed that students did not perform better on vocabulary learning via MALL than their counterparts who used traditional methods of paper-based or textbook-based study (Alemi et al., 2012; Dehghan et al., 2017; Nikoopour et al., 2014; Zhang et al., 2011). However, these results were not consistent with the findings of most studies (e.g. Azabdaftati & Mozaheb, 2012; Başoğlu & Akdemir, 2010; Basal et al., 2016; Bensalem, 2018; Jafari & Chalak, 2016; Kim, 2011; Motallebzadeh et al, 2011; Ornprapat & Wiwat, 2015; Ou-Yang & Wu, 2017; Tabatabaei & Goojani, 2012; Wu, 2014).

Secondly, few studies have explored the effects of mobile technologies on vocabulary retention, but those that have studied retention obtained completely opposite results (Alemi et al., 2012; Zhang et al., 2011). According to Thornbury (2002), learning is, in fact, remembering. Thus, vocabulary learning is actually vocabulary retention. So for further understanding of the effects of mobile technologies, both vocabulary learning and vocabulary retention are included in the present study.

Thirdly, few researchers (Agca & Özdemir, 2013; Makoe & Shandu, 2018; Ou-Yang & Wu, 2017; Wu, 2015) have developed mobile apps especially for vocabulary learning, or showed their benefits in facilitating vocabulary learning, except that Makoe and Shandu (2018) did not explore the app's effectiveness. Nevertheless, EFL learners' perceptions of vocabulary learning via mobile apps were explored only by Agca and

Özdemir (2013). Furthermore, according to Afzali et al. (2017) and Burston (2013), studies on the effects of self-developed mobile apps on EFL vocabulary learning are still rare in an EFL context, and EFL learners' perceptions of mobile apps need to be further explored.

The present study proposes to fill the gaps above. It also aims to use mobile apps as a means for improving vocabulary learning and retention, as well as to test its effects. In addition, the students' perceptions of mobile apps are explored, for their perceptions of the apps have a direct influence on their language learning (Yu, 2019).

2.7 Summary

Chapter two presents an overall picture of the present state of research on vocabulary learning and retention and the effectiveness of mobile apps for vocabulary use through a review of the literature related to a theoretical framework, vocabulary knowledge as well as retention, Mobile-assisted Language Learning (MALL), and EFL vocabulary learning and retention via MALL. Firstly, the theoretical framework is presented to provide theoretical support for the present study. Next, vocabulary knowledge, including vocabulary definitions, the two dimensions of vocabulary knowledge, and related research, are introduced. Then, incidental and intentional vocabulary learning are demonstrated and these are followed by vocabulary retention. Additionally, MALL is presented, and related studies on MALL are reviewed. Finally, the research on EFL vocabulary learning, as well as vocabulary retention via MALL, is presented and the present gaps are pointed out.

Research Methodology

This chapter introduces the methodology used in the present study. It starts with the research design, and then introduces the population and samples of the study, the research instruments, and the procedure of the experiment, which is followed by the data collection and the data analysis. Finally, it concludes with a summary.

3.1 Research Design

The current study aims to investigate the effects of using a mobile app on EFL learners' vocabulary learning and retention, and also to explore their perceptions of the mobile app.

According to Creswell and Creswell (2017), for an experiment in which only a convenient sample is possible, and when subjects are not randomly assigned, the procedure is called a quasi-experiment. The researchers (Charles & Mertler, 2002; Thomas, 2003; Wiersma & Jurs, 2005) agreed that a quasi-experiment is a kind of experimental research for dealing with the relationship between cause and effect. It might compare outcomes for one group receiving program tasks with outcomes for another similar group not receiving program tasks (Moore, 2008). A quasi-experimental design is applied in the present study because the purpose of this research was to explore the effects of the mobile app on vocabulary learning, and two sample classes were chosen based on convenience.

Furthermore, a mixed-method approach is employed in the present study. According to Tashakkori and Teddlie (1998, 2010), it is more efficient to answer research questions by mixed methods than by either a quantitative or a qualitative method alone. Besides, Creswell and Creswell (2017) claimed that the weaknesses/shortcomings of one research method could be offset by the strengths/advantages of another research method. For one thing, the weakness of a qualitative method means sometimes leaving out contextual sensitivities and focusing more on meanings and experiences (Silverman, 2010), which may be offset by one strength of a quantitative method. Its findings are likely to be generalized to a whole population or a sub-population because it involves a larger sample (Carr, 1994). For another, the weaknesses of a quantitative method: leaving out the common meanings of social phenomenon (Denzin & Lincoln, 1998), failing to ascertain deeper underlying meanings and explanations (Rahman, 2016), and cannot account for how the social reality is shaped and maintained, or how people interpret their actions and others' actions (Blaikie, 2007), would be offset by the strengths of a qualitative method: producing the thick description of participants' feelings, opinions, and experiences and interpreting the meanings of their actions (Denzin, 1989), holistically understanding the human experience in specific settings (Denzin & Lincoln, 2002), and allowing the researchers to discover the participants' inner experiences and to figure out how meanings are shaped through and in culture (Corbin & Strauss, 2008).

The triangulation of data means that data is collected through multiple sources, such as interviews, observations, and document analysis, to ensure internal validity (Creswell & Creswell, 2017). According to Muller-Cajar and Mukundan (2007), triangulation of one study means triangulating the study from the perspectives of data, theories, investigators, methodologies and so on. For the current study, theoretical triangulation and methodological triangulation are applied.

Theoretical triangulation involves the design principles for MALL (Mobile-assisted Language Learning) as recommended by Stockwell and Hubbard (2013), dual coding theory (Paivio, 2007, 1986, 1971), cognitive theory of multimedia learning (Mayer,

2005, 1997), a memory-based strategic framework for vocabulary learning (Ma, 2014a), providing the study with theoretical support.

Methodological triangulation involves collecting data with a mixed-method approach for the study. The benefits of applying triangulation can increase the validity of a study (Robson, 2002). Interpreting statistical data could be enhanced with the help from a qualitative description. In turn, a qualitative finding could be improved from quantitative evidences (Robson, 2002).

3.2 The Population and Samples

According to Frankfort-Nachmias and Nachmias (1996), the term "population" is identified as the entire set of relevant units of analysis or data. The population in a single study usually has the same or the similar features. Nevertheless, commonly, it is not practical to research into the whole population for a researcher in one study, for the population is typically too many to handle (Cohen et al., 2000). Therefore, for representing the population, a sample is often chosen for the study.

The population for this study was made up of 850 newcomers in 17 classes of arts students in Anshun University for the academic year 2019 in China. Next, two intact classes with 114 non-English major first-year students out of 850 counterparts were chosen as samples based on convenience and availability for the present study. According to Mackey and Gass (2005), intact classes are employed for convenience. Creswell (2009: 155) stated that "in many experiments, only a convenient sample is possible because the investigator must use naturally formed groups, such as a classroom, an organization or a family unit". Thus, applying intact classes is not only more authentic for students but also more reliable and convenient for the researcher to study.

The demographic information of the two classes, including the number, period of learning English, age, gender, and English proficiency, is shown in Table 3.1 below.

Table 3.1 The demographic information for the two classes in the study

	Average Age	Gender	Length of Learning English	English Proficiency (150 full points)	T-value	Sig.
Secretary class (N=56)	19	Male(26)	10~11 years	$\overline{X}$ = 94.27/150	1.092	.927
		Female(30)				
Chinese language class (N=58)	18	Male(25)	10~12 years	$\overline{X}$ = 94.52/150		
		Female(33)				

Table 3.1 demonstrates that both classes have similar features in number, age, the proportion of males/females, and period of English learning. Furthermore, the mean of English proficiency from two classes was at a similarly low level, as the mean for the Secretary class was 94.27 points and that for the Chinese language class 94.52 points by English test of NCEE (National College Entrance Exam) with 150 full points. This indicated that neither class was proficient in English. Their English proficiency was obtained from the English scores of NCEE in China, which is held yearly for screening out students for universities all over the country, being well known for having high reliability and validity. Furthermore, an independent-samples t-test illustrated few differences in English proficiency between the two classes ($P = 0.927 > 0.05$). This signifies that the two classes had almost the same levels of English proficiency before the experiment and that they were suitable for the experiment. Therefore, the Secretary class was randomly assigned as the experiment group and the Chinese language class as the control group.

3.3 Research Instruments

The instruments employed in the present study were the following: the target words, the mobile app, the size of the vocabulary test, the knowledge scale of the vocabulary, a questionnaire, semi-structured interviews, and diaries.

3.3.1 The Target Words

Based on the low pass rate in CET-4 which ranges from 4.11% to 6.82% for the years 2015—2018 at Anshun university, improving their vocabulary is a must for university students because they all have to take the nationally recognized CET-4 and passing CET-4 is a prerequisite for a bachelor's degree in China (Zhang et al., 2011).

Also, based on the eight weeks' schedule of the freshmen in the academic year 2019, eighty words were picked out as target ones from CET-4 vocabulary in terms of frequency. To decide on 80 target words, a corpus containing CET-4 test papers (2014—2018) was compiled by the researcher. Then, an online software Word Frequency Counter was applied to count the frequency of words appearing in the corpus. Next, the top 80 high-frequency CET-4 words were listed (Appendix A) for students to learn after the researcher checking three CET-4 vocabulary books (Liu, 2017; Ma, 2009; Yu, 2008).

Moreover, the 80 words were divided into eight packages randomly with ten words per package to be covered in eight weeks with one package per week. The reasons for choosing ten words per package for students to learn each time were as follows. According to Miyake and Shah (1999), working memory is responsible for holding information temporarily with a limited capacity. A quantification of the working memory capacity limit is the "magical number seven" put forward by Miller (1956). According to Miller (1956), the information-processing capacity of young adults is around 5 to 9 elements or "chunks" (seven plus/minus two), regardless of words, letters, digits, or other units. This claim has been approved and shared in various studies (Baddeley, 1992; Miller & Cohen, 2001; Neisser, 2014). Therefore, in order not to surpass the capacity of students' working memory, ten words were selected for each package for them to learn every time.

Furthermore, every target word was provided with a phonetic symbol, its part of speech, a Chinese definition, an example in a sentence, a picture, an audio file, and exercises. The Chinese definitions, parts of speech, and phonetic symbols were extracted from the Oxford Advanced Learner's English-Chinese Dictionary (2014), and the sentences, as well as the exercises, were from the three CET-4 vocabulary books mentioned above. Next, the pictures and audio files were extracted from one search engine, Baidu, which is the most popular and dominant one of searching engines in China. Finally, all the materials concerning the target words were added to the mobile app, and then the learning sections as well as the retrieval sections of the app were set up. In order to clearly illustrate the descriptions above, sample screenshots in the mobile app are shown in Section 3.3.2, and the sample wordlist with the same ten words is displayed in Appendix D.

3.3.2 The Mobile App

The mobile app was designed with the assistance of an associate professor holding a Master of Science degree with fifteen years' teaching experiences. An introduction to the interface of the mobile app and two main sections (learning sections and retrieval sections of CET-4 words) were designed step by step with the illustration of the word on the app.

Step 1: The homepage of the mobile app appears after students log in with their ID number, as shown in Figure 3.1 below. The time allocated to each time learning is around 15 minutes for students, which refers to the pilot study.

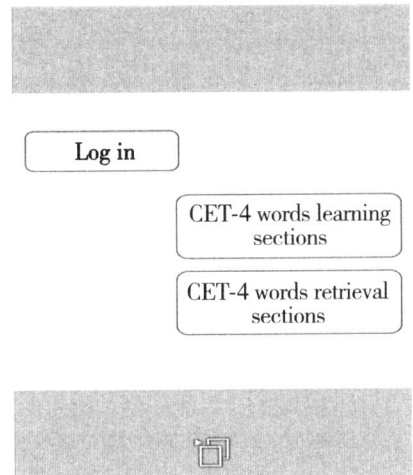

Figure 3.1 The interface of the mobile app homepage

Step 2: The interface of the learning sections, including eight separate sections, pops out after clicking on, as illustrated in Figure 3.2 below. According to the 8-week schedule for the students, they click on the appropriate learning section in order.

Figure 3.2 Screenshot of learning sections interface

Step 3: In the first week, the interface of Learning section 1 shows up with ten words one by one after students' click on Learning section 1, which is illustrated by Figure 3.3 with the first word "involve".

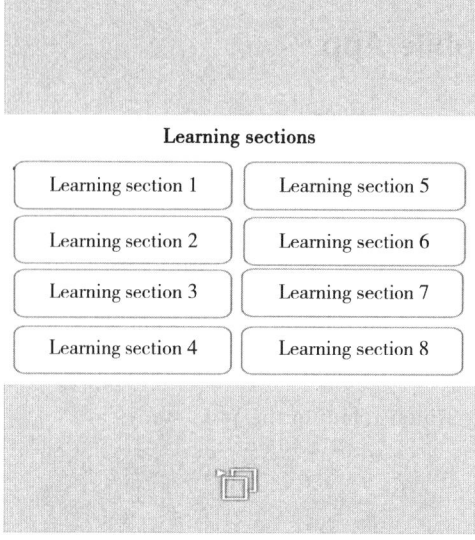

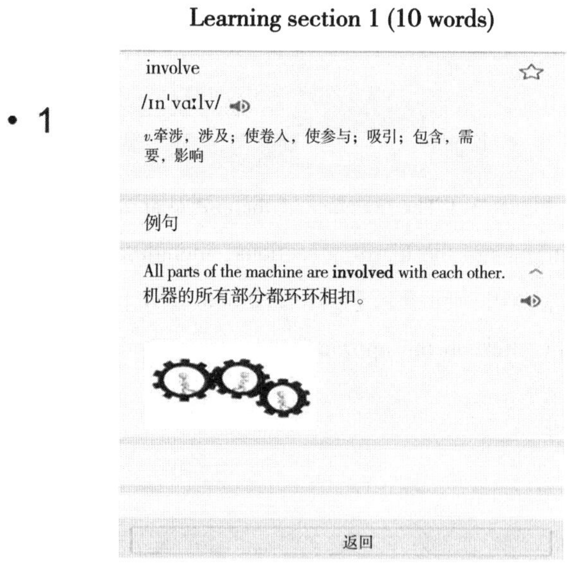

Figure 3.3 Screenshot of the word "involve" in Learning section 1

Step 4: The interface of the retrieval sections appears after the students finish Learning section 1 and click on the retrieval sections on the homepage, as shown in Figure 3.4.

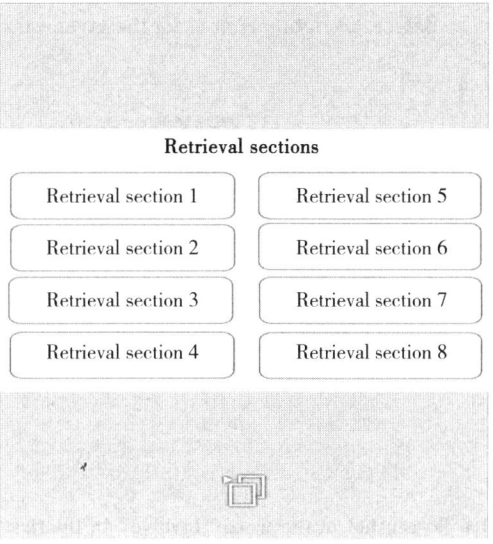

Figure 3.4 Screenshot of retrieval sections

Step 5: The page of Retrieval section 1 containing three types of exercises appears after students click on Retrieval section 1. There are three types of exercises, students "Select the right meaning for the given word" "Select the right word for given meaning" and "Spell the right word on given meaning", respectively. Figure 3.5 below demonstrates the descriptions above.

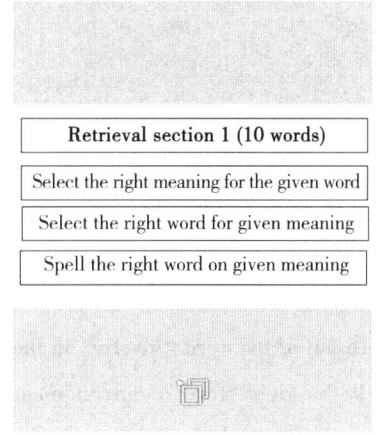

Figure 3.5 Screenshot of Retrieval section 1

Step 6: The page of "select the right meaning for the given word" appears after clicking on the first column, as illustrated by Figure 3.6 with the first word "involve".

Select the right meaning for the given word

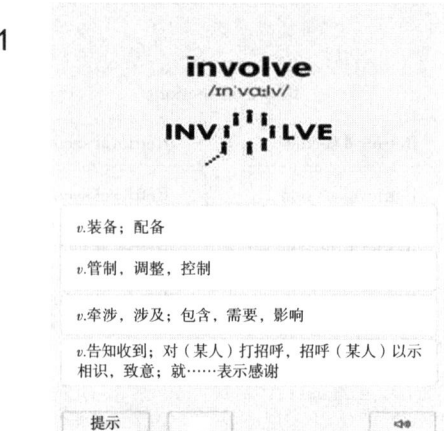

Figure 3.6 Screenshot of the word "involve" in the first column

Step 7: The page of "Select the right word for given meaning" shows up after students finish the first type of exercise and click on the second column, as shown in Figure 3.7 with the word "involve".

Select the right word for given meaning

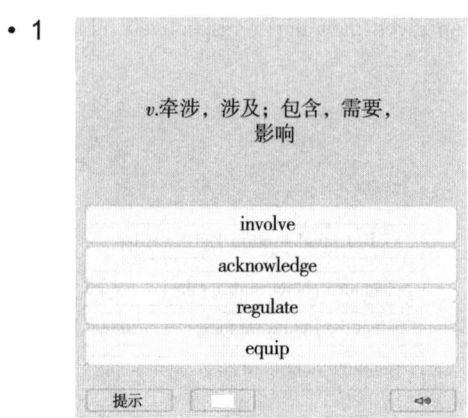

Figure 3.7 Screenshot of the word "involve" in the second column

Step 8: The page "Spell the right word on given meaning" appears after students finish the second type of exercise and click on the third column, as demonstrated by Figure 3.8 with the word "involve".

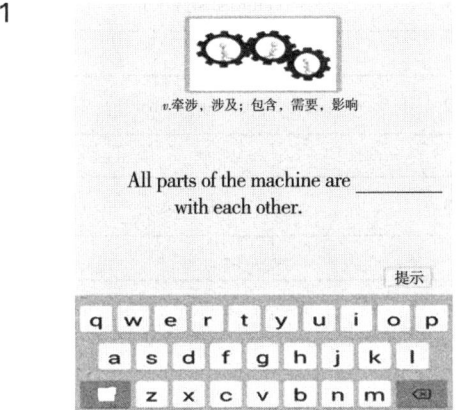

Figure 3.8 Screenshot of the word "involve" in the third column

Step 9: The app automatically logs out each time when students finish the third type of exercise "Spell the right word on given meaning".

Developing the Mobile App's Contents: With respect to the programme and steps for developing the contents of the app, an introduction is given by the researcher, who consulted the computer engineer of the app. Firstly, the Android operating system takes 52% of about two million apps worldwide (Joorabchi et al., 2013), and 98% of the participants in the present study use smartphones with the Android operating system. Therefore, the Android operating system was used for developing the contents of the app.

Then, steps to develop the contents for both the learning and retrieval sections are demonstrated by flowcharts and figures. See a sample word below.

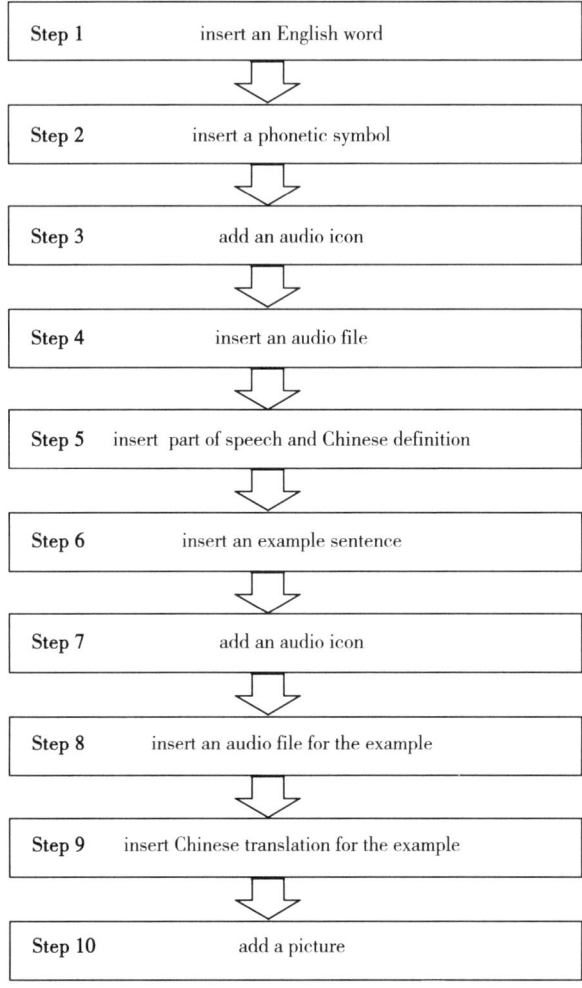

Flowchart 3.1 Steps for designing learning sections of one word in the app

Based on Flowchart 3.1 above and Figure 3.9 with the second word "discharge" in Learning section 1 below, more explicit introductions were given. Firstly, the word followed by a phonetic symbol, by its part of speech as well as a simple Chinese definition is presented with pictures and audio files at the same time. The reason why a simple Chinese definition is provided next to the word is because this is the most effective method for vocabulary learning (Ellis, 1995), and it helps learners learn a word more quickly if the meaning of the word is conveyed by the first language translation (Nation, 1982). In the present study, a simple Chinese definition refers to the primary meanings of the word extracted from the *Oxford Advanced Learner's English-Chinese Dictionary* (2014). Later, the example sentence with a Chinese translation is provided to help the students obtain the word meaning in context more easily (Groot, 2000).

Learning section 1 (10 words)

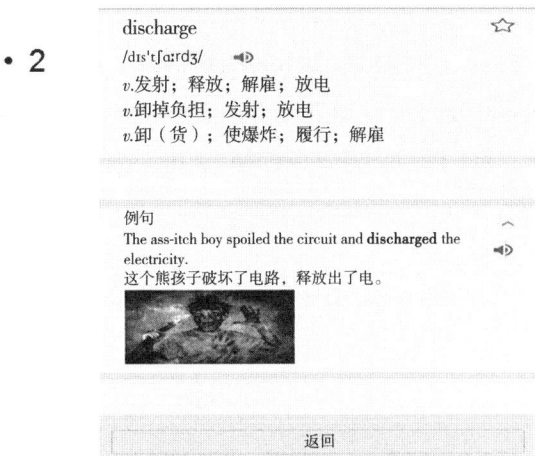

Figure 3.9 Screenshot of "discharge" in Learning section 1 of the app

As mentioned above, in the retrieval sections of the app, there are three types of exercises: two multiple-choice exercises and one spelling exercise for each word. The steps for designing each exercise are presented with flowcharts below.

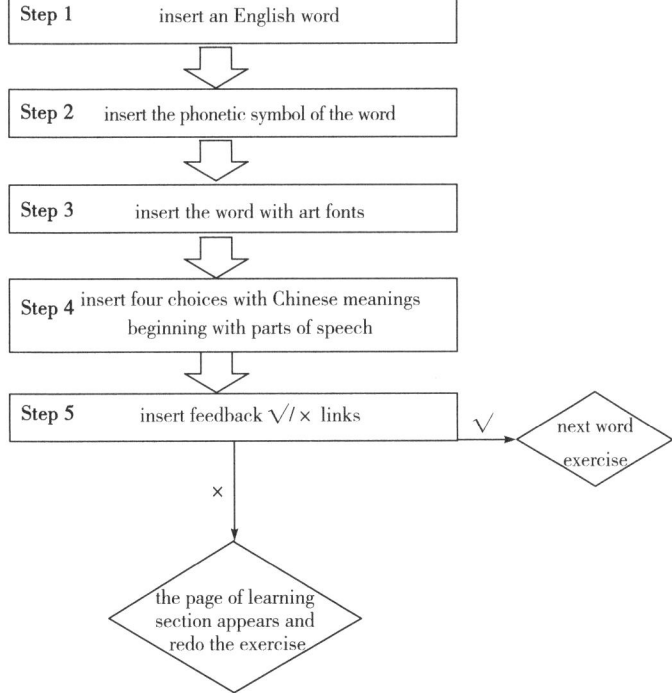

Flowchart 3.2 Steps for designing the first multiple-choice exercise in the app

In terms of Flowchart 3.2 above and Figure 3.10 below, the steps for designing the first multiple-choice exercise are presented. For the first multiple-choice exercise, students need to choose the corresponding Chinese meaning from four choices based on a given English word. When they select the right choice, they see a "√" feedback, and then the page will jump to another word exercise. When they select the wrong choice, they see a "×" feedback, and the learning section of the word appears. After the word is learned again, a link "return" brings students back to the interface of the previous exercise.

Select the right meaning for the given word

· 2

discharge
/dɪsˈtʃɑːrdʒ/
diScharge

v.解雇；放电

n.框，构架，结构，体格；v.构成，制定

n.竞争对手，参赛者

n.盾，防护物；v.保护

提示

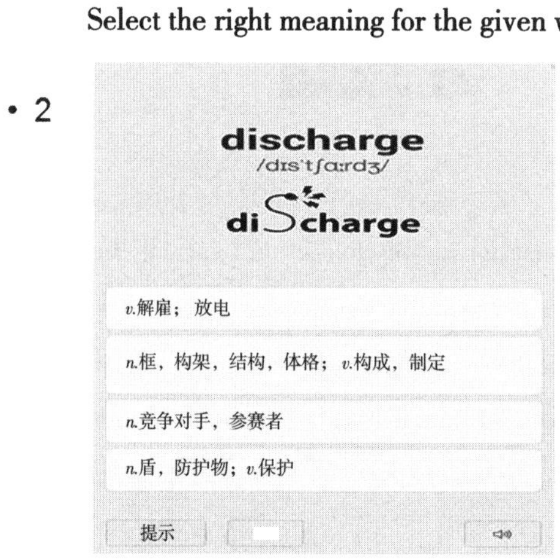

Figure 3.10 Screenshot of "discharge" in the first multiple-choice exercise

As shown in Flowchart 3.3 and Figure 3.11 below, in the second multiple-choice exercise, students choose the corresponding English word from four words based on the given Chinese meaning. When they select the right word, the "√" feedback is seen, and then the page jumps to another word exercise. When they select the wrong word, the "×" feedback appears, and the learning section of the word pops up. As in the first type of exercise, a link "return" in the learning section helps students return to the page of the previous exercise.

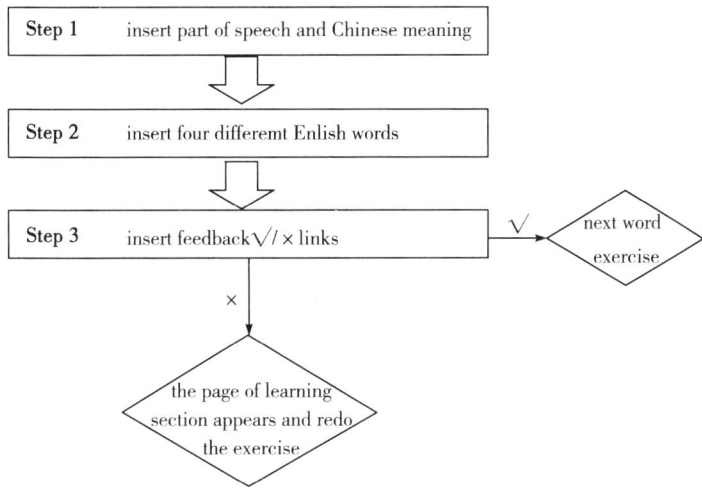

Flowchart 3.3 Steps for designing the second multiple-choice exercise in the app

Select the right word for given meaning

Figure 3.11 Screenshot of "discharge" in the second multiple-choice exercise

In respect to the third type of exercise, students spell the missing word in a sentence based on the given information. The steps for developing this type of exercise can be seen clearly in Flowchart 3.4, combined with Figure 3.12 below. Firstly, if students cannot recall the spelling of the word, they select the tips icon to relearn the word. After relearning, they select the link "return" to go back to the page of the spelling exercise. Next, if students spell the word correctly, the "√" feedback pops up, and the page of another word spelling exercise appears. If the spelling is incorrect, the " × " feedback pops up, and then the page of the learning section appears for students who want to check or relearn the word. As mentioned for the two types of exercise above, the link "return" brings them back to the interface for the spelling exercise.

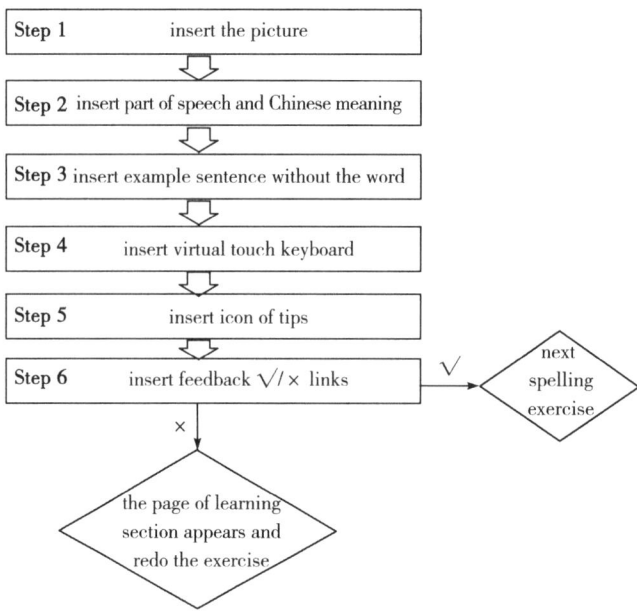

Flowchart 3.4 Steps for designing spelling exercise

Spell the right word on given meaning

• 2

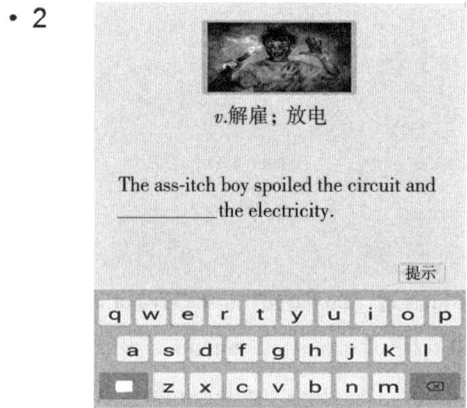

Figure 3.12 "discharge" in spelling exercise

3.3.3 Vocabulary Size Test

  Vocabulary Size Test (VST) (Nation & Beglar, 2007) was selected as a measurement for both groups before the treatment. The reasons for choosing VST were as follows. Firstly, VST was constructed by Nation and Beglar (2007) as a proficiency measurement of total vocabulary size for ESL/EFL learners. This is suitable for the present study, which examines if there is a difference of students' vocabulary size between 2 groups before the treatment.

Secondly, VST is a reliable instrument with a high reliability to measure vocabulary size. For validating VST, a Rasch-based test was done by Beglar (2010), and revealed 3 features summarized by Nguyen and Nation (2011: 89): "① It can be used with learners with a vast range of proficiency levels; ② It measures a single factor (probably written receptive vocabulary knowledge), and other factors play a minor role in performance in the test; ③ It performs consistently and reliably, even though circumstances change. These changes include comparing the performance of male subjects with female subjects, comparing the 70-item version of the test with the 140-item version, and comparing learners of various proficiency levels." Finally, it was found that the reliability was 0.96.

VST contains 140 items with 10 items representing each of fourteen 1,000-word levels from the British National Corpus. That is to say, his/her vocabulary size is likely to reach the 14,000-word level if he/she gets 140 full points. And its format is equipped with multiple choices, which is demonstrated in Figure 3.13 with an excerpt from VST (Appendix E).

Instructions: In each item, you should choose the right meaning from a, b, c, d to go with the word in CAPITAL letters by clicking the small circle.

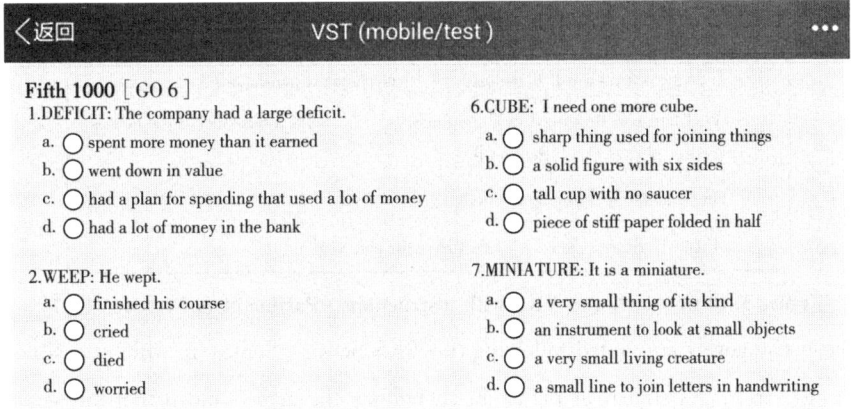

Figure 3.13 Screenshot of 5,000-word level in VST (Nation & Beglar, 2007)

Each item stands for a 100-word family and ten items represent every 1,000-word frequency level. Therefore, his/her vocabulary size can be deduced in the test by using the formula below.

$$\text{Vocabulary size} = \text{Total scores} \times 100$$

3.3.4 Vocabulary Knowledge Scale

Vocabulary Knowledge Scale (VKS) was selected as the instrument for measuring vocabulary learning and retention of the study (Paribakht & Wesche, 1993). The reasons for selecting VKS were as follows. Firstly, it measured a broad range of knowledge types: noticing word forms, knowing the link between the word's form with meaning, and using the word to make sentences in different contexts, which matched well with the stages and exercises of the words' learning via the app in the present study.

Secondly, the reliability of VKS was found to be high (0.89) by Wesche and Paribakht (1996), and it has also proven to be useful in measuring vocabulary learning and retention (Paribakht, 2005; Wesche & Paribakht, 2009). So the Vocabulary Knowledge Scale is employed in the present study (Appendix F).

Paribakht and Wesche's (1997) VKS uses a five-point elicitation scale that comprises five items. It is demonstrated in Figure 3.14 below.

Instructions: choose the most suitable one (I — V) going with the bold word to fill in the bracket, and do as told if you choose one from III to V.

```
I. I don't remember having seen the word before.
II. I have seen this word before, but I don't know what it means.
III. I have seen this word before, and I think it means _____. (synonym or translation)
IV. I know this word. It means _____. (synonym or translation)
V. I can use this word in a sentence: _____. (write a sentence) (If you do this section, please also do Section IV.)
One example is shown how to do it.
E.G.    drive ( V )    I can drive the car. 驾驶
```

Figure 3.14 Screenshot of VKS with instructions (Paribakht & Wesche, 1997)

These categories are coded following the VKS Scoring Scale, in which possible points range from 1 to 5. As shown in Figure 3.15 below, the arrows mean that the selection of category I results in 1 point and the selection of category II results in 2 points. For categories III — V, various points can be awarded based on the quality of the answers provided. The full points for the VKS are 400 points.

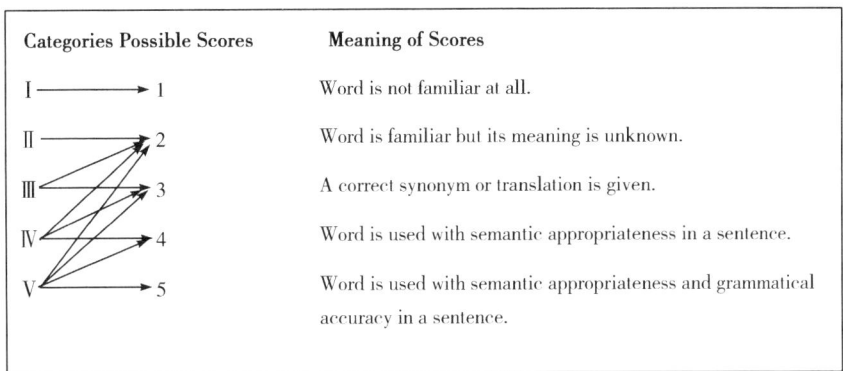

Figure 3.15 VKS Scoring Scale (Paribakht & Wesche, 1997: 181)

For the study, the Target Words Knowledge Scale (Appendix F) was adapted from VKS (Paribakht & Wesche, 1997) and its reliability was tested. Moreover, the reliability was obtained by using reliability statistics with SPSS (18.0 version), as shown in Table 3.2 below.

Table 3.2 Reliability statistics of Target Words Knowledge Scale

Cronbach's Alpha	Number of Items
.89	80

As demonstrated in Table 3.2 above, Cronbach's Alpha of the words knowledge scale is .89 ($\alpha = 0.89$). The knowledge scale can be accepted as reliable in the study, since a good reliability of a scale can be found, if Alpha is higher or equal to 0.7 (Deniz & Alsaffar, 2013).

3.3.5 The Questionnaire on Students' Perceptions

According to the researchers (Gass & Selinker, 2008; Krashen, 1981, 1982), within second language acquisition, an affective filter would indicate a learner's attitudes or perceptions of learning and suggest his/her level of language learning. So for probing into the subjects' perceptions of the current app, a questionnaire was administered in the study.

As for the construction of the questionnaire, items (2,5,6, and 8) were adapted from Chang et al. (2012), and items (3,7,11, and 13) from Wang (2015). The remainder of the questionnaire items were developed by the researcher.

The questionnaire consists of two parts: (1) students' background information;

(2) students' perceptions of vocabulary learning via the app. The first part includes age, gender, period of learning English, English scores in NCEE, and experiences of English learning through a smartphone. Such data is necessary to provide the participants' demographic information. The second part includes 16 items to elicit students' perceptions of vocabulary learning via the app with a Five-point Likert Scale (5: strongly agree; 4: agree; 3: not sure; 2: disagree; 1: strongly disagree).

To examine the questionnaire content validity, the index of item-objective congruence (IOC) for checking content validity of developing items from Rovinelli and Hambleton (1977) was applied. Firstly, the IOC and IOC index can be calculated by the formula in Figure 3.16 below.

$$IOC = ÓR/N$$

ÓR: the total score from experts

N: the number of experts

IOC index: IOC/the number of items

Figure 3.16 The formula for IOC and IOC index

Then, three English teachers rated each item to see whether it was congruent with the objective (congruent = 1, uncertain = 0, incongruent = −1). The background information of the three teachers is shown in Table 3.3 below.

Table 3.3 Background information of the three English teachers

	Age	Gender	Title	Years of English Teaching
TA	44	female	Associate professor	15
TB	41	female	Associate professor	17
TC	52	male	Associate professor	30

The records of IOC for checking the items of the draft questionnaire are shown (see Appendix G), and its content validity was calculated as 0.875. According to Rovinelli and Hambleton (1977), an acceptable value for content validity should be higher or equal to 0.5. The IOC index (0.875) of the study, which meant that most of the items in the draft questionnaire were acceptable. The result of the IOC check revealed that four items (items 2, 5, 8, 13) in the draft questionnaire needed to be revised. After revision, the present questionnaire in an English version (Appendix H) was made.

For testing the questionnaire reliability, it was trialed in one of the first-year non-English major classes with 55 students. The categories of "Analyze" "Scale" and "Reliability Analysis" were used in SPSS (18.0 version) and Cronbach's Alpha value is shown in Table 3.4 below.

Table 3.4 **Reliability statistics of the questionnaire**

Cronbach's Alpha	Number of Items
.913	16

According to Cronbach and Shevelson (2004), the coefficient of Cronbach's Alpha ranges from 0 to 1 by value. The larger the value is, the more reliable the questionnaire is. Besides, according to Deniz and Alsaffar (2013), good reliability of a questionnaire can be confirmed, if Alpha is higher than or equal to 0.7 ($\alpha \geqslant 0.7$). Therefore, it is reasonable to regard the questionnaire of the study as reliable because its Cronbach's Alpha is .913 ($\alpha = 0.913$).

3.3.6 Interview

An interview was selected as one way of data collection of students' perceptions for the study. According to Holstein and Gubrium (2004), an interview is a helpful instrument to generate information of personal perspectives and experiences for studies. Also, according to Creswell (2009: 175), "as a qualitative research instrument, an interview enables an understanding of the meaning that the participants hold about the problem, not the meaning that the researchers bring to the research or writers express in the literature."

Furthermore, Fontana and Frey (2005) claimed that interviews would contain three types: unstructured interviews, semi-structured interviews, and structured interviews based on the degree of structuring. An unstructured interview is an interview without predetermined questions or answers (Minichiello et al., 1990; Punch, 1998). A semi-structured interview is in the middle between an unstructured interview and a structured interview. A structured interview is one where the interviewer asks each interviewee the same questions in the same order to collect consistent and comparable data (Patton,

2002). In the study, a semi-structured interview was decided, and the reasons for choosing it are listed as follows.

Firstly, according to Bernard (1988), in a semi-structured interview, the interviewer not only controls the process of getting information from interviewees, but also follows newly arising leads. Secondly, based on Denzin and Lincoln (1994), in practice, every interviewee is different, and the interviewer must be flexible enough to make appropriate adjustments for unanticipated developments. The semi-structured interview has the potential of flexibility to meet the interviewer's demands. Therefore, the way of semi-structured interview was decided for the study to collect data that could not be wholly or directly observed, such as beliefs, feelings, and perceptions, that the questionnaire would not necessarily cover.

With regard to what questions should be asked in the semi-structured interview, 11 questions were from the researcher referring to the questionnaire of students' perceptions to find in-depth answers to the third research question. Then, item-objective congruence (IOC) (Rovinelli & Hambleton, 1977) was applied for checking if interview questions could evaluate what they were supposed to assess.

A list of 11 interview questions and an evaluation form were delivered to three experienced English teachers who rated the items of the questionnaire in Section 3.3.5 above. The IOC and IOC index of three experts rating each question with the formula in Figure 3.17 below are shown in detail (Appendix I).

$$IOC = ÓR/N$$

ÓR: the total score from experts

N: the number of experts

IOC index: IOC/the number of items

Figure 3.17 The formula for IOC and IOC index

The IOC index was calculated as 0.88 (see Appendix I). According to Rovinelli and Hambleton (1977), an acceptable value for content validity should be higher or equal to 0.5 (validity ≥ 0.5). Thus, most questions in the interview were valid and relevant with aims of the study. As a result, all interview questions were set (Appendix J, English version) after questions 8 and 10 were revised. In order to avoid any misunderstandings of the interview questions, the interviews were conducted in Chinese (Appendix J, Chinese version).

3.3.7 Diary

Students from two groups were required for keeping diaries about recording the length of time they learned and to provide feedback each week. Both of the groups reviewed each package of ten words based on 9 hours', 1 day's, 2 days' and 6 days' intervals from the first time they studied each week. The format of the diary is shown in Table 3.5 below. In addition to recording the vocabulary learning each time, students were free to write comments, reflections, or anything relevant to their vocabulary study.

Table 3.5 **The format of the diary for the experiment and the control group**

Name:		Student ID:		Major:	
5 times/ week( )	First time (on Monday)	Second time (on Tuesday)	Third time (on Wednesday)	Fourth time (on Thursday)	Fifth time (on Friday)
10 words/time	suitable time for learning words	9 hours' interval from 1st time	1 day's interval from 1st time	2 days' interval from 1st time	6 days' interval from 1st time
Starting to finishing time					
My feelings towards learning and reviewing words on week( )					

3.4 Procedure of the Experiment

In Week 1, the purposes of the study were introduced briefly to the participants of the two groups in the classroom. At the same Week 1, the students from the experiment group received a consent form (Appendix B) and signed it voluntarily. Also, the students from the control group signed a similar consent form (Appendix C). Then, the students from the two groups took the Vocabulary Size Test and the Vocabulary Knowledge Scale Test as pre-tests in the classroom which the researcher monitored. Next, in the same week, an introduction to the mobile app, including the eight packages with 80 target words, was made to the experiment group and then installed into their mobile phones. But the list of the same eight packages was distributed to the control group on sheets of paper (Appendix D).

In Week 2, the students from both groups were required to learn one package for the first time every Monday and review it four times outside the classroom in one week for eight successive weeks. In addition, the students were required to keep diaries on the length of time of their vocabulary learning each time and their feelings, and then to hand in the diaries once a week.

In Week 10, both groups took the Vocabulary Knowledge Scale Test as well as the pre-test but in a different order which the researcher monitored. In the same week, the experiment group completed the questionnaire on their perceptions (Appendix H, Chinese version), and the selected 19 participants were interviewed by the researcher individually based on the interview questions (Appendix J, Chinese version).

In Week 14, both groups took the Vocabulary Knowledge Scale Test but in a different order as a delayed post-test which the researcher monitored. According to Ebbinghaus (1885), after four weeks, the information kept in mind would stay for a long time without much loss and in a stable state, so the delayed post-test was held four weeks after the post-test. Table 3.6 below illustrates the timetable of the procedure.

Table 3.6 **Timetable for two groups in the experiment**

Week	Control group	Experiment group
1	①The researcher's introduction to the purpose of the research (10 minutes) ②Take Vocabulary Size Test (40 minutes), Vocabulary Knowledge Scale Test (45 minutes)	
	The researcher handed out the paper-based wordlists (25 minutes)	The researcher's introduction and students' installation of the mobile app (30 minutes)

(续表)

Week	Control group	Experiment group
2—9	①Learn and review the respective wordlist by paper-based method outside the classroom by week ② Write and hand in the respective week's diaries	①Learn and review the respective package of words via the app outside the classroom by week ② Write and hand in the respective week's diaries
10	Take Vocabulary Knowledge Scale Test (45 minutes)	① Take Vocabulary Knowledge Scale Test (45 minutes), complete the questionnaire of perceptions (20 minutes) ② 19 interviewees take the semi-structured interviews, with about 10 minutes for every interviewee
11—13	Attend classes as usual without learning target words or reviewing	
14	Take Vocabulary Knowledge Scale Test (45 minutes)	

3.5 Data Collection

In order to collect the data, the Vocabulary Size Test, Vocabulary Knowledge Scale Test, the questionnaire, the semi-structured interview, and diaries were introduced.

3.5.1 Vocabulary Size Test

For examining if a difference in vocabulary size can be detected between two groups before the experiment, they were pre-tested with the Vocabulary Size Test (Nation & Beglar, 2007). So at the first week in the first semester of 2019 academic year, both groups took a Vocabulary Size Test in the classroom without any means of reference which the researcher monitored. It took the students 40 minutes to complete the Vocabulary Size Test. The students were only allowed to leave the classroom after they handed in the test sheet. The recovery rate of the Vocabulary Size Test sheet was 100%, which meant the researcher handed out a fixed number of test sheets for students to finish and later all test sheets were collected back.

3.5.2 Vocabulary Knowledge Scale Test

To find out how much the two groups knew the target words before the treatment, and to measure their performances on learning vocabulary and on retention, the Vocabulary Knowledge Scale Test, which was adapted from the VKS (Paribakht & Wesche, 1993, 1997) was employed in three tests: pre-test, post-test, and delayed post-test.

Firstly, in the first week, the VKS was handed out to both groups to finish within 45 minutes in a closed-book test which the teacher monitored. Secondly, in the tenth week after eight weeks' vocabulary learning, the two groups were assessed in a post-test by using the same Vocabulary Knowledge Scale as in the pre-test but in a different order in the English classroom which an English teacher monitored. Finally, the delayed post-test was finished four weeks after the post-test. The VKS of the post-test was the same as that of the delayed post-test but in a different order. All the tests were completed using paper and pencil, and the recovery rate of the VKS test sheets in the pre-test, post-test, and delayed post-test was 100%.

3.5.3 The Questionnaire on Perceptions

In the tenth week, after the students from the experiment group had finished the post-test, they filled out the questionnaires and returned the questionnaires to the researcher within 20 minutes in the classroom. After all questionnaires were collected back by the researcher, they were number coded.

3.5.4 The Semi-structured Interview

According to the criteria for selecting the number of interviewees from the Alberta Municipal Health and Safety Association (AMHSA, 2010), a representative amount of the interview sample was decided on (Appendix K). The criteria present the minimum number of interviewees relying on different amounts of participants, which would represent the sample size of interview (Shen & Suwanthep, 2011).

Based on the criteria above, the number of 19 out of 56 students in the experiment group would be a minimum amount and proper for the semi-structured interview. So, 19 interviewees were selected based on purposive sampling in terms of their responses to the questionnaire and diaries.

After the students from the experiment group finished the post-test and the questionnaire in the 10th week, the selected 19 interviewees were called into a classroom, and individual interviews were conducted in another classroom by the researcher. In the process of interviewing, the responses from the students were recorded by a tape recorder. To make all interviewees understand interview questions and elaborate their thoughts clearly, their mother language: Chinese language was used. Notes were also taken in case the tape recorder failed to work.

3.5.5 The Diary

From the second week on, the students from the two groups handed in their diaries to the researcher on every Sunday evening for eight successive Sunday evenings. Then, the researcher would check the vocabulary learning diary of every student carefully and give some reminders if anyone had not done the vocabulary learning or review as the schedule.

3.6 Data Analysis

For this section, the methods of how to analyze data are described. Table 3.7 below demonstrates the employed data analysis.

Table 3.7 **Data analysis and its objective**

Data from	Data analysis	Objectives
VST	Mean and S. D. analysis Paired-samples t-test Independent-samples t-test	To examine the difference in vocabulary size between two groups before the experiment

(续表)

Data from	Data analysis	Objectives
VKS	Mean and S. D. analysis Paired-samples t-test Independent-samples t-test	To identify students learning of words and retention
Questionnaire	Percentage analysis	To explore students' perceptions of the app by triangulation
Semi-structured interview	Thematic analysis	
Diaries	Thematic analysis	

3.6.1 Analyzing the Data of VST

Firstly, after the data of VST was collected, descriptive statistics were performed with SPSS (18.0 version) for gaining an overview about the data. Secondly, an independent-samples t-test was used to examine if a huge difference in the mean vocabulary size existed between the two groups, and whether they were qualified for the experiment.

3.6.2 Analyzing the Data of VKS

3.6.2.1 The Data from the VKS in the Pre-test

Firstly, the mean and standard deviation were applied to describe the VKS with the help of SPSS (18.0 version). Secondly, to see whether a significant difference existed in the knowledge of the target words between two groups, the mean of knowledge of the target words was analyzed by an independent-samples t-test.

3.6.2.2 The Data from the VKS in the Post-test

Firstly, the mean and standard deviation were employed to describe the VKS by SPSS (18.0 version). Next, a paired-samples t-test was applied to examine if any difference in mean of knowledge of the words existed between the pre-test and post-test for each group. Then, an independent-samples t-test was used to examine if a difference existed between two groups in mean of knowledge of the words from the post-test. The data analyses were used to answer the first research question.

3.6.2.3 The Data from the VKS in the Delayed Post-test

At first, M and S. D. were for describing the students' knowledge of the words by SPSS (18.0 version). Then, a paired-samples t-test was performed to explore if a difference was exhibited between the delayed post-test and the post-test in mean for each group. Next, an independent-samples t-test was done for examining whether a difference in students' knowledge of the words was exhibited for delayed post-test of 2 groups. The aim of data analyses was for answering the second research question.

3.6.3 Analyzing the Data of the Questionnaires

The data of the questionnaire was analyzed by using descriptive statistics. To be precise, the percentages in the descriptive statistics of SPSS (18.0 version) were used for analyzing students' questionnaires and the percentage of each item was calculated. Because six students did not complete all the items of their questionnaires, the remaining fifty students' questionnaires were analyzed. The results of the questionnaires combined with those of the semi-structured interviews and the diaries were sufficient to answer the third research question.

3.6.4 Analyzing the Data of the Semi-structured Interviews

Firstly, the researcher transcribed the responses of the interviewees to produce a written version. Later, the transcripts were translated properly into English if they were expressed in Chinese. Thirdly, the translations and transcripts were read very carefully by the researcher and three English teachers with more than fifteen years' teaching experiences mentioned in Section 3.3.5 in order to form the first impressions.

As Dörnyei (2007) argued, those impressions affect the way one researcher perceives and codes the data eventually. Reading the transcripts reflectively, the researcher sifts data line by line. This is the time when coding begins as the first step to categorize the raw data.

Fourthly, coding needs to be followed by key concepts so that these can develop into final themes step by step. Finally, the summarized themes out of questionnaires and diaries revealed the in-depth reasons as part of answers to the third research question.

3.6.5 Analyzing the Data of the Diaries

Diaries can be a kind of qualitative data, for they record things subjectively (Walsh, 2003). As for the current study, students' dairies would offer the researcher much in-depth information concerning their feelings, opinions, feelings, reflections, and the unknown.

After students' diaries were all collected, they were number coded in ascending order of the students' IDs each week. Then, based on the "open coding" [1] technique proposed by Punch (1998) and the "axial coding" [2] technique proposed by Strauss and Corbin (1998), the raw data was reduced by coding and synthesis to find the categories and themes. These categories and themes were used to verify the answers to the first and second questions, and then to further answer the third research question with the data from the questionnaire, as well as from the interviews.

3.7 Implications from Pilot Study and Adjustments for Main Study

It has been claimed that "a pilot study is a small-scale trial of the proposed procedures, materials, and methods, and sometimes also includes coding sheets and analytic choices" (Mackey & Gass, 2005: 43). They also claimed that a pilot study is useful for researchers to test the feasibility of the proposed research project and to fix the uncovered problems for the main study. Thus, the pilot study was done for examining the plausibility of the research project, and to explore if any adjustment was necessary before the main study.

---

[1] "Open coding" is the process of breaking down, examining, comparing, conceptualizing, and categorizing data; it is the part of the analysis that pertains specifically to the naming and categorizing of phenomena through close examination of data (Punch, 1998: 207 – 211).

[2] "Axial coding" is a set of the process whereby data are put back together in new ways after open coding paradigms involving conditions, context, interactional strategies and consequences (Strauss & Corbin, 1998: 61 – 62).

A pilot study was done for two classes, with 116 Chinese EFL newcomers who were picked out by the researcher's availability and convenience at the first semester of 2018 academic year. The detailed report of the pilot study is attached (see Appendix L). Furthermore, the results of the pilot study proved that the current research project was plausible. Moreover, several implications from the pilot study were listed, and corresponding adjustments were made for the main study as follows.

Firstly, when students filled in the questionnaire, ten students did not understand "the clues of images" in item 12: "I can learn the words easier based on the clues of images and example sentences in the app." Moreover, eight students asked what "the contexts of example sentences" meant in item 15: "the contexts of example sentences help me learn how to use the words appropriately." Later, "the clues of images" was changed into "the pictures" in item 12, and "the contexts of example sentences" was changed into "the example sentences" in item 15. These changes helped students understand more quickly and clearly. The revised questionnaire for the main study is shown in Appendix J.

Secondly, during the interviews, some interviewees just responded with "yes" and did not say anything else in answer to the interview questions (5, 6, 7, and 8), because all the questions began with "Is it ...?" Thus, to elicit more responses from the interviewees, the above questions were revised as open-ended questions, and adjusted accordingly. The revised list of interview questions is shown in Appendix J.

Finally, the students' diaries were added as another research instrument in the main study. Because the improved vocabulary learning and retention of the experiment group in the pilot study might have something to do with the greater number of times used for vocabulary learning via the mobile app than for the paper-based wordlist, to reduce the effects of the unequal times, the two groups were required to learn the target words five times within one week and to keep diaries on the length of time they spent each time. Another aim of adding diaries as an instrument was to triangulate the answers to the third research question with students' unseen writings, by combing the questionnaires and the interviews.

3.8 Summary

To sum up, this chapter describes the research methodology for the study in detail. At the beginning, the research design was explained. Then, the population and samples in the study were introduced. Later, the research instruments were presented respectively, which comprised the target words, the mobile app, the vocabulary size test, the vocabulary knowledge scale, the questionnaire, the semi-structured interview, and the students' diaries. Next, the procedure of the experiment was introduced, which was then followed by the data collection. Additionally, the processes of data analysis were described in order to answer the three research questions. Finally, some adjustments were done to the main study from the researcher's pilot study. In Chapter 4, the results of the data analyses and the discussion are presented.

Chapter 4

Results and Discussion

This chapter presents the results and then makes discussions in reference to the research, theories relevant to the results of the present study. Firstly, the results of the Vocabulary Size Test for two groups are presented. Then, the results of the pre-test and post-test on the students' knowledge of the target words are illustrated to answer the first research question which is followed by a discussion. Next, the results of the delayed post-test concerning knowledge of the target words are used to answer the second question, which is followed by a discussion. Later, the results of the questionnaires, the interviews, and the students' diaries from the experiment group are used to answer the third research question which is followed by a discussion. Additionally, the results of the students' diaries from the control group and the related discussion are presented. Finally, this chapter concludes with a summary.

4.1 Results of the Vocabulary Size Test

The Vocabulary Size Test (VST) was developed by Nation and Beglar (2007) as a proficiency measurement of total vocabulary size for EFL/ESL learners. VST is made up of 140 items (Appendix E), and has been proved as a reliable measurement with a reliability value of 0.96 (Beglar, 2010).

In order to examine whether there were significant differences in students' vocabulary levels between two groups and to assess whether they were suitable for the experiment, descriptive statistics and an independent-samples t-test were employed. Then, Table 4.1 below illustrates what is found.

Table 4.1 **An independent-samples t-test of vocabulary size from two groups**

Vocabulary Size Test				
Group	$\overline{X}$	Standard Deviation (S.D.)	T-value	Sig. (2-tailed)
EG (N=56)	1989.29	644.044	15.057	.293
CG (N=58)	2110.34	578.470		

EG: Experiment Group; CG: Control Group (Significant level $p < 0.05$)

As shown by Table 4.1, the mean of the vocabulary size from the experiment group is 1989.29 (S.D. =644.044), and the mean of the vocabulary size from the control group is 2110.34 (S.D. =578.470). However, no significant difference between the mean of EG and the mean of CG was detected ($p = 0.293$) from an independent-samples t-test. Furthermore, in terms of the mean of the two groups, their average vocabulary size was around 2,000 words, which was far from the requirement of 4,500 words for CET-4 in China. The results disclosed that two groups stayed at a similarly low level in terms of vocabulary size, indicating that both of them lacked sufficient vocabulary knowledge and needed to learn more vocabulary in order to pass the CET-4. Therefore, the students from both groups were suitable for the experiment.

4.2 The Effects of Using the App on Students' Vocabulary Learning

This section provides the results for answering 1st question (RQ1): What are the effects of using a mobile app on EFL students' vocabulary learning achievement? To answer RQ1, descriptive statistics, a paired-samples t-test, and an independent-samples t-test of the Target Words Knowledge Scale Test were conducted.

4.2.1 Results of an Independent-samples T-test of the Pre-tests for Two Groups

The Target Words Knowledge Scale Test (Appendix F) was adapted from the Vocabulary Knowledge Scale (Paribakht & Wesche, 1997), and the Knowledge Scale Test proved to be reliable with a reliability of 0.89 based on Deniz and Alsaffar (2013).

From CET-4 vocabulary, the top 80 high-frequency words were chosen for two groups' learning. To examine whether the target words were suitable for them to learn, and whether there was a difference of knowledge of the target words between them, the Target Words Knowledge Scale Test was administered as a pre-test for both groups.

Table 4.2 An independent-samples t-test of the pre-test for two groups

Test	Group		Full points (400)	$\overline{X}$	S.D.	T-value	Sig. (2-tailed)
Pre-test	EG (N=56)	Highest score	172/400	145.88	28.258	39.316	.662
		Lowest score	95/400				
	CG (N=58)	Highest score	184/400	143.82	22.707		
		Lowest score	85/400				

EG: Experiment Group; CG: Control Group (Significant level p < 0.05). The total scores of the Target Words Knowledge Scale Test were 400 points.

According to Table 4.2, the mean score of the pre-test from the experiment group was 145.88 (S.D. = 28.258), with their scores ranging from 95 to 172. The mean score of the pre-test from the control group was 143.82 (S.D. = 22.707), with their scores ranging from 85 to 184. This indicated that the target words were unknown to the students from either group, so they could be used for them to learn. Next, after an independent-samples t-test, no significant difference between the mean of EG and that of CG was identified (p = 0.662). It meant that two groups exhibited a similar level concerning their knowledge of the target words which suggested they were suitable for the treatment.

4.2.2 Results of the Post-test and a Paired-samples T-test for EG

The post-test of target words was carried out after eight weeks' treatment. With descriptive statistics, the results of post-test for experiment group are shown in Table 4.3 below. Later, a paired-samples t-test was performed for experiment group to determine the difference between mean of pre-test and that of post-test, as demonstrated by Table 4.4.

Table 4.3 Descriptive statistics of the post-test for EG

EG (N=56)		$\overline{X}$	S.D.
Highest score	365/400	328.16	44.978
Lowest score	309/400		

EG: Experiment Group. The total scores of the Target Words in the Knowledge Scale Test were 400 points.

Table 4.4 A paired-samples t-test of the pretest and the post-test for EG

Tests	$\overline{X}$	S.D.	T-value	Sig. (2-tailed)
Pre-test	145.88	28.258	12.386	.000
Post-test	328.16	44.978		

EG: Experiment Group (Significant level p < 0.05). The total scores of the Target Words in the Knowledge Scale Test were 400 points.

According to Table 4.3 above, mean of post-test from experiment group was 328.16 (S.D = 44.978), with scores ranging from 309 to 365. Furthermore, according to Table 4.4 above, mean of experiment group changed from 145.88 for the pre-test to 328.16 for the post-test, an increase of 182.28. In addition, the result of the paired-samples t-test disclosed that a significant difference between mean of pre-test and mean of post-test was detected (p = 0.000 < 0.05). It suggested that learning achievements of the target words were improved noticeably for those students who used the app after an eight-week treatment.

4.2.3 Results of the Post-test and a Paired-samples T-test for CG

The results of post-test for control group after using descriptive statistics are given in Table 4.5 below. Next, a paired-samples t-test was performed for control group to determine the statistical difference between mean of post-test and that of pre-test, as demonstrated in Table 4.6 below.

Table 4.5 **Descriptive statistics of the post-test for CG**

CG (N =58)		$\overline{X}$	S. D.
Highest score	281/400	242.20	34.550
Lowest score	196/400		

CG: Control Group. The total scores of Target Words in the Knowledge Scale Test were 400 points.

Table 4.6 **A paired-samples t-test of the pre-test and the post-test for CG**

Tests	$\overline{X}$	S. D.	T-value	Sig. (2-tailed)
Pre-test	143.82	22.707	11.203	.000
Post-test	242.20	34.550		

CG: Control Group (Significant level $p < 0.05$). The total scores of the Target Words in the Knowledge Scale Test were 400 points.

According to Table 4.5 above, mean of post-test for control group was 242.20 (S.D = 34.550), with their scores ranging from 196 to 281. As illustrated by Table 4.6 above, mean of control group changed from 143.82 on the pre-test to 242.20 on the post-test, which is an increase of 98.38. By further analysis, the result of the paired-samples t-test showed that a significant difference between mean of pre-test and mean of post-test was identified ($p = 0.000 < 0.05$). These results indicated that the students' learning achievements of the target words improved significantly for the students using the paper-based wordlist for eight weeks.

4.2.4 Results of an Independent-samples T-test of the Post-tests for Two Groups

An independent-samples t-test was performed to detect the statistical difference between two groups' mean of post-tests. Moreover, the results of the independent-samples t-test are presented in Table 4.7 below.

Table 4.7 **An independent-samples t-test of the post-tests for two groups**

Test	Group	$\overline{X}$	S. D.	T-value	Sig. (2-tailed)
Post-test	EG (N =56)	328.16	44.978	40.472	.000
	CG (N =58)	242.20	34.550		

EG: Experiment Group CG: Control Group (Significant level $p < 0.05$). The total scores of the Target Words in the Knowledge Scale Test were 400 points.

As displayed by Table 4.7 above, the mean score of the post-test for the experiment group (M = 328.16; S.D. = 44.978) is much higher than that of the control group (M = 242.20; S.D. = 34.550). By further analysis with an independent-samples t-test, a statistically significant difference was detected ($p = 0.000 < 0.05$). This meant that the students learned more words by using the app compared with those using the paper-based wordlist, indicating that the app was more effective in improving students' vocabulary learning.

4.3 Discussion about the Effects of the App on Vocabulary Learning

As mentioned above, those students with the mobile app learned more words than their peers by the wordlist. Similarly, Wang and Shih (2015) showed that the students with a mobile app scored significantly higher in the vocabulary post-test than their counterparts, indicating that the app was effective in improving EFL vocabulary learning. As found by Poláková and Klímová (2019), the students using a mobile app obtained higher scores than the students using traditional methods on vocabulary learning tests. According to Chen et al. (2019), the performance in vocabulary learning by EFL students using a mobile app was significantly better than that of their counterparts. Nevertheless, the results were different from those of Dehghan et al. (2017) who did not find any significant difference in vocabulary learning between the WhatsApp group and the textbook-based wordlist group. The reason for this might be that the students using WhatsApp were often distracted from vocabulary learning while chatting with friends or listening to music or something unrelated to the task online, since WhatsApp has a reputation as an entertaining communication app (Church & de Olivia, 2013). To look closely at findings from the study, however, the four reasons below may account for the experiment students' more significant performances.

Firstly, the merits of a multimedia environment in the app were displayed in helping the students with learning vocabulary. The combination of pictures and texts helped learners understand words easily and stimulated their motivation, because they gave the learners a role as a knowledge constructor, who could select and connect pieces of information from visual and verbal sources (Gonulal, 2019; Mayer, 1997). Also, Kim and Gilman (2008) found that a multimedia environment was likely to motivate students to concentrate on EFL vocabulary learning. Moreover, Matsuoka and Hirsh (2010) highlighted that a deep understanding of vocabulary due to the multimedia environment would facilitate a better transfer of vocabulary knowledge to authentic contexts and leave deep impressions on learners. They also argued that the multimedia environment can help L2 learners remember the words faster and it is superior to the learning of words in isolation. These results are consistent with the research (e.g. Al-Seghayer, 2016; Govindasamy et al., 2019; Mayer & Fiorella, 2014; Ramezanali, 2017; Rusanganwa, 2015), which revealed that a multimedia presentation of words by texts, sound, and pictures, could help learners learn the words faster and retain them longer.

Secondly, the immediate corrective feedback in the app assisted students to adjust their vocabulary learning, and then helped them store the correct meanings as well as the forms of the words in their minds. The researchers (Henderson, 2019; Soria et al., 2020; Sprenger, 2018) found that immediate corrective feedback helped considerably in developing students understanding of vocabulary, monitoring their vocabulary learning, and correcting any incorrect guess before they stored the right vocabulary knowledge in their long-term memory. According to Mollakhan et al. (2013), the corrective feedback was beneficial for Iranian EFL students to realize and revise errors when they were learning new vocabulary. Besides, it was identified that corrective feedback when offered promptly would increase learning, for it could help learners correct their mistakes and maintain right responses (Pashler et al., 2005; Roediger & Butler, 2011).

Thirdly, the students' more significant achievements in vocabulary learning may be due to their enjoyment of using a new app. According to Green (1993), there was a positive correlation between the enjoyment induced by something and good impacts on learning. As stated by Sandberg et al. (2011), using a mobile app brought much enjoyment and fun to the students, which motivated them to use the app in their spare time and benefited their EFL learning. Additionally, according to Hsu et al. (2017), the enjoyment of using mobile apps among senior high school EFL students could improve their relaxation levels and sustained their attention levels on vocabulary learning. Thus, the students exhibited substantial vocabulary learning achievements, regardless of gender. Therefore, it is reasonable to believe because of enjoyment, happiness, and fun that an app brings, students like the activity of learning vocabulary with the app, which, in turn, contributes to increasing achievements of the vocabulary test.

Lastly, the audios of words in the app helped students' with right pronunciations, which might result in better vocabulary learning. According to the researchers (Celce-Murcia, 2001; Laufer, 1998), the right pronunciation of a new word was quite significant for L2 vocabulary learning. As claimed by Min (2013), many EFL learners could not learn words very well, for their misspelled words were probably due to the words being mispronounced. Besides, according to He et al. (2015), and Kaplan-Rakowski and Loranc-Paszylk (2019), EFL learners improved their pronunciation of words by listening to audio recording which facilitated the rate of delivering and retrieving words, for they could learn EFL words better from the similarities between the orthographic and the acoustic of the words, as disclosed by Hennings (2000) and McCarthy (1994). These findings are in agreement with those of the studies (Karousou & Nerantzaki, 2020; Trofimovich & Issacs, 2012), which revealed that the students with access to recordings and phonology were better at remembering and retrieving lexical items. Moreover, EFL university students generally reported that the opportunities to practice pronunciation via a mobile app was the one most motivating and beneficial features of learning vocabulary (Kohnke, 2020).

4.4 The Effects of Using the App on Students' Vocabulary Retention

This section presents the results for answering the second research question (RQ2):

What are the effects of employing a mobile app on EFL students' vocabulary retention? To answer RQ2, descriptive statistics, a paired-samples t-test, and an independent-samples t-test of the Target Words in the Knowledge Scale Test were employed.

4.4.1 Results of the Delayed Post-test and a Paired-samples T-test for EG

The delayed post-test of the target words in the Knowledge Scale Test was conducted four weeks after the post-test. The results of the delayed post-test for the experiment group are presented in Table 4.8 below. Next, a paired-samples t-test was performed for the experiment group to examine the statistical difference between the mean score of the post-test and that of the delayed post-test, as shown in Table 4.9 below.

Table 4.8 **Descriptive statistics of the delayed post-test for EG**

Test	EG (N=56)	Full points (400)	$\overline{X}$	S.D.
Delayed Post-test	Highest score	331/400	292.22	48.067
	Lowest score	278/400		

EG: Experiment Group. The total scores of the Target Words in the Knowledge Scale Test were 400 points.

Table 4.9 **A paired-samples t-test of the post-test and the delayed post-test for EG**

Group	Tests	$\overline{X}$	S.D.	T-value	Sig. (2-tailed)
EG (N=56)	Post-test	328.16	44.978	12.215	.229
	Delayed Post-test	292.22	48.067		

EG: Experiment Group (Significant level $p < 0.05$). The total scores of the Target Words in the Knowledge Scale Test were 400 points.

According to Table 4.8 above, mean of delayed post-test for experiment group was 292.22 (S.D =48.067), with their scores ranging from 278 to 331. Next, as displayed in Table 4.9 above, for the experiment group, its mean decreased from 328.16 on the post-test to 292.22 on the delayed post-test, which is a reduction of 35.94. Moreover, from a paired-samples t-test, no significant difference between mean of delayed post-test and that of post-test was identified ($p = 0.229 > 0.05$). It indicated that experiment students' retention of the words declined slightly after four weeks.

4.4.2 Results of the Delayed Post-test and a Paired-samples T-test for CG

Similarly, after using descriptive statistics, the results of the delayed post-test for the control group are shown in Table 4.10 below. Then, a paired-samples t-test was conducted for the control group to determine the statistical difference between the mean score of the post-test and that of the delayed post-test, as shown in Table 4.11.

Table 4.10 **Descriptive statistics of the delayed post-test for CG**

Test	CG (N = 58)	Full points (400)	$\overline{X}$	S.D.
Delayed Post-test	Highest score	265/400	174.65	36.843
	Lowest score	134/400		

CG: Control Group. The total scores of the Target Words in the Knowledge Scale Test were 400 points.

Table 4.11 **A paired-samples t-test of the post-test and delayed post-test for CG**

Group	Tests	$\overline{X}$	S.D.	T-value	Sig. (2-tailed)
CG (N = 58)	Post-test	242.20	34.550	21.456	.000
	Delayed Post-test	174.65	36.843		

CG: Control Group (Significant level $p < 0.05$). The total scores of the Target Words in the Knowledge Scale Test were 400 points.

As revealed by Table 4.10 above, mean of delayed post-test for control group is 174.65 (S.D = 36.843), with their scores ranging from 134 to 265. From Table 4.11 above, mean of control group decreased from 242.20 on the post-test to 174.65 on the delayed post-test, with a decrease of 67.55. By further analysis of a paired-samples t-test, a significant difference between mean of post-test and that of delayed post-test was detected ($p = 0.000 < 0.05$). This meant that the control group students' retention of the words declined considerably four weeks later.

4.4.3 Results of an Independent-samples T-test for the Delayed Post-test

An independent-samples t-test was performed to determine the statistical difference between the mean score of the delayed post-test for the experiment group and that for the control group. The results of the independent-samples t-test are illustrated in Table 4. 12 below.

Table 4. 12 **An independent-samples t-test of the delayed post-test for the two groups**

Test	Group	$\overline{\text{X}}$	S. D.	T-value	Sig. (2-tailed)
Delayed Post-test	EG (N = 56)	292.22	48.067	32.475	.001
	CG (N = 58)	174.65	36.843		

EG: Experiment Group; CG: Control Group; Significant level p < 0.05. The total scores of the Target Words in the Knowledge Scale Test were 400 points.

According to Table 4. 12 above, mean of delayed post-test for experiment group (M = 292.22; S. D. = 48.067) was much higher than that of the control group (M = 174.65; S. D. = 36.843). Through further analysis with an independent-samples t-test, a significant difference was detected in mean of delayed post-tests from two groups (p = 0.001 < 0.05). This meant that the students using the app could retain more words than the students who used the paper-based wordlist, suggesting that the app was more effective in students' retention of the words.

4.5 Discussion of the Effects of the App on Vocabulary Retention

As presented above, the app was effective in maintaining students' memory of the words. The results concur well with the findings of the studies (Kohnke et al., 2019; Poláková & Klímová, 2019), which showed that using mobile apps could enhance students' vocabulary retention effectively. Nevertheless, these results are different from the findings of Zhang et al. (2011), which showed that no significant difference was detected on vocabulary retention between the group using SMS (Short Message Service) and the group employing a paper-based wordlist. The reasons could be related to the shortcomings of SMS of mobile phones, which have a limited memory capacity, difficulties in learning words, and reviewing. In the present study, the three reasons below can be considered as causal factors for a more enduring memory of words among the students using the app.

At first, the spaced review by the retrieval sections of the app probably strengthens students' memory of the words. According to Kang (2016), the spaced vocabulary review means having the initial study and subsequent repetitions of words being spaced over time. In the present study, this spacing was implemented by the students' reviewing the target words four times at intervals of 9 hours, 1 day, 2 days and 6 days after they first encountered them in one week. According to the researchers (Daloğlu et al., 2009; Epp & Phirangee, 2019; Kang, 2016; Namaziandost et al., 2019), it was discovered that the spaced repetitions of vocabulary had facilitating influences on transferring learners' knowledge of the learned vocabulary from short-term memory to long-term memory. Besides, students' spaced review of the exercises in the app would be helpful, as the exercises were part of the vocabulary learning which also led to effective vocabulary retention (Stockwell, 2010; Zimmerman, 1997). Furthermore, these findings are supported by Ma's (2014a) study, which showed that each time the words were retrieved for practice in the students' review, the memory trace for the words would be strengthened. Moreover, it is highlighted that retrieval exercises in the vocabulary review often produce more substantial gains in long-term memory compared to repeated learning (Barcroft, 2006; Candry et al., 2020; Carrier & Pashler, 1992; Roediger & Karpicle, 2005; Roediger & Butler, 2011).

Next, dual coding systems of the words in the app led to better recall. According to Paivio (2007), dual coding systems mean the verbal system and the visual system, which processes, stores linguistics information (such as texts and sound) and visual information (such as pictures and videos), respectively. In addition, three different processing levels: representational, referential, and associative processing, often take place within or between verbal and nonverbal/visual systems to intensify the memory of the information (Clark & Paivio, 1991; Paivio, 1986). Further details can be seen in Section 2.1.2. As claimed by Lin, the dual association of verbal and visual modes is very useful in recalling related information, since "when one memory trace is lost, the other remains and is accessible" (2009: 24). Furthermore, according to Boers et al. (2017), presenting words in two or more modes can attract more attention to the words from EFL students' and hence promotes their retention of vocabulary. They explained further that the visual, as well as verbal illustrations of new words, enhances the quality of processing, and thus makes the words more memorable. These findings substantiate those of Kanellopoulou et al. (2019), which demonstrated that bimodal presentations of new words can improve learners' long-term memory of them.

Finally, students' greater involvement in the exercises of the app resulted in their better retention of the words. As highlighted by Hulstijn and Laufer (2001), the words processed with a greater involvement are retained better than those of their counterparts who processed the words with a lower involvement. This is also supported from the levels of processing theory by Craik and Lockhart (1972), who claimed that the chance of a single piece of information to be stored into the long-term memory was decided by its processing levels initially. According to Douglas (2016), ESL students performed better on vocabulary learning with the load of involvement being heavier on task-induced activities. Their long-term retention of vocabulary, however, proved to be relatively limited. The reason might have something to do with the small number of participants, with only five students taking part in the whole process of research. Moreover, Bagheri et al. (2020) found that Iranian EFL learners' retention of idioms would increase when their involvement load was more engaged in the tasks.

4.6 The Students' Perceptions of the App

To answer the third research question (RQ3): What are the EFL learners' perceptions of vocabulary learning via a mobile app? The responses from the questionnaire, the interview, and the diaries of the experiment group, were examined together. The results are presented below.

4.6.1 Results of the Questionnaire

The questionnaire was adapted from Chang et al. (2012) and Wang (2015) (see details in Section 3.3.5). The questionnaire was valid and reliable, as its content validity was 0.875 and its reliability 0.913. First, according to the students' responses to the questionnaire, the results were obtained using descriptive analysis on SPSS (18.0

version). Then, the results were summarized into five categories, namely, attitudes towards using, perceived convenience, perceived ease of use, perceived usefulness, and continued intention to use, based on the studies of Chang et al. (2012) and Davis (1989). Table 4.13 below shows a summary.

Table 4.13 **Responses to the questionnaire with numbers and percentages**

Items	Categories (average)	Strongly Disagree	Disagree	Not sure	Agree	Strongly Agree
4. It is a good method to learn vocabulary via the app.	Attitude towards using (36/50, 72%)	0%	4,8%	8,16%	29,58%	9,18%
5. I prefer the app to the traditional wordlist for learning vocabulary.		0%	6,12%	10,20%	21,42%	13,26%
2. Learning vocabulary via the app is convenient, for I can choose place and time to learn new words.	Perceived convenience (42/50, 84%)	0%	2,4%	10,20%	27,54%	11,22%
11. The app makes vocabulary learning more convenient outside the classroom.		0%	0%	4,8%	32,64%	14,28%
1. The vocabulary learning app is easy to use.	Perceived ease of use (37/50, 74%)	0%	3,6%	7,14%	32,64%	8,16%
3. It is easier for me to learn vocabulary via the app.		0%	5,1%	18,36%	21,42%	6,12%
12. I can learn the words easier based on the clues of images and examples sentences in the app.		0%	3,6%	4,8%	29,58%	14,28%

(续表)

Items	Categories (average)	Strongly Disagree	Disagree	Not sure	Agree	Strongly Agree
6. The vocabulary learning app motivates me to learn new words.	Perceived usefulness (31/50, 62%)	0%	6,12%	16,32%	19,38%	9,18%
7. The app is useful for me to learn vocabulary.		0%	2,4%	9,18%	29,58%	10,20%
8. The learning sections in the app help me learn vocabulary more effectively.		0%	0%	9,18%	31,62%	10,20%
9. The immediate feedback in the app can push me to monitor and adjust my vocabulary learning.		0%	3,6%	12,24%	23,46%	12,24%
10. The retrieval sections in the app enable me to review and remember the vocabulary well.		0%	0%	18,36%	27,54%	5,10%
13. The example sentences in the app can consolidate knowledge of the words.		0%	5,10%	16,32%	20,40%	9,18%
14. The vocabulary learned via the app is not easily forgotten.		0%	7,14%	29,58%	12,24%	2,4%
15. The example sentences help me learn how to use the words appropriately.		0%	3,6%	18,36%	21,42%	8,16%

(续表)

Items	Categories (average)	Strongly Disagree	Disagree	Not sure	Agree	Strongly Agree
16. In the future, I will continue to use the app to learn vocabulary.	Continued intention to use(40/50, 80%)	0%	2,4%	8,16%	23,46%	17,34%

As demonstrated in Table 4.13 above, firstly, 42 out of 50 students (84%) agreed that the mobile app was convenient to use for vocabulary learning, as illustrated by the responses to two items (i.e. items 2 and 11). The number of 84% in the bracket is the mean percentage of the total percentage concerning the choices "agree" and "strongly agree" for items 2 and 11, and this formula is also applicable to the following. In addition, 40 out of 50 students (80%) expressed their intention of continuing to use the app for learning vocabulary in the future, as shown by the responses to item 16. Moreover, 37 out of 50 students (74%) reported that the mobile app made their vocabulary learning easy, as can be seen from the responses to three items (i.e. items 1, 3 and 12). Besides, according to their responses to two items (i.e. items 4 and 5), 36 out of 50 students (72%) held positive attitudes towards the usage of the app. Last, 31 out of 50 students (62%) believed that it was useful to learn and retain the vocabulary by using the mobile app, as demonstrated in the responses to eight items (i.e. items 6, 7, 8, 9, 10, 13, 14 and 15).

4.6.2 Results of the Semi-structured Interview

For the semi-structured interview, eleven questions were from the researcher who referred to the questionnaire of the students' perceptions. The questions in the interview were valid and relevant to the objectives of the present study, since the content validity was 0.88 (see details in Section 3.3.6). Next, a thematic analysis was employed to analyze the data from the interview of the present in terms of Dörnyei (2007). To find the themes from the data, the responses of the interviewees were used. In the beginning, 19 students (ten males and nine females) selected on purposive sampling from the experiment group were numbered according to the order of being interviewed. For instance, St. 1 stood for the first student to be interviewed. To ensure the accuracy of the transcriptions and translations by the researcher, the interview conversations were recorded by a digital recorder as well as a notebook, and cross-checked by two experienced English teachers. Later, through thematic analysis, three themes (i. e. fondness, advantages, and challenges of the app) arose from five categories below, which were summarized from the interviewees' responses (Appendix O). Table 4.14 below demonstrates the five categories.

Table 4.14 **Categories found from interviewees' responses**

Categories(number, percentage)	Interviewees' responses
1. Fondness for the app (18/19, 94.7%)	
-in learning words	St.19:"...it is easier to learn words with the app than using the traditional wordlist, so I am fond of it..."
2. Usefulness/Helpfulness (19/19, 100%)	
-in understanding and expanding words	St.9:"...the example sentences make me understand the new words and also expand other words..."
-in remembering words	St.5:"...the app left a deep impression on me..."
-in improving listening	St.8:"...it can practice and then improve my listening skill..."
-in adjusting words' learning	St.13:"...the feedback made me correct my errors and adjust my learning..."
-in correcting pronunciation	St.16:"...it can improve my pronunciation of words when I read them wrong..."
-in recalling words	St.17:"...the relevant pictures and sentences would come to my mind for helping me recall the words..."
-in practicing four skills	St.19:"...it can help me practice my speaking, listening, reading and translation..."
-in arousing interest in learning words	St.4:"...interesting sentences and pictures of the app arouse my interest in learning the words..."

(续表)

Categories (number, percentage)	Interviewees' responses
3. Convenience (19/19, 100%)	
-in time	St. 11: "…*I can use the fragment time to learn vocabulary via the app…*"
-in place	St. 14: "…*I can learn words anywhere I want…*"
-in size	St. 1: "…*I can learn words conveniently, for it is lighter to carry a mobile phone than to carry a textbook…*"
4. Innovation (17/19, 89.5%)	
-in the way of learning words	St. 2: "…*using this app to learn words is an innovation, for I have never employed such a method for learning vocabulary before…*"
5. Drawbacks (4/19, 21.1%)	
-in the irrelevant information popping out	St. 8: "…*when I was in the process of learning words via the app, other information popping out distracted me from study…*"
-in the exercise designing	St. 11: "…*the exercise of making sentences should be added into the app for strengthening the usage of vocabulary…*"
-in the network connection	St. 13: "…*sometimes the network connection was unstable, made me feel frustrated, and then gave up learning words…*"
-in covering the words of textbooks	St. 17: "…*it would make make me better if textbooks' words were involved in the app, for I was not ready for CET-4 words with low proficiency…*"

Firstly, 18 out of 19 (94.7%) interviewees were fond of the mobile app mainly for its advantages in learning words, as shown in Table 4.14 above. These lend support to the students' responses to the questionnaire concerning their attitudes. Nevertheless, St. 7 said:

"*I prefer to use a traditional wordlist to learn words, for I have used it for a long time and I am used to it. Besides, there are many temptations in the mobile phone, and it easily distracts me, for I am not a self-disciplined person.*"

Next, the three categories showing the advantages of the app and the last category exhibiting the challenges faced by students are displayed as follows.

(1) All interviewees (100%) considered that using the app was useful/helpful in

eight aspects, which included: "in understanding and expanding words" "in remembering words" "in improving listening" "in adjusting words' learning" "in correcting pronunciation" "in recalling words" "in practicing four skills" "in arousing interest in learning words". These findings offer vital evidence for the students' responses to the questionnaire regarding the app's usefulness.

(2) All interviewees (100%) regarded the app as convenient for them to learn and review words in three aspects: "in time" "in place" and "in size". These aspects match well with the students' responses to the questionnaire about convenience.

(3) 17 out of 19 interviewees (89.5%) referred to using the app as an innovative way of learning words.

(4) Finally, 4 out of 19 interviewees (21.1%) displayed their challenges by describing the drawbacks of the app, which were "in the irrelevant information popping out" "in the exercise designing" "in the network connection" "in covering the words of textbooks". In other words, these aspects should be improved in the future.

4.6.3 Results of the Students' Diaries from EG

Experiment group learners began to keep a diary on the length of time for learning the target words, their feelings concerning their learning words or reviews every week from the second week (W2) to the ninth week (W9). Therefore, eight weeks later, 448 diaries were collected from 56 students of experiment group. Next, the diaries were numbered. The diaries (D) per week (W) in the experiment group (EG) were numbered in ascending order of students' ID numbers, such as D1W2EG, D2W2EG, D3W2EG…, D1W3EG, D2W3EG, D3W3EG…, and the like. For instance, the code D1W2EG meant the first student's diary in the second week from the experiment group, and D1W3EG meant the first student's diary in the third week from experiment group, and the like.

Then, the diaries were first translated from Chinese into English by the researcher and then the translations were cross-examined by two experienced English teachers. Later, the translations of the diaries were grouped and categorized to form themes. Table 4.15 below demonstrates the length of time, study time, and the feelings expressed in the diaries of the experiment group (Appendix P).

Table 4.15 **Time length, studying time for ten words/week, and feelings from EG**

Times/week	The 1st time	The 2nd time	The 3rd time	The 4th time	The 5th time	Total time/week
Average time length (minutes)	20	18	17	10	10	75
1. Studying time (number, percentage)	Students' writings					
-in early morning (43/56, 76.7%)	D6W2EG: "...when I woke up at 6:00 a.m. before getting up, I would switch on smartphone and use the app to learn words..."					
-between two classes (34/56, 60.7%)	D28W5EG: "...usually I use the app to review words during the 20 minutes' break time between two classes..."					
-during meals (35/56, 62.5%)	D31W4EG: "...I often learn the words through the app while I am queuing or eating in the canteen..."					
-while going-out (45/56, 80.4%)	D18W9EG: "...when I go outside and take a bus, I like using the app to learn words to kill time..."					
-late at night (51/56, 91.1%)	D42W7EG: "...After 11:00 p.m., I got on the bed and could not fall asleep easily. Then I turned on the smartphone to learn words via the app..."					
2. Feelings by category (number, percentage)	Students' writings					
(1) Preferable (46/56, 82.1%)						
-in memorizing words	D54W6EG: "...I prefer the app, for it helps me remember many words..."					
(2) Convenient (51/56, 91.1%)						
-in time and place	D39W3EG: "...as long as the smartphone is on me, I can learn and review words via the app anytime, anywhere..."					
(3) Effective (44/56, 78.6%)						
-in memory of words	D31W2EG: "... Words are memorized repeatedly, which effectively enhances the memorization of the word..."					

(续表)

Times/week	The 1st time	The 2nd time	The 3rd time	The 4th time	The 5th time	Total time/week
(4) Reasonable (50/56, 89.3%)						
-in learning ten words at a time	D31W2EG: "…using the app to learn ten words per time outside the class is reasonable and easy…"					
-in a five-time schedule per week	D38W5EG: "…The teacher gave us the five-time schedule of the app so that we didn't have any pressure to learn words…"					
(5) Satisfied (41/56, 73.2%)						
-with an increase in vocabulary size	D6W7EG: "…It's another full week, and my vocabulary size increases day by day. I feel very satisfied…"					
(6) Fun (43/56, 76.8%)						
-in the process of learning words	D14W8EG: "…In the process of memorizing words, …This will alleviate the boring of reciting words and add more fun…"					
-in the process of remembering words	D8W5EG: "… I feel that memorizing words has also become a fun thing, easy and fun…"					
(7) Easy (38/56, 67.9%)						
-in memorizing words	D46W9EG: "…It feels easy to memorize a lot of words through the app. The words which once cost me a long time to memorize only need a while to stay in my mind now…"					
(8) Useful (47/56, 83.9%)						
-in the pronunciation of words	D31W3EG: " … using the app to review words could correct my pronunciation…"					
-in increasing interest in English	D43W4EG: "…after using the app for three weeks, my interest in English learning is much improved…"					
-in memorizing words	D38W5EG: "…I think using this app to remember words is very helpful, and it suits me very well …"					
-in increasing confidence in English	D25W2EG: "…After using the app, my heart has lighted a raging fire, and my confidence in English comes back…"					

(续表)

Times/week	The 1st time	The 2nd time	The 3rd time	The 4th time	The 5th time	Total time/week
(9) Willing to persist (46/56, 82.1%)						
-in learning words via the app	D32W6EG: "…*Memorizing words is getting more relaxed, and more vocabulary is accumulated. I hope I can persist in learning words via the app…*"					
(10) Difficult (11/56, 19.6%)						
-in sticking to the schedule during military training	D43W4EG: "…*Because of military training* [1], *the arrangement each day was full. It was challenging to stick to the five-time schedule to learn words…*"					
-in remembering the pronunciations and meanings of all words	D24W6EG: "…*but it was difficult to remember the pronunciation and meanings of every word completely…*"					
-in recalling the words	D52W7EG: "…*I felt I could not recognize the words after seeing them if I switched off the smartphone…*"					

As displayed in Table 4.15 above, the students' length of time spent on the ten words was 15 minutes per time making a total of 75 minutes every week. Next, their studying time ranged from early morning to late in the evening. To be precise, the popularity of the students' study time via the app ranked from high to low was "late at night" (51/56, 91.1%), "while going-out" (45/56, 80.4%), "in early morning" (43/56, 76.7%), "during meals" (35/56, 62.5%), "between two classes" (34/56, 60.7%).

Furthermore, with respect to students' feelings about the app, four themes (i.e. preference, merits, willingness to persist, difficulties in using the app) are formed from nine categories of their diaries, which are displayed as follow.

---

1 In China, every newcomer in the university has to take military training, which often lasts from two weeks to four weeks. It usually begins in September of the first semester. During the military training, all courses of the freshmen stop, and all they have to do is to take the military training led by military instructors from 6:00 a.m. to 9:00 p.m. every day with several breaks a day.

First, 46 out of 56 students (82.1%) showed their preferences for the app, because they felt it was "convenient" "effective" "reasonable" "satisfying" "fun" "easy" "useful" in learning and remembering the words via the app. These findings further confirm the students' positive attitudes towards the app which were found from the questionnaire and the interview. Next, the seven categories about the merits of the app are presented as follows.

(1) 51 out of 56 students (91.1%) thought it was convenient to learn and review words via the app.

(2) 44 out of 56 students (78.6%) described the app as effective in enhancing their memory of words.

(3) 50 out of 56 students (89.3%) believed that it was reasonable for them to learn 10 words via the app independently using the five-time schedule within one week.

(4) 41 out of 56 students (73.2%) expressed their satisfaction with the app, for they could feel their vocabulary size increasing after using the app.

(5) 43 out of 56 students (76.8%) mentioned that learning and memorizing words via the app was enjoyable for them.

(6) 38 out of 56 students (67.9%) claimed that they felt that it was easy to keep the words in mind through the app.

(7) 47 out of 56 students (83.9%) perceived the app as useful in correcting the pronunciation of words, increasing their interest in English, memorizing words, and improving their confidence in English.

Additionally, 46 out of 56 students (82.1%) expressed their willingness to persist in using the app in the future.

Finally, 11 out of 56 students (19.6%) mentioned their difficulties in using the app while following the schedule during military training, remembering the pronunciations and meanings of all the words, and recalling the words.

4.7 Discussion on the Students' Perceptions of the App

First, according to the students' responses to the questionnaire, it was discovered that 36 out of 50 students (72%) held positive attitudes towards the app. This finding is supported by 18 out of 19 interviewees (94.7%), who showed their fondness for the app. Also, 46 out of 56 students (82.1%) mentioned in their diaries that they preferred learning and remembering vocabulary via the app. These findings match well with the studies (Bensalem, 2018; Deris & Shukor, 2019; Gonulal, 2019; Klimova & Polakova, 2020; Kohnke, 2020; Ornprapat & Wiwat, 2015), which revealed that most of EFL students held positive attitudes towards learning EFL vocabulary helped by mobile apps. Additionally, according to Creswell (2017), the triangulation of data from multiple sources: the questionnaire, interview, and diary, can ensure the internal validity of the data. Therefore, the reasons for the students' positive attitudes towards the app from the questionnaires, interviews, and diaries, were reliable. They are further discussed as follows.

(1) According to the results from the questionnaires, interviews, and diaries, one common reason, the convenience of the app is mentioned, although the amount and percentage of students expressing this view are slightly different (42 of 50 students or 84% from the questionnaires; 19 interviewees or 100% from the interviews; 51 of 56 students or 91.1% from the diaries). As shown by Kim et al. (2013), students positively accepted the use of mobile apps for language learning, for the convenience offered by the apps increased their learning opportunities. Also, Soleimani et al. (2014) ascertained positive responses from EFL students to a mobile app due to its great convenience. Moreover, Deris and Shukor (2019) discovered that their students considered it convenient to learn EFL vocabulary via a mobile app, since it was accessible in any place and at any time. As a consequence, they were able to use the app based on their preferred place and time, which made their vocabulary learning very effective. The findings above

are further confirmed by Klimova and Polakova (2020), who highlighted that EFL students appreciated the convenient accessibility of learning vocabulary with smartphone apps more than with the traditional textbooks. Additionally, Kohnke (2020) disclosed that EFL university students regarded the anytime, anywhere flexibility of the app as strengths to learn vocabulary, which they often employed on the way to university.

(2) 37 out of 50 students (74%) from the questionnaires and 43 of 56 students (76.8%) from the diaries claimed that it was easy and fun to learn and review vocabulary via the app. As identified by Wang (2015), Thai EFL students found the mobile app attractive and interesting for learning vocabulary. One reason why mobile learning had a positive effect on students' engagement was provided by Hargis et al. (2014), who explained that mobile technologies brought EFL learners' more fun and thus motivated them to more proactive involvement. Also, Kwangsawad (2019) stated that EFL students found employing smartphones more fun and productive in English classes. Additionally, the students liked using the mobile app to learn new EFL words, since they felt that learning words from the app rather than from textbooks was more fun, less stressful, and easier to use (Klimova & Polakova, 2020).

(3) The usefulness/helpfulness of the app was identified from 31 of 50 students' (62%) responses to the questionnaire, 19 interviewees (100%), and 47 out of 56 students' (83.9%) diaries. According to Tabatabaei and Goojani (2012), the Short Message Service (SMS) of mobile phones was useful in facilitating EFL vocabulary learning among Iranian high school learners. Similarly, Ornprapat and Wiwat (2015) found that the app SMS of mobile phones helped contribute to the success of Thai EFL students' vocabulary learning and increased their learning motivation. Similarly, Makoe and Shandu (2018) learned that the self-developed mobile app was helpful in enhancing EFL learners' vocabulary learning and forming their habits of autonomous learning in South Africa. Next, exploring the experiences of Chinese older adults' (aged from 45 to 85) learning EFL vocabulary with various mobile apps, Wang and Christiansen (2019) revealed that using mobile apps was very useful in improving their vocabulary and motivation for learning English. This lends support to the studies of Yu (2019) and Chen

(2020), who found that using mobile technologies could increase learners' confidence and motivation in learning a foreign language.

(4) 17 out of 19 interviewees (89.5%) regarded it as innovative to learn vocabulary via the app. As demonstrated by Basal (2012), mobile learning can enrich EFL traditional teaching and learning methods creatively by setting a flexible, hands-on way learning both inside and outside the classroom. Pavlik (2015) argued that mobile technologies were transforming teaching and learning methods by challenging educational notions of space, time, content, processes, and outcomes. As a result, teachers and learners were experiencing innovative changes, which included the direction of communication, interactivity, the media of teaching and learning, the constraints on the learning process and output. Next, Sung et al. (2016) showed that MALL had great potential for reforming teaching and learning methods with innovations. This is consistent with the study of Basal et al. (2016), which identified that using apps was innovatively shaping the way EFL teachers taught and students learned by offering them many new opportunities. Moreover, it was revealed that learning vocabulary via the mobile app provided an innovative opportunity and experience for Saudi Arabian EFL students (Shahbaz & Khan, 2017).

(5) 44 out of 56 students (78.6%) in the diaries described the app as effective. Hu (2013) argued that regular SMS (Short Message Service) on mobile phones might act as an effective way for EFL learners to exercise their autonomous vocabulary learning. As noted by Rezaei et al. (2014), it was an effective way to improve EFL vocabulary learning through the mobile app, for it helped visualize the meanings of words by multimedia and hence left a deep impression on them. Next, Wu (2015) attested that the self-developed app was effective in facilitating Chinese EFL learners' vocabulary learning in a natural environment with its great convenience and easiness. Also, it was discovered by Ma (2019) that the dictionary apps could significantly improve the efficiency of ESL learners' vocabulary learning by offering multiple functions and rich resources. Moreover, EFL learners felt that it was challenging and time-consuming to learn academic EFL vocabulary, yet they felt that mobile apps could enhance their academic vocabulary

learning more efficiently (Kohnke, 2020).

(6) 50 out of 56 students (89.3%) in the diaries mentioned that it was reasonable for them to learn ten words at one time five times per week with the mobile app. As claimed by Paas et al. (2004), working memory (short-term memory) could only perform a few tasks or hold a limited number of information each time. Undertaking more information than working memory can process at one time would lead to memory fatigue or even failure (Ginns, 2006; Merckelbach et al., 2000). Other causes might be that the limits of short-term memory capacity for an adult were seven ± two objects (Miller, 1956), and that learners' working memories were more likely to experience confusion with a high cognitive load induced by dealing with many objects at one time (Sweller, 2016). In addition, according to Nation (1990, 2001), EFL learners needed to be exposed to a word 5 ~ 16 times to acquire it thoroughly, and frequent re-encountering of the word was crucial for learners to keep the vocabulary in long-term retention. Thornbury (2002) stated that one important factor that improved retention was spaced learning of the words. This means that the words learned over spaced periods were kept better than those counterparts learned in concentrated bursts. This is verified by the findings of Thornton and Houser (2005) that spaced practice exhibited more beneficial impacts on vocabulary learning and retention than massed practice.

(7) 41 out of 56 students (73.2%) in the diaries wrote that they were satisfied with the app. Santos et al. (2016) highlighted that EFL learners with various mother languages were satisfied with an Augmented Reality (AR) App as it enabled students to better retain words. Next, as discovered by Wang (2017), Taiwanese EFL learners were satisfied with his/her self-developed app to learn vocabulary because they found it relaxing and convenient. By developing an Augmented Reality (AR) App for Malaysian EFL learners, Che Hashim et al. (2018) found that students and teachers were content with the app due to its learnability and ease of use. Additionally, it was noted that EFL university students were satisfied with a mobile game-based English vocabulary learning app because they enjoyed using it and became more involved (Chen et al., 2019). Moreover, Kohnke (2020) found that in general EFL students were satisfied with the app to learn vocabulary.

(8) 40 out of 50 students (80%) from the questionnaires and 46 out of 56 students (82.1%) in the diaries expressed their willingness to persist in using the app to learn vocabulary in the future. As identified by Kim et al. (2013), ESL learners became more willing to use mobile technologies for English learning in their lives, since it could bring them many learning opportunities. Wang et al. (2015) found that EFL learners' willingness to use the Word Power App for future study was influenced by their classroom learning experience. In addition, according to Wang and Hsu (2020), EFL learners' future behavioral intentions closely correlated with their satisfaction with the app. In other words, when the learners were satisfied with the app, they were more likely to continue to use it in the future.

Nevertheless, 4 out of 19 interviewees (21.1%) mentioned the drawbacks of apps, and 11 out of 56 students (19.6%) described their difficulties in using the app. As argued by Wang and Higgins (2006), the barriers that constrained the use of mobile technologies for language learning were related to psychological, pedagogical, and technological factors. They also claimed that it was time-consuming for EFL learners to embrace mobile technologies, and that it was impossible to expect all of them to accept Mobile-assisted Language Learning at the same pace. The disadvantage of using mobile apps for language learning identified in the studies (Li & Li, 2011; Viberg & Grönlund, 2013) was that some students might be distracted easily from unrelated information on their smartphones or prefer to do something else. Besides, challenges concerning the costs of the Internet and mobile devices for language learning were faced by parents, students, teachers, and educational institutions (Oberg & Daniels, 2013; Oz, 2014). Additionally, Wu (2015) pointed out that a lack of interaction and updating of contents were two shortcomings of the app she developed for EFL vocabulary learning. It was discovered that one limitation affecting the usability of mobile technologies for language learning was the dependency on networks (Elaish et al., 2017). This is substantiated by Makoe and Shandu (2018) who explained that EFL learners would experience frustration and barriers hindering their vocabulary learning when there was no network or the Internet unstable. Moreover, as revealed by Taghizadeh and Porkar (2018), the reasons for the negative attitudes of some students towards using mobile technologies for EFL vocabulary learning could be the result of technical problems, the small batteries on mobile devices, and the possible harm to their eyes.

4.8 Results of the Diaries from CG and Discussion

Like students of experiment group, control group counterparts also wrote diaries on the time length of their learning target words, their feelings about the learning words or reviews every week from the second week (W2) to the ninth week (W9). Consequently, 464 diaries were collected from 58 students of the control group after eight weeks. Then, the diaries were numbered. The diaries (D) per week (W) in the control group (CG) were numbered in ascending order of students' ID numbers, such as D1W2CG, D2W2CG, D3W2CG..., D1W3CG, D2W3CG, D3W3CG..., and the like. For example, the code D1W2CG meant the first student's diary in the second week from the control group, and D1W3CG meant the first student's diary in the third week from the control group, and the like.

Later, the diaries were translated from Chinese into English by the researcher and then cross-checked by two teachers with college English teaching experiences. Next, the translations were grouped and categorized into themes. Table 4.16 illustrates the length of time for studying found from the students' diaries of the control group.

Table 4.16 **Time length, studying time for ten words/week from CG**

Times/week	The 1st time	The 2nd time	The 3rd time	The 4th time	The 5th time	Total time/week
Average time length (minutes)	18	17	16	14	15	80
Studying time (number, percentage)	Students' writings					
-before the first class of the day (48/58, 82.8%)	D7W4CG: "...I often use the time before the first class beginning to recite the wordlist on the paper sheet..."					

(续表)

Times/week	The 1st time	The 2nd time	The 3rd time	The 4th time	The 5th time	Total time/ week
-after class and before meals (41/58, 70.7%)	D16W3CG: "...After class, I usually spent some time on the wordlist before I went to the crowded canteen..."					
-during the night (50/58, 86.2%)	D43W7EG: "...After having dinner, I prefer to go to the library to recite the wordlist..."					

As shown in Table 4.16, the length of time students spent on the ten words was 16 minutes per time which made a total of 80 minutes every week. Next, the study time of the control group varied from morning to night. Table 4.17 below presents the similarities and differences on the length of time and studying time between the two groups.

Table 4.17 **Similarities/differences on time length, studying time of the two groups**

Groups	Times/week	The 1st time	The 2nd time	The 3rd time	The 4th time	The 5th time	In total
EG	Time length (minutes)	20	18	17	10	10	75
CG		18	17	16	14	15	80
	Studying time (number and percentage, ranking from high to low)						
EG		Late at night (51/56, 91.1%)	During going-out periods (45/56, 80.4%)	In early morning (43/56, 76.7%)	During the meals (35/56, 62.5%)	Between two classes (34/56, 60.7%)	
CG		During the night (50/58, 86.2%)	Before the first class of the day (48/58, 82.8%)	After class and before meals (41/58, 70.7%)			

According to Table 4.17 above, the average length of time spent on the ten words by the experiment group was 15 minutes at a time, which was close to that of the control group (16 minutes/time). Next, the students of the experiment group spent 75 minutes in total on the ten words every week, which was a similar amount of time to that of the control group (80 minutes/week). Nevertheless, the periods of study time for experiment group were more varied than control group, which suggested that the app was more convenient than the paper-based wordlist for learning the target words.

Table 4.18 Students' feelings about the paper-based wordlist from CG

Feelings by category (number, percentage)	Students' writings
1. Good(36/58, 62.1%)	
-with the five-time schedule	D14W2CG: "…when I first saw the words, I had a strong sense of strangeness. By the third time, I became familiar with the words, and I remembered the words. By the fifth time, I was thoroughly familiar with them. So this five-time schedule was good for us to be familiar with the words…"
2. Tedious(38/58, 65.5%)	
-in learning words	D33W5CG: "…it was annoying and painful for me to spend much time learning the wordlist…"
-in reviewing words	D40W3CG: "…the review process with the wordlist is annoying…"
3. Weak(42/58, 72.4%)	
-in retaining words	D5W3CG: "…The meanings of words were easy to be confused with others. Hence it was difficult to remember the words. Missing or reversed letters often happened to me when I tried to spell the words…"
-in efficiency	D51W5CG: "…I found that I learned vocabulary slowly and forgot them quickly. The effectiveness of memorizing words with the wordlist was very low…"
-in pronouncing words	D10W2CG: "… when reading words, I felt my tongue was not smooth. And the pronunciation of the words was challenging for me, and it was not accurate…"

Furthermore, as illustrated by Table 4.18, three categories: satisfaction with the five-time schedule, tediousness, and weaknesses of the paper-based wordlist, are summarized from the students' diaries of the control group (Appendix Q). First, 36 out of 58 students (62.1%) mentioned that it was good for them to learn the ten words according to the five-time schedule. This is consistent with the findings of previous studies (e.g. Ginns, 2006; Merckelbach et al., 2000; Miller, 1956; Nation, 1990, 2001;

Sweller, 2016; Thornbury, 2002; Thornton & Houser, 2005), who revealed that it was reasonable for language learners to learn a small number of words at a time based on a spacing effect.

Next, 38 out of 58 students (65.5%) considered it tedious to learn and review vocabulary using the paper-based wordlist. According to Hanafiah (2015), the students became bored easily with learning from a wordlist and then lost interest in vocabulary learning or even in studying English as a subject. As pointed out by Gadanecz (2018), EFL students considered it dull to learn vocabulary with the paper-based wordlist, which had a negative influence on their self-efficacy and motivation for language learning. Also, it was found that the Iranian EFL students of the control group perceived wordlists as a tedious method to learn vocabulary (Taghizadeh & Porkar, 2018). Additionally, according to the pilot study of the researcher, it showed that EFL learners were likely to feel stressed and tired from looking at wordlists, especially long wordlists from English textbooks, which could affect their learning motivation.

Lastly, 42 out of 58 students (72.4%) claimed that they felt there were three weaknesses in learning paper-based wordlists, which were their retention of the words, learning efficiency, and pronunciation of the words. These findings concur with the study of Mondria and Wit-de-Boer (1991), who found that memorizing vocabulary by using wordlists caused them to become confused and forgetful. Also, Oxford and Scarcella (1994) disclosed that only offering students a wordlist was undoubtedly not an effective method for vocabulary instruction. This is confirmed by Zheng et al. (2015), who demonstrated that it was not effective for Chinese EFL university students to memorize new words using the traditional method of wordlists. Additionally, Icht and Mama (2019) found that the non-production of words (words read silently) was less durable and showed more memory decay than the production of words (words read out) over time. So it can be deduced that the weakness of the students' pronouncing words from a wordlist could negatively influence their vocabulary learning and memory. However, Nation (1993) and Clipperton (1994) argued that learners could directly remember the spelling, pronunciation, and meanings of the words on a wordlist. The reason for this may be that the learners received help with the pronunciation when learning the words, while learners of control group in the study had to learn the wordlist by themselves.

4.9 Summary of the Results and Discussion

To sum up, the result of an independent-samples t-test showed that a statistically significant difference was detected on the post-test between the control group and the experiment group. It indicated that students achieved more words via the mobile app compared with those from the control group, and demonstrated that the app was more effective than paper-based wordlist in improving students' vocabulary learning. These are in line with the findings of the studies (Bensalem, 2018; Chen et al., 2019; Poláková & Klímová, 2019; Wang & Shih, 2015). Besides, the students' more vocabulary achievements via the app could be due to four aspects, which referred to the multimedia environment (Al-Seghayer, 2016; Gonulal, 2019; Kim & Gilman, 2008; Matsuoka & Hirsh, 2010; Mayer, 1997; Mayer & Fiorella, 2014; Ramezanali, 2017; Rusanganwa, 2015), the immediate corrective feedback (Henderson, 2019; Mollakhan et al., 2013; Pashler et al., 2005; Roediger & Butler, 2011; Soria et al., 2020; Sprenger, 2018), the enjoyment induced by the app (Green, 1993; Hsu et al., 2017; Sandberg et al., 2011), the audios of words in the app (Celce-Murcia, 2001; He et al., 2015; Hennings, 2000; Kaplan-Rakowski & Loranc-Paszylk, 2019; Karousou & Nerantzaki, 2020; Laufer, 1998; McCarthy, 1994; Min, 2013; Trofimovich & Issacs, 2012).

Secondly, the results of the delayed post-test disclosed that the students' retention of the words decreased for both groups. The paired-samples t-test for the experiment group showed an insignificant difference between the post-test and the delayed post-test, suggesting a slight reduction of words memory. However, through the paired-samples t-test for the control group, a significant difference was detected between the post-test and the delayed post-test, indicating a considerable memory decay of words. By a further independent-samples t-test, a statistically significant difference was identified on the delayed post-test between the two groups. This meant that the students using the app could retain more words than the students employing the paper-based wordlist, indicating that the app was more effective in maintaining students' retention of the words. These findings are consistent with those of the studies (Kohnke et al., 2019; Poláková & Klímová, 2019). In addition, three factors may account for students retaining more words by using the mobile app, which were the spaced review (Barcroft, 2006; Candry et al., 2020; Carrier & Pashler, 1992; Daloǧlu et al., 2009; Epp & Phirangee, 2019; Kang, 2016; Namaziandost et al., 2019; Roediger & Karpicle, 2005; Roediger & Butler, 2011; Stockwell, 2010; and Zimmerman, 1997), dual coding systems of the words (Boers et al., 2017; Clark & Paivio, 1991; Kanellopoulou et al., 2019; Lin, 2009; Paivio, 1986, 2007), the involvement loads induced by the exercises (Bagheri et al., 2020; Craik & Lockhart, 1972; Douglas, 2016; Hulstijn & Laufer, 2001).

Thirdly, 36 out of 50 students (72%) held positive attitudes towards the app based on their responses to the questionnaire. Also, 18 out of 19 interviewees (94.7%) showed that they liked the app. Also, 46 out of 56 students (82.1%) mentioned in their diaries that they preferred the app. These findings lend support to previous studies (Bensalem, 2018; Deris & Shukor, 2019; Gonulal, 2019; Klimova & Polakova, 2020; and Ornprapat & Wiwat, 2015), which reported that most of the students held positive attitudes towards using mobile apps to learn EFL vocabulary. Additionally, the reasons why most students held positive attitudes towards the app could be the convenience (Deris & Shukor, 2019; Kim et al., 2013; Klimova & Polakova, 2020; Soleimani et al., 2014), ease and enjoyment of using (Deris & Shukor, 2019; Hargis et al., 2014; Klimova & Polakova, 2020; Kwangsawad, 2019; Wang, 2015), the usefulness of the apps (Chen, 2020; Makoe & Shandu, 2018; Ornprapat & Wiwat, 2015; Tabatabaei & Goojani, 2012; Wang & Christiansen, 2019; Yu, 2019), their innovative features (Basal, 2012; Basal et al., 2016; Pavlik, 2015; Shahbaz & Khan, 2017; Sung et al., 2016), their effectiveness (Hu, 2013; Ma, 2019; Rezaei et al., 2014; Wu, 2015), their practicality (Ginns, 2006; Merckelbach et al., 2000; Nation, 1990, 2001; Paas et al., 2004; Sweller, 2016), their satisfaction (Che Hashim et al., 2018; Chen et al., 2019; Santos et al. , 2016; Wang, 2017), and their willingness to persist in using the app (Kim et al. , 2013; Wang & Hsu, 2020; Wang et al. , 2015).

Fourthly, 4 out of 19 interviewees (21.1%) mentioned the drawbacks of the app, and 11 out of 56 students (19.6%) described their difficulties in using the app. The reasons for this may have something to do with psychological factors (Wang & Higgins, 2006), the easily distracted attention (Li & Li, 2011; Viberg & Grönlund, 2013), the costs of mobile devices and of the Internet usage (Oberg & Daniels, 2013; Oz, 2014), the lack of interaction and of the contents' updating (Wu, 2015), the technical problems (Elaish et al. , 2017; Makoe & Shandu, 2018; Taghizadeh & Porkar, 2018), and the possible damage to their eyes (Taghizadeh & Porkar, 2018).

Lastly, as regards the control group, 38 out of 58 students (65.5%) considered it tedious to learn and review vocabulary using the paper-based wordlist. The reasons for this could be that they found the wordlist boring (Gadanecz, 2018; Hanafiah, 2015; Taghizadeh & Porkar, 2018), and the stress, as well as the tiredness induced by the wordlist found from the pilot study of the researcher. Furthermore, 42 out of 58 students (72.4%) pointed out the weaknesses of learning vocabulary by using a paper-based wordlist, which were the difficulty in retaining words (Mondria & Wit-de-Boer, 1991), the low efficiency of the wordlist (Oxford and Scarcella, 1994; Zheng et al. , 2015), and the lack of help in learning how to pronounce the words (Icht & Mama, 2019).

Chapter 5

Conclusion, Implications and Recommendations

This chapter is organized into four sections. Firstly, the procedure and the main findings of the current study are presented. Then, the implications of the present study are shown. Next, the recommendations for further research are proposed. Lastly, a summary of this chapter is given.

5.1 Conclusion of the Study

The study was proposed and done for the purpose of adding to the existing research on mobile app-assisted vocabulary learning in this mobile technology-driven era. A mobile app was developed especially for the vocabulary learning of Chinese EFL learners which was based on four theories: the ten design principles for MALL (Stockwell & Hubbard, 2013), the dual coding theory (Paivio, 2007, 1986, 1971), the cognitive theory of multimedia learning (Mayer, 2014), and the memory-based strategic framework for vocabulary learning (Ma, 2014a). Then, together with exploring the effectiveness of the app on students' vocabulary learning and retention, their perceptions of the app were probed. Next, a mixed methods approach was used to collect data in the study. A quantitative methodology was employed to assess the students' vocabulary size in a pre-test, their knowledge of the target words from the pre-test, post-test and the delayed post-test, as well as their perceptions of the mobile app. In addition, in order to triangulate the students' performances above, a qualitative method was applied to analyze the data from the interviews and the diaries in terms of Creswell (2017). Moreover, to achieve the objectives, three research questions were formulated as below.

(1) What are the effects of using a theory-based mobile app on EFL students' vocabulary learning achievement?

(2) What are the effects of employing a theory-based mobile app on EFL students' vocabulary retention?

(3) What are the EFL learners' perceptions of vocabulary learning via a theory-based mobile app?

To answer the research questions, a quasi-experimental design was made for the study. The duration of the experiment was 14 weeks throughout the first semester of the academic year 2019. First, two classes were chosen to be the participants based on convenience and availability. One secretary class with 56 students was assigned as the experiment group and a Chinese language class with 58 counterparts as the control group at random. Then, in week 1, the two groups were briefed in the classroom about the purpose of the study. Next, in the same week, after both groups had finished the Vocabulary Size Test (VST) and the Vocabulary Knowledge Scale (VKS), the mobile app with eight packages of 80 target words was introduced and then installed into the smartphones of the experiment group. In contrast, the wordlists of the same eight packages on paper sheets were given out for control group weekly.

Moreover, from the second week on, both groups started to learn one package of ten words by the proposed schedule on their own every week. Also, the diaries of both groups about the time for learning and the students' feelings were collected once a week. Eight weeks later, in week 10, both groups completed the VKS as in the pre-test. In the same week, the students from the experiment group finished the questionnaire, and in terms of their responses to the questionnaire and the diaries, 19 participants were selected purposely and interviewed individually. Additionally, four weeks later, both groups took the delayed post-test. Lastly, after the data was collected, descriptive statistics, the independent-samples t-test, and the paired-samples t-test were performed by SPSS (18.0 version) to analyze the quantitative data. Next, the data from the semi-structured interview, as well as the diaries, were analyzed qualitatively.

The main findings of the current study can be summarized as follows.

Firstly, the mobile app was more effective in improving students' vocabulary learning than a paper-based wordlist. This concurs well with a recent study of Poláková and Klímová (2019), which revealed that the experiment group using a mobile app learned more words than the control group using traditional methods. In the present study, four main reasons may account for the experiment students' higher achievements in vocabulary learning.

(1) The multimedia environment in the app had the advantages of facilitating students' understanding of the words quickly, helping them learn faster, and strengthening their memory of the words. These are consistent with the findings of the studies (e.g. Al-Seghayer, 2016; Gonulal, 2019; Govindasamy et al., 2019; Matsuoka & Hirsh, 2010; Mayer & Fiorella, 2014; Ramezanali, 2017; Rusanganwa, 2015).

(2) Corrective feedback in the app was offered promptly which was useful in helping students' to adjust their methods and timing for vocabulary learning, and memorizing the correct meanings as well as the forms of words. As demonstrated in the studies (Henderson, 2019; Soria et al., 2020; Sprenger, 2018), instant corrective feedback helped students' considerably in monitoring their vocabulary learning and correcting any mistaken guesses before they stored their vocabulary knowledge correctly.

(3) The enjoyment from using the app motivated and increased students' vocabulary learning, which resulted in more significant achievements in their vocabulary learning. This lends support to the studies by Green (1993) and Poláková and Klímová (2019), which indicated that the enjoyment of using mobile apps could enhance their effectiveness in learning.

(4) The audio recordings of words in the app improved students' pronunciation,

which led to improved vocabulary learning. According to the researchers (He et al., 2015; Kaplan-Rakowski & Loranc-Paszylk, 2019; Karousou & Nerantzaki, 2020; Trofimovich & Issacs 2012), by listening to audio recordings of words, students would improve pronunciation, which was likely to facilitate their memorizing and retrieval of the words.

Secondly, the students using the app retained more words than those using the paper-based wordlist in the long-term. This result is in agreement with other studies (Kohnke et al., 2019; Poláková & Klímová, 2019), which revealed that using mobile apps could enhance students' vocabulary retention effectively over time. In the present study, this may be attributed to three reasons as follow.

(1) The spaced review of the exercises in the app strengthened the words in students' long-term memories. This is consistent with the research findings (Candry et al., 2020; Daloğlu et al., 2009; Epp & Phirangee, 2019; Ma, 2014a; Namaziandost et al., 2019), which substantiated that spaced repetitions of retrieval had a positive impact on transferring vocabulary knowledge from the short-term to the long-term memory.

(2) Dual coding of the words in the app contributed to better recall of them. This corroborates the studies (Clark & Paivio, 1991; Lin, 2009; Paivio, 1986, 2007), which showed that the words presented in both verbal and visual modes were recalled effectively because "when one memory trace is lost, the other remains and is accessible" (Lin, 2009: 24).

(3) More involvement loads induced by the exercises of the app resulted in their better retention of the words. These are line with the findings of the studies (Bagheri et al., 2020; Craik & Lockhart, 1972; Douglas, 2016; Hulstijn & Laufer, 2001), which unveiled that learners' retention of words become higher with increasing involvement loads induced by the tasks (exercises).

Thirdly, based on students' responses obtained from the questionnaire, it was highlighted that 72% of the students held positive attitudes towards app-assisted vocabulary learning. This is verified by the 18 interviewees' responses of their 19 counterparts and 82.1% of the students' diaries from the experiment group. Also, the results above match well with the findings of other studies (Bensalem, 2018; Gonulal, 2019; Kohnke, 2020; Ornprapat & Wiwat, 2015). To analyze these responses more closely, six advantages may explain why most of the students liked the app in the present study: they were "convenient" (Godwin-Jones, 2008; Huang et al., 2012; Jee, 2011; Kohnke, 2020; Ma, 2019; Younus, 2014), "easy" (Wang, 2015), "useful" (Kim, 2011, 2013; Ornprapat & Wiwat, 2015; Wang & Christiansen, 2019; Tabatabaei & Goojani, 2012), "entertaining" (Başoğlu & Akdemir, 2010; Aga & Özdemir, 2013; Poláková & Klímová, 2019), "effective" (Basal et al., 2016; Gonulal, 2019; Ma, 2019; Kohnke, 2020), and "increasing confidence and motivation in English" (Chen, 2020; Yu, 2019).

At last, three weaknesses with the paper-based wordlist learning were disclosed by the present study, which were in the following. (1) Students considered it difficult to clearly remember the words because they were often confused between different words and some were lost from memory. This is verified by the study of Mondria and Wit-de-Boer (1991), which highlighted that remembering vocabulary using a wordlist easily led to confusion and even memory loss. (2) The efficiency was low in learning vocabulary with the wordlist. This is supported by Zheng et al. (2015), who revealed that the traditional mode of learning words from a wordlist made university EFL students learn slowly and forget quickly. (3) The students' difficulties in pronouncing the words negatively affected their memory of the learned words. This is confirmed by the study of Icht and Mama (2019), which found that the non-production of words (words read silently) was less durable in the memory, and showed more memory decay than the production of words (words read out) over time. However, Clipperton (1994) and Nation (1993) claimed that learners could directly remember the spelling, pronunciation, and meanings of the words from a wordlist. The possible reason was that the students received help with the pronunciation when they were learning words in the studies of Clipperton (1994) and Nation (1993).

5. 2 Pedagogical Implications from the Present Study

As the present study has examined the effects of the mobile app on EFL students' vocabulary learning, vocabulary retention, and on their perceptions of the app, several pedagogical implications emerged as follows.

First, the mobile app can be applied to assist vocabulary teaching and learning under the COVID-19, for at the special period, students' learning in classroom is not allowed or impossible in many countries around the world.

Second, the mobile app was beneficial in improving the students' vocabulary learning and retention more effectively than the paper-based wordlist, and also most of the Chinese EFL learners enjoyed using it. This indicates the possibility of re-judging the English vocabulary teaching practices for Chinese EFL learners. So, an alternative to learn or teach EFL vocabulary may be desirable. In turn, this would generate implications for EFL teachers and different stakeholders, such as educational directors and policy-makers. They should consider two points: replicating this study by a larger scale for checking the generalizability of current results and supporting the development of other English language skills, such as listening, grammar, and reading with well-designed mobile apps. For instance, English teachers can design listening comprehension activities well and add them into the mobile app for students to learn and practice anywhere, anytime. As described in diary D21W8EG of the present study, this kind of learning method via the app was not only suitable for vocabulary development but also for the improvement of other English language skills.

Third, students could form their autonomous habit of learning vocabulary via the app. In a mobile technology era, it is not necessary for students to depend heavily on teachers like the traditional model of the past. Also, it is not sufficient for university students to learn vocabulary within a limited classroom time. As claimed by the researchers (Chumcharoensuk, 2013; Ko & Goranson, 2014; Schmitt, 1998a, 2000), vocabulary learning and retention are time-consuming in EFL settings, as the acquisition of vocabulary knowledge is both a continuous and incremental process. So the advantages of the mobile app can be fully exploited by learners to develop their vocabulary on their own. Nevertheless, teachers should conduct monitoring during students' vocabulary learning via mobile apps. Some evidence for this was found in the present study. For example, St. 7 in the interview said: "…there are many temptations in the mobile phone, and it easily distracts me to other things for I am not a self-disciplined person…". Also, another interviewee (St. 11) suggested, "…Adding a time alarm setting in the app, like reminding us to memorize words when every time is up…". Similarly, one student described in diary D18W6EG "…What I find the hardest thing to remember is not words, but easy to forget memorizing the words next time…".

Lastly, the findings could have impacts on the layout, design and online/offline learning concerning mobile apps. In the current study, the mobile app proved to be both a useful resource and to some extent frustrating, which is consistent with the findings of Makoe & Shandu (2018). It was a useful resource because it offered students convenient and easy access to the vocabulary learning contents with advantages as mentioned above. It was, however, frustrating for the students when the mobile phones hindered access to the contents, such as when there was no network. Therefore, app developers should consider developing apps that meet all the needs, both academic and technological, of the students.

5.3 Recommendations for Further Research

There are three recommendations for future research as follow.

Firstly, the present study was a preliminary attempt to improve Chinese EFL learners' vocabulary learning and retention in a local university. Therefore, to further validate the effectiveness of using a mobile app for EFL learners, a large-scale replication study is needed with an increase of the sample size from different grades and at various universities in China.

Secondly, future researchers should conduct a thorough needs analysis of their learners to establish individual differences before selecting vocabulary content and developing mobile apps. The present study revealed that different students from both groups had different feelings towards the same ten words in the same week. For instance, in the eighth week, one student of the experiment group in diary D19W8EG described: "…it was easy to learn and remember the words this week". While in the same week, another student in diary D32W8EG wrote: "…I found it very difficult to learn and memorize the words this week". Similarly, in the fifth week, one student of the control group in diary D53W5CG mentioned: "…the words this week were not complicated for me so that I could remember them quickly and clearly…". But in the same week, another student in diary D6W5CG wrote: " the words had many meanings this week, even though I spent longer time learning them, I still found it difficult to store them in my mind". These difficulties may have had to do with the different amounts of vocabulary known to the students, as well as their English proficiency. Consequently, researchers need to choose words and design exercises in the apps at different levels of difficulty for students so that they will be able to learn vocabulary more effectively.

Thirdly, besides vocabulary learning, many further studies should be carried out concerning the impacts of mobile apps on other English language skills in EFL settings especially during the COVID-19. The fifth-generation mobile network (5G) arrived in our daily lives in 2019 with the strengths: reduced latency, high data rates, energy savings, increased system capacity, reduced costs, large-scale device connectivity, and it will become widespread from 2020 onwards. A report from the Ministry of Industry and Information Technology (MIIT) of China on October 31 of 2019 announced three important communications operators (China Telecom, China Mobile, China Unicom) and 5G commercial packages. These 5G commercial packages were officially launched on November 1 in the whole of China, which means that China has now stepped into the era of 5G. As a result, research focusing on the impacts of 5G mobile technology on the teaching of English language skills will be urgently needed.

Finally, further research could be conducted through the iOS system-based mobile apps, for in the present study the mobile app was only operated for smartphones with the Andriod systems to learn vocabulary and then its widespread usage could be limited.

5.4 Summary of the Chapter

This chapter draws a conclusion to the current study. In the first section, the main results of the study were summarized. In the second section, the pedagogical implications gained from the study were presented. Finally, four recommendations were offered for future research.

REFERENCES

[1] Adolphs S, Schmitt N. Lexical coverage of spoken discourse [J]. Applied linguistics, 2003, 24 (4): 425 –438.

[2] Afshari S, Tavakoli M. The relationship between depth and breadth of vocabulary knowledge and Iranian EFL learners' listening comprehension [J]. International journal of research studies in language learning, 2016, 5 (5): 13 –24.

[3] Afzali P, Shabani S, Basir Z, et al. Mobile-assisted vocabulary learning: a review study [J]. Advances in language and literary studies, 2017, 8 (2): 190 –195.

[4] Agca R K, Özdemir S. Foreign language vocabulary learning with mobile technologies [J]. Procedia-social and behavioral sciences, 2013, 83:781 –785.

[5] Aldukhayel D. Vlogs in L2 listening: EFL learners' and teachers' perceptions [J]. Computer assisted language learning, 2019, 34(8): 1 –20.

[6] Alemi M, Sarab M R A, Lari Z. Successful learning of academic word list via MALL: mobile assisted language learning [J]. International education studies, 2012, 5 (6): 99 –109.

[7] Al-Fahad F. Students' attitudes and perceptions towards the effectiveness of mobile learning in King Saud University, Saudi Arabia [J]. The Turkish online journal of educational technology, 2009, 8 (2): 111 –119.

[8] Alfotais A. Investigating the effect of spaced versus massed practice on vocabulary retention in the EFL classroom [D]. University of Essex, Essex, United Kingdom, 2019.

[9] Alm A. Socially multilingual: an exploration of informal language learning practices through Facebook [C]. In Proceedings of the World CALL Conference, Glasgow, 2013:1 –3.

[10] Al-Seghayer K. The effect of multimedia annotation modes on L2 vocabulary acquisition: a comparative study [J]. Language learning & technology, 2001, 5 (1): 202 –232.

[11] Al-Seghayer K. ESL/EFL instructors' perceptions of the importance of computer-assisted reading in L2 reading instruction [J]. Theory and practice in language

studies, 2016, 6 (9): 1753 – 1761.

[12] Al-Wasy B Q, Mahdi H S. The effect of mobile phone applications on improving EFL learners' self-editing [J]. Journal of education and human development, 2016, 5(3): 149 – 157.

[13] Alzu'bi M, Akram M, Sabha N, et al. Using mobile-based email for English foreign language learners [J]. The Turkish online journal of educational technology, 2013, 12(1): 178 – 186.

[14] AMHSA. Criterion for determining a representative interview sample [OL]. http://www.amhsa.net., 2010.

[15] Rinne L, Gregory E, Hardiman M, et al. Why arts integration improves long-term retention of content [J]. Mind, brain, and education, 2011, 5(2): 89 – 96.

[16] Anshun University. The admission scores and the enrollment plan of Anshun University [OL]. http://zsgzw.asu.edu.cn/., 2018.

[17] Atkinson R C, Shiffrin R M. Human memory: a proposed system and its control processes//Spence K W. The psychology of learning and motivation: advances in research and theory [M] New York: Acadamic Press.

[18] Averell L, Heathcote A. The form of the forgetting curve and the fate of memories [J]. Journal of mathematical psychology, 2010, 55(1): 25 – 35.

[19] Behrooz A, Amin M M. Comparing vocabulary learning of EFL learners by using two different strategies: mobile learning vs. flashcards [J]. The EuroCALL review, 2012, 20(2): 47 – 59.

[20] Azar A S, Nasiri H. Learners' attitudes toward the effectiveness of mobile assisted language learning (MALL) in L2 listening comprehension, international conference on current trends in ELT [J]. Procedia-social and behavioral sciences, 2014, 98: 1836 – 1843.

[21] Baddeley A. Working memory [J]. Science, 1992, 255(5044): 311 – 324.

[22] Bagheri N R, Mohammad H R, Sarbandi F M. The impact of involvement load on Iranian EFL learners' retention of idiomatic expressions [J]. Language related

research, 2020, 10(6): 55 – 86.

[23] Bahrick H P. Stabilized memory of unrehearsed knowledge[J]. Journal of experimental psychology: General, 1992, 121(1): 112 – 113.

[24] Barbour M K, Grzebyk T Q, Eye J. Any time, any place, any pace-really? Examining mobile learning in a virtual school environment [J]. Turkish online journal of distance education, 2014, 15(1): 114 – 127.

[25] Barcroft J. Can writing a new word detract from learning it? More negative effects of forced output during vocabulary learning [J]. Second language research, 2006, 22(4): 487 – 497.

[26] Barcroft J. Effects of synonym generation on incidental and intentional L2 vocabulary learning during reading [J]. TESOL quarterly, 2009, 43(1), 79 – 103.

[27] Barrow J, Nakashi Y, Ishino H. Assessing Japanese college students' vocabulary knowledge with a self-checking familiarity survey [J]. System, 1999, 27(2): 223 – 247.

[28] Basal A. Authoring tools for developing content in language education [J]. International journal on new trends in education and their implications, 2012, 3(4): 164 – 169.

[29] Basal A, Yilmaz S, Tanriverdi A, et al. Effectiveness of mobile applications in vocabulary teaching [J]. Contemporary educational technology, 2016, 7(1): 47 – 59.

[30] Başoğlu E B, Akdemir Ö. A comparison of undergraduate students' English vocabulary learning: using mobile phones and flash cards [J]. The Turkish online journal of educational technology, 2010, 9(3): 1 – 7.

[31] Beglar D. A Rasch-based validation of the vocabulary size test [J]. Language testing, 2010, 27(1): 101 – 118.

[32] Bensalem E. The impact of WhatsApp on EFL students' vocabulary learning [J]. Arab world English journal, 2017, 9(1): 23 – 38.

[33] Bernard H R. Research methods in cultural anthropology [M]. Newbury Park, CA: Sage, 1988.

[34] Bird S. Effects of distributed practice on the acquisition of second language English syntax [J]. Applied psycholinguistics, 2010, 31(4): 435-452.

[35] Blaikie N. Approaches to social enquiry [M]. 2nd ed. Cambridge: Polity Press, 2007.

[36] Boers F, Eyckmans J, Kappel J, et al. Formulaic sequences and perceived oral proficiency: putting a lexical approach to the test [J]. Language teaching research, 2006, 10 (3): 245-261.

[37] Boers F, Warren P, Grimshaw G, et al. On the benefits of multimodal annotations for vocabulary uptake from reading [J]. Computer assisted language learning, 2017, 30(7): 709-725.

[38] Brown P C, Roediger H L, McDaniel M A. Make it stick [M]. Belknap Press, 2014.

[39] Burston J. Language learning technology MALL: future directions for BYOD applications [J]. The IALLT journal for language learning technologies, 2013, 43(2): 89-96.

[40] Burston J. Twenty years of MALL project implementation: a meta-analysis of learning outcomes [J]. ReCALL, 2014, 27(1): 4-20.

[41] Butcher K R. The multimedia principle [M]. 2nd ed. //Mayer R E. The Cambridge handbook of multimedia learning. New York: Cambridge University Press, 2014: 174-205.

[42] Butler A C, Roediger H L. Feedback enhances the positive effects and reduces the negative effects of multiple-choice testing [J]. Memory & cognition, 2008, 36(3): 604-616.

[43] Cahill L, McGaugh J L. A novel demonstration of enhanced memory associated with emotional arousal [J]. Consciousness and cognition, 1995, 4(4), 410-421.

[44] Cai J G. The evidence of China college English diminishes and its trends [J]. Foreign language research, 2012, 3: 46-52.

[45] Candry S, Decloedt J, Eyckmans J. Comparing the merits of word writing and

retrieval practice for L2 vocabulary learning [J]. System, 2020, 89 (102206): 1-11.

[46]Carey B. How we learn: the surprising truth about when, where, and why it happens [M]. New York: Random House, 2014.

[47]Carpenter S K, Cepeda N J, Rohrer D, et al. Using spacing to enhance diverse forms of learning: review of recent research and implications for instruction [J]. Educational psychology review, 2012, 24(3): 369-378.

[48] Carr L T. The strengths and weaknesses of quantitative and qualitative research: what method for nursing? [J] Journal of advanced nursing, 1994, 20(4): 716-721.

[49]Carrier M, Pashler H. The influence of retrieval on retention [J]. Memory & cognition, 1992, 20(6):633-642.

[50] Cavus N, Ibrahim D. M-Learning: an experiment in using SMS to support learning new English language words [J]. British journal of educational technology, 2009, 40 (1): 78-91.

[51]Celce-Murcia M. Teaching English as a second or foreign language [M]. 3rd ed. Boston: Thomson Learning, 2001.

[52]Cepeda N J, Pashler H, Vul E, et al. Distributed practice in verbal recall tasks: a review and quantitative synthesis [J]. Psychological bulletin, 2006, 132(3): 354-380.

[53] Chang C C, Yan C F, Tseng J S. Perceived convenience in an extended technology acceptance model: mobile technology and English learning for college students [J]. Australasian journal of educational technology, 2012, 28(5): 809-826.

[54] Chapelle C. Multimedia CALL: lessons to be learned from research on instructed SLA [J]. Language learning & technology, 1998, 2(1): 22-34.

[55]Charles C M, Mertler C A. Introduction to educational research [M]. Boston: Allyn and Bacon, 2002.

[56]Che Hashim N, Abd Majid N A, Arshad H, et al. User satisfaction for an augmented reality application to support productive vocabulary using speech recognition

[J]. Advances in multimedia, 2018:1-10.

[57] Chen C H. AR videos as scaffolding to foster students' learning achievements and motivation in EFL learning [J]. British journal of educational technology, 2020, 51(3): 1-16.

[58] Chen C M, Liu H M, Huang H B. Effects of a mobile game-based English vocabulary learning app on learners' perceptions and learning performance: a case study of Taiwanese EFL learners [J]. ReCALL, 2019, 31(2): 170-188.

[59] Chen C M, Hsu S H. Personalized intelligent mobile learning system for supporting effective English learning [J]. Journal of educational technology & society, 2008, 11(3), 153-180.

[60] Chen H. Use of Praat in visualization of English pronunciation teaching [J]. Journal of Lanzhou institute of education, 2013, 29(9): 53-58.

[61] Chen X B. Tablets for informal language learning: student usage and attitudes [J]. Language learning & technology, 2013, 17(1): 20-36.

[62] Chen Y, Carger C L, Smith T J. Mobile-assisted narrative writing practice for young English language learners from a fund of knowledge approach [J]. Language learning & technology, 2017, 21(1): 28-41.

[63] Chen Y Y. A study on the correlation between breadth and depth of vocabulary knowledge of high school students and English writing [J]. Nanjing Normal University, 2011.

[64] Cheung S K. A study on the use of mobile devices for distance learning [J]. Lecture notes in computer science, 2012, 74(11): 89-98.

[65] Chinnery G M. Emerging technologies going to the MALL: mobile assisted language learning [J]. Language learning & technology, 2006, 10(1): 9-16.

[66] Chumcharoensuk N. A comparative study of English learning motivation types between Thai and Cambodian first-year undergraduate English majors [J]. Thammasat University, 2013.

[67] Chun D M. L2 reading on the web: strategies for accessing information in

hypermedia [J]. Computer assisted language learning, 2001, 14(5): 367－403.

[68] Chun D M, Plass J L. Effects of multimedia annotations on vocabulary acquisition [J]. Modern language journal, 1996, 80(2), 183－198.

[69] Chun D M, Plass J L. Facilitating reading comprehension with multimedia [J]. System, 1996, 24(4): 503－519.

[70] Church K, Oliver N. Understanding mobile web and mobile search use in today's dynamic mobile landscape[P]. Proceedings of the 13th International Conference on Human-computer Interaction with Mobile Devices and Services (pp. 67－76), ACM, 2011.

[71] Church K, Oliveira R. de. What's up with WhatsApp? Comparing mobile instant messaging behaviors with traditional SMS [P]. Proceedings of the 15th International Conference on Human-computer Interaction with Mobile Devices and Services(pp. 352－361), ACM, 2013.

[72] Clark J M, Paivio A. Dual coding theory and education [J]. Educational psychology review, 1991, 3(3): 149－210.

[73] Clipperton R. Best paper by a graduate student award: explicit vocabulary instruction in French immersion [J]. Canadian modern language review, 1994, 50(4): 736－749.

[74] Coady J, Huckin T. Second language vocabulary acquisition: a rationale for pedagogy [M]. Cambridge: Cambridge University Press, 1997.

[75] Cohen L, Manion L, Morrison K. Research methods in education [M]. London: Routledge, 2000.

[76] Conway M, Cohen G, Stanhope N. Very long-term memory for knowledge acquired at school and university [J]. Applied cognitive psychology, 1992, 6(6): 467－482.

[77] Corbin J M, Strauss A. Basics of qualitative research [M]. London: Sage Publications Ltd., 2008.

[78] Craik F I M, Lockhart R S. Levels of processing: a framework for memory

research [M]. Journal of verbal learning and verbal behavior, 1972, 11: 671 – 684.

[79] Creswell J W. Research design: qualitative, quantitative, and mixed methods approaches [M]. 3rd ed. London: Sage Publications Ltd. , 2009.

[80] Creswell J W, Creswell J D. Research design: qualitative, quantitative, and mixed methods approaches [M]. 4th ed. London: Sage Publications Ltd. , 2017.

[81] Cronbach L J. My current thoughts on coefficient alpha and successor procedures [J]. Educational and psychological measurement, 2004, 64(3): 391 – 418.

[82] Crothers E, Suppes S. Experiments in second-language learning [M]. New York: Academic Press, 1967.

[83] Dai J H. A study on the vocabulary size of non-English majors at CET-4 level [J]. Journal of Chongqing University of technology (social science), 2013, 27(1): 118 – 123.

[84] Daloǧlu A, Baturay M, Yildirim S. Designing a constructivist vocabulary learning material [M]. //Marriott R C V & Torres P L. Handbook of research on e-learning methodologies for language acquisition. Hershey, PA: Information Science, 2009: 186 – 203.

[85] Dashti F A, Aldashti A A. EFL college students' attitudes towards mobile learning [J]. International education studies, 2015, 8(8): 13 – 20.

[86] Douglas Jr V. Enhancing English academic vocabulary acquisition and retention in intensive English programs with the involvement load hypothesis [J]. Theory and practice in language studies, 2016, 6(12): 2237 – 2244.

[87] David P. Verizon: How much do you charge now? [OL]. New York Times. http://www.nytimes.com/2009/11/12/technology/personal tech/12 pogue-email. html. , 2009.

[88] Davis F D. Perceived usefulness, perceived ease of use, and user acceptance of information technology [J]. MIS quarterly, 1989, 13(3): 319 – 340.

[89] Dehghan F, Rezvani R, Fazeli S. Social networks and their effectiveness in learning foreign language vocabulary: a comparative study using WhatsApp [J]. CALL-EJ, 2017, 18(2): 1 – 13.

[90] Deniz M S, Alsaffar A A. Assessing the validity and reliability of a questionnaire on dietary fibre-related knowledge in a Turkish student population [J]. Journal of health, population, and nutrition, 2013, 31(4): 497-503.

[91] Denzin N K, Lincoln Y S. Handbook of qualitative research [M]. Thousand Oaks: Sage Publications Ltd., 1994.

[92] Denzin N K, Lincoln Y S. Collecting and interpreting qualitative materials [M]. Thousand Oaks: Sage Publications Ltd., 1998.

[93] Denzin N K, Lincoln Y S. The qualitative inquiry reader [M]. London: Sage Publications Ltd., 2002.

[94] Deris F D, Shukor N S A. Vocabulary learning through mobile apps: A phenomenological inquiry of student acceptance and desired apps features [J]. International journal of interactive mobile technologies, 2019, 13(7): 129-140.

[95] Diamond L, Gutlohn L. Teaching vocabulary [OL]. http://www.Reading rockets.org/article/teaching-vocabulary., 2006.

[96] Dongale T D, Pawar P S, Tikke R S, et al. Mimicking the synaptic weights and human forgetting curve using hydrothermally grown nanostructured CuO memristor device [J]. Journal of nanoscience and nanotechnology, 2018, 18(2): 984-991.

[97] Dörnyei Z. Questionnaires in second language research: construction, administration, and processing [M]. Mahwah, NJ: Lawrence Erlbaum Associates Inc, 2003.

[98] Dörnyei Z. Creating a motivating classroom environment. In international handbook of English language teaching [M]. Springer, Boston, MA, 2007: 719-731.

[99] Dukic Z, Chiu D K, Lo P. How useful are smartphones for learning? Perceptions and practices of library and information science students from Hong Kong and Japan [J]. Library Hi Tech, 2015, 33(4): 545-565.

[100] Duman G, Orhon G, Gedik N. Research trends in mobile assisted language learning from 2000 to 2012 [J]. ReCALL, 2014, 27(2): 197-216.

[101] Ebadi S, Rahimi M. Exploring the impact of online peer-editing using Google

Docs on EFL learners' academic writing skills: a mixed methods study [J]. Computer assisted language learning, 2017, 30(8): 787-815.

[102] Ebbinghaus H. Memory: a contribution to experimental psychology [M]. Dover, New York, 1885.

[103] Elaish M M, Shuib L, Ghani N A, et al. Mobile learning for English language acquisition: taxonomy, challenges, and recommendations [J]. IEEE access, 2017, 5: 19033-19047.

[104] Elgort I, Warren P. L2 vocabulary learning from reading: Explicit and tacit lexical knowledge and the role of learner and item variables [J]. Language learning, 2014, 64 (2): 365-414.

[105] Elias T. Universal instructional design principles for mobile learning [J]. International review of research in open and distance learning, 2011, 12(2): 143-156.

[106] Ellis N. Vocabulary acquisition research group virtual library [J]. The language teacher, 1995, 19(2): 12-16.

[107] Ellis R. SLA research and language teaching [M]. New York: Oxford University Press, 1997.

[108] Epp C D, Phirangee K. Exploring mobile tool integration: design activities carefully or students may not learn [J]. Contemporary educational psychology, 2019, 59: 1-17.

[109] Faqe C K. The influences of mobile learning applications on students' learning of English language: Soran University as an example [J]. International journal of education and research, 2015, 3(1): 551-559.

[110] Farjami F, Aidinlou N A. Analysis of the impediments to English vocabulary learning and teaching [J]. International journal of language and linguistics, 2013, 1(4): 1-5.

[111] Fletcher J D, Tobias S. The multimedia principle [M]. // Mayer R E. The handbook of multimedia learning. New York: Cambridge University Press, 2005: 117-133.

[112]Folse K. Is explicit vocabulary focus the reading teacher's job? [J]. Reading in a foreign language, 2010, 22(1):139-160.

[113]Folse K. Applying L2 lexical research findings in ESL teaching [J]. TESOL quarterly, 2011, 45(2): 362-369.

[114] Fontana A, Frey J H. The interview: from neutral stance to political involvement[M]. 3rd ed. // Denzin N K & Lincoln Y S. The sage handbook of qualitative research. Thousand Oaks, CA: Sage Publications Ltd., 2005: 695-728.

[115]Nachmias D. Research methods in the social sciences [M]. New York: Worth Publishers, 1981.

[116]Fujimoto C. Perceptions of mobile language learning in Australia: How ready are learners to study on the move? [J]. The JALT CALL journal, 2012, 8(3): 165-195.

[117]Gairns R, Redman S. Working with words: a guide to teaching and learning vocabulary [M]. New York: Cambridge University Press, 1986.

[118]Gass S. Discussion: incidental vocabulary learning [J]. Studies in second language acquisition, 1999, 21(2): 319-333.

[119] Gass S, Selinker L. Second language acquisition: an introductory course [M]. Mahwah, NJ: L, 2001.

[120]Gass S, Selinker L. The role of the native language: an historical overview [M]. Gass S. Second language acquisition: an introductory course. New York: Tayler & Francis, 2008: 89-120.

[121] Gathercole S E, Baddeley A D. Phonological working memory: a critical building block for reading development and vocabulary acquisition [J]. European journal of psychology of education, 1993, 78: 259-272.

[122]Geddes S J. Mobile learning in the 21st century: benefits for learners [J]. Knowledge tree e-journal, 2004, 30(3): 214-228.

[123]Ginns P. Integrating information: a meta-analysis of the spatial contiguity and temporal contiguity effects [J]. Learning and instruction, 2006, 16: 511-525.

[124] Godwin-Jones R. Emerging technologies: Web-writing 2.0: Enabling, documenting, and assessing writing online [J]. Language learning & technology, 2008, 12(2): 7-13.

[125] Godwin-Jones R. Emerging technologies: mobile apps for language learning [J]. Language learning and technology, 2011, 15(2): 2-11.

[126] Gonulal T. The use of Instagram as a mobile-assisted language learning tool [J]. Contemporary educational technology, 2019, 10(3): 309-323.

[127] Govindasamy P, Yunus M M, Hashi H. Mobile assisted vocabulary learning: examining the effects on students' vocabulary enhancement [J]. Universal journal of educational research, 2019, 7(12A): 85-92.

[128] Green J M. Student attitudes toward communicative and non-communicative activities: Do enjoyment and effectiveness go together? [J]. The modern language journal, 1993, 77(1): 1-10.

[129] Greidanus T, Nienhuis L. Testing the quality of word knowledge in a second language by means of word associations: types of distractors and types of associations [J]. The modern language journal, 2001, 85(4): 567-577.

[130] Groot P J. Computer assisted second language vocabulary acquisition [J]. Language learning & technology, 2000, 4(1): 60-81.

[131] Guo J L. A study of correlations among non-English majors' breadth of vocabulary knowledge, depth of vocabulary knowledge and speaking competence[D]. Xi'an International Studies University, 2017.

[132] Gürkan S. Effect of annotation preferences of EFL students' on their level of vocabulary recall and retention [J]. Journal of educational computing research, 2019, 57(6): 1436-1467.

[133] Hadi M S, Emzir E. Improving English speaking ability through mobile assisted language learning (Mall) learning model [J]. International journal of language education and cultural review, 2016, 2(2): 71-74.

[134] Haebig E, Leonard L B, Deevy P, et al. Retrieval-based word learning in

young typically developing children and children with development language disorder Ⅱ: a comparison of retrieval schedules [J]. Journal of speech, language, and hearing research, 2019, 62(4): 944-964.

[135] Hanafiah A. The effect of teaching vocabulary through guessing games and wordlist on 7th grade students' vocabulary achievement [D]. Widya Mandala Catholic University, 2015.

[136] Har A L C, Abidin M J Z, Saibon J S. The benefits and drawbacks of using tablet-based digital storytelling in vocabulary learning among Malaysian young English as a second language (ESL) learners [J]. Asia Pacific journal of educators and education, 2019, 34: 17-47.

[137] Hargis J, Cavanaugh C, Kamali T, Soto M. A federal higher education iPad mobile learning initiative: triangulation of data to determine early effectiveness [J]. Innovative higher education, 2014, 39(1): 45-57.

[138] Harley H. Subject, events and licensing [D]. Massachusetts Institute of Technology, Cambridge, USA, 1995.

[139] Hashimoto B J, Egbert J. More than frequency? Exploring predictors of word difficulty for second language learners [J]. Language learning, 2019, 69(4): 839-872.

[140] Hayati A, Jalilifar A, Mashhadi A. Using Short Message Service (SMS) to teach English idioms to EFL students [J]. British journal of educational technology, 2013, 44(1): 66-81.

[141] Hazaea A N, Alzubi A A. The effectiveness of using mobile on EFL learners' reading practices in Najran University [J]. English language teaching, 2016, 9(5): 8-21.

[142] He B, Puakpong N, Lian A. Factors affecting the normalization of CALL in Chinese senior high schools [J]. Computer assisted language learning, 2015, 28(3): 189-201.

[143] He S R, Chen T T, Zhang L F. On the thinking of vocabulary teaching of college English [J]. Home drama, 2017, 1: 196-198.

[144] He W W, Duan J Y. The effect of productive vocabulary size and depth of vocabulary knowledge on English majors' writing quality [J]. Journal of Zhaotong Teacher's College, 2012, 34(1): 62–66.

[145] Heift, T. Learner control and error correction in ICALL: browsers, peekers, and adamants [J]. CALICO journal, 2013, 19(2), 295–313.

[146] Henderson C. The effect of feedback timing on L2 Spanish vocabulary acquisition in synchronous computer-mediated communication [J]. Language teaching research, 2019, 25(2).

[147] Hennings D G. Contextually relevant word study: adolescent vocabulary development across the curriculum [J]. Journal of adolescent & adult literacy, 2000, 44(3): 268–279.

[148] Henriksen B. Three dimensions of vocabulary development [J]. Studies in second language acquisition, 1999, 21(2): 303–317.

[149] Herrington A, Herrington J, Mantei J. New technologies, new pedagogics: mobile learning in higher education [M]. Wollongong: University of Wollongong, 2009.

[150] Hirsh D, Nation P. What vocabulary size is needed to read unsimplified texts for pleasure? [J]. Reading in a foreign language, 1992, 8(2): 689–696.

[151] Hockly N. Interactive whiteboards [J]. ELT journal, 2013, 67(3): 354–358.

[152] Holstein J A, Gubrium J F. The Active Interview [M]. 2nd ed. // Silverman D. Qualitative research: theory, method and practice. Thousand Oaks, CA: Sage Publications Ltd., 2004: 140–161.

[153] Horst M, Cobb T, Meara P. Beyond a clockwork orange: acquiring second language vocabulary through reading [J]. Reading in a foreign language, 1998, 11: 207–223.

[154] Hou X M. A tentative study of the effects of vocabulary knowledge on non-English majors' reading comprehension and English writing [D]. Shangdong University, 2016.

[155] Hsu C F, Chen C M, Cao D. Effects of design factors of game-based English

vocabulary learning app on learning performance, sustained attention, emotional state, and memory retention[C]. The 6th IIAI International Congress on Advanced Applied Informatics (IIAI-AAI), Hamamatsu, Japan, 2017.

[156] Hu M, Nation I S P. Unknown vocabulary density and reading comprehension [J]. Reading in a foreign language, 2000, 13(1): 403 –430.

[157] Hu S G, Liu Y, Chen T P, et al. Emulating the Ebbinghaus forgetting curve of the human brain with a NiO-based memristor [J]. Applied physics letters, 2013, 103(13): 1 –4.

[158] Hu Z. Vocabulary learning assisted by mobile phones: perceptions of Chinese adult learners [J]. Journal of Cambridge studies. 2013, 8(1): 139 –154.

[159] Huang H M. Toward constructivism for adult learners in online learning environments [J]. British journal of educational technology, 2002, 33(1): 27 –37.

[160] Huang X P. On the correlation between vocabulary knowledge and CET- 4 [J]. Foreign language teaching abroad, 2003, (4): 48 –53.

[161] Huang Y M, Huang S H, Lin Y T. A ubiquitous English vocabulary learning system: evidence of active/passive attitudes vs. usefulness/ease-of-use [J]. Computers & education, 2012, 58(1): 273 –282.

[162] Hubbard P. Making a case for learner training in technology enhanced language learning environments [J]. CALICO journal, 2013, 30(2): 163 –178.

[163] Huckin T, Coady J. Incidental vocabulary acquisition in a second language: a review [J]. Studies in second language acquisition, 1999, 21(2): 181 –193.

[164] Hulstijn J. Retention of inferred and given word meanings: experiments in incidental vocabulary learning [J]. Vocabulary & applied linguistics, 1992: 113 –125.

[165] Hulstijn J H, Laufer B. Some empirical evidence for the involvement load hypothesis in vocabulary acquisition [J]. Language learning, 2001, 51(3): 539 –558.

[166] Hwang G J, Tsai C C. Research trends in mobile and ubiquitous learning: a review of publications in selected journals from 2001 to 2010 [J]. British journal of educational technology, 2011, 42(4): 65 –70.

[167] Icht M, Mama Y. The effect of vocal production on vocabulary learning in a second language [J]. Language teaching research, 2019.

[168] Immordino-Yang M H, Damasio A. We feel, therefore, we learn: the relevance of affective and social neuroscience to education [J]. Mind, brain and education, 2007, 1(1): 3–10.

[169] Jackson H, Amvela E Z. Words, meaning and vocabulary [M]. Trowbridge: The Cromwell Press, 2000.

[170] Jafari S, Chalak A. The role of WhatsApp in teaching vocabulary to Iranian EFL learners at junior high school [J]. English language teaching, 2016, 9(8): 85–92.

[171] Jaradat R M. Students' attitudes and perceptions towards using m-learning for French language learning: a case study on Princess Nora University [J]. International journal of learning management systems, 2014, 2(1): 33–44.

[172] Jarvis H, Krashen S. Is CALL obsolete? Language acquisition and language learning revisited in a digital age [J]. TESL-EJ, 2014, 17(4):1–6.

[173] Jee M J. Web 2.0 Technology meets mobile-assisted language learning[J]. IALLT journal of language learning technologies, 2011, 41 (1): 161–175.

[174] Jiang L R. The analysis on how to improve the passing rate of CET-4 among Chinese universities [J]. Rural economy and technology, 2016, 27(10): 239–240.

[175] Joorabchi M E, Mesbah A, Kruchten P. Real challenges in mobile app development [J]. Empirical software engineering and measurement, 2013: 15–24.

[176] Joyce B, Weil M. Models of teaching model [M]. Boston: A Liyn Dan Bacon, 1972.

[177] Kachroo J N. Report on an investigation into the teaching of vocabulary in the first year of English [J]. Bulletin of the central institute of English, 1962, 2: 67–72.

[178] Kanellopoulou C, Kermanidis K L, Giannakoulopoulos A. The dual-coding and multimedia learning theories: film subtitles as a vocabulary teaching tool [J]. Education sciences, 2019, 9(3): 210.

[179] Kang S H. Spaced repetition promotes efficient and effective learning: policy implications for instruction [J]. Policy insights from the behavioral and brain sciences, 2016, 3(1): 12-19.

[180] Kang S H K, McDermott K B, Roediger H L. Test format and corrective feedback modify the effect of testing on long-term retention [J]. The European journal of cognitive psychology, 2007, 19(4-5): 528-558.

[181] Kaplan-Rakowski R, Loranc-Paszylk B. The impact of verbal and nonverbal auditory resources on explicit foreign language vocabulary learning [J]. System, 2019, 85 (102114): 1-10.

[182] Karousou A, Nerantzaki T. Phonological memory training and its effect on second language vocabulary development [J]. Second language research, 2020, 38(1).

[183] Karpicke J D, Roediger H L. The critical importance of retrieval for learning [J]. Science, 2008, 319(TN. 5865): 966-968.

[184] Karpicke J D, Zaromb F M. Retrieval mode distinguishes the testing effect from the generation effect [J]. Journal of memory and language, 2009, 62(3): 227-239.

[185] Katemba C V. Students' vocabulary enhancement at grade 10: a comparative study using CALL & MALL in Indonesia [J]. CALL-EJ, 2019, 20(1): 87-114.

[186] Kennedy C, Levy M. L'italiano al telefonino: using SMS to support beginners' language learning [J]. ReCALL, 2008, 20(3): 315-330.

[187] Kilickaya F. The effect of computer assisted language learning on Turkish learners' achievement on the TOEFL exam [J]. Teaching English with technology, 2007, 7(1): 1-25.

[188] Kim B. Social Constructivism [M]. //Orey M. Emerging perspectives on learning, teaching, and technology. North Charleston: CreateSpace, 2010.

[189] Kim, H S. Effects of SMS text messaging on vocabulary learning [J]. Multimedia assisted language learning, 2011, 14(2): 159-180.

[190] Kim H S. Emerging mobile apps to improve English listening skills[J]. Multimedia assisted language learning, 2013, 16(2): 11-30.

[191] Kim J, Ilon L, Altmann J. Adapting smartphones as learning technology in a Korean university [J]. Journal of integrated design and process science, 2013, 17 (1): 1-18.

[192] Klimova B, Polakova P. Students' perceptions of an EFL vocabulary learning mobile application [J]. Education Sciences, 2020, 10(2): 37-44.

[193] Klopfer E, Squire K, Jenkins H. Environmental detectives: PDAs as a window into a virtual simulated world[D]. IEEE International Workshop, 2002: 95-98.

[194] Ko M H. Glossing and second language vocabulary learning [J]. TESOL quarterly, 2012, 46(1): 56-79.

[195] Ko M H, Goranson J. Technology-assisted vocabulary learning and student learning outcomes: a case study [J]. Multimedia assisted language learning, 2014, 17 (1): 11-33.

[196] Koester M. Science teachers who draw: the red is always there [M]. Wisconsin, United States: Deep University Press, 2015.

[197] Kohnke L, Zhang R, Zou D. Using mobile vocabulary learning apps as aids to knowledge retention: business vocabulary acquisition [J]. Journal of Asia TEFL, 2019, 16(2): 683-690.

[198] Kohnke L. Exploring learner perception, experience and motivation of using a mobile app in L2 vocabulary acquisition [J]. International journal of computer-assisted language learning and teaching IJCALLT, 2020, 10(1): 15-26.

[199] Krashen S. Second language acquisition and second language learning [M]. Oxford: Pergamon Press, 1981.

[200] Krashen S. Principles and practice in second language acquisition [M]. Oxford: Pergamon Press, 1982.

[201] Krashen S. Principles and practice in second language acquisition [M]. New York: Prentice Hall, 1987.

[202] Krashen S. We acquire vocabulary and spelling by reading: additional evidence for the input hypothesis [J]. The modern language journal, 1989, 73 (4): 440 – 464.

[203] Kukulska-Hulme A. Mobile language learning now and in the future [M]. // Svensson P. From vision to practice: language learning and IT. Sweden: Swedish Net University, 2006: 295 – 310.

[204] Kukulska-Hulme A. Will mobile learning change language learning? [J] ReCALL, 2009, 21(2): 157 – 165.

[205] Kukulska-Hulme A. Re-skilling language learners for a mobile world [M]. Monterey, CA: The International Research Foundation for English Language Education, 2013.

[206] Kukulska-Hulme A, Shield L. An overview of mobile assisted language learning: from content delivery to supported collaboration and interaction [J]. ReCALL, 2008, 20(3): 271 – 289.

[207] Kwangsawad T. University students' perceptions of MALL in EFL classes [J]. Studies in English language teaching, 2019, 7(1): 75 – 82.

[208] Laufer B. A factor of difficulty in vocabulary learning: deceptive transparency [J]. AILA Rreview, 1989, 6: 10 – 20.

[209] Laufer B. The development of passive and active vocabulary in a second language: same or different? [J]. Applied linguistics, 1998, 19(2): 255 – 271.

[210] Laufer B. Reading, word-focused activities and incidental vocabulary acquisition in a second language [J]. Prospect, 2001, 16(3): 44 – 54.

[211] Laufer B. Vocabulary acquisition in a second language: Do learners really acquire most vocabulary by reading? Some empirical evidence [J]. Canadian modern language review, 2003, 59(4): 567 – 587.

[212] Laufer B. Second language vocabulary acquisition from language input and from form-focused activities [J]. Language teaching, 2009, 42(3): 341 – 354.

[213] Laufer B, Hulstijn J. What leads to better incidental vocabulary learning:

comprehensible input or comprehensible output? Pacific Second Language Research Forum, Tokyo, 1998.

[214] Laufer B, Nation P. Vocabulary size and use: lexical richness in L2 written production [J]. Applied linguistics, 1995, 16(3): 307-322.

[215] Laufer B, Nation P. A vocabulary-size test of controlled productive ability [J]. Language testing, 1999, 16(1): 33-51.

[216] Laufer B, Shmueli K. Memorizing new words: Does teaching have anything to do with it? [J] RELC journal, 1997, 28(1): 89-108.

[217] Lee P, Lin H. The effect of the inductive and deductive data-driven learning (DDL) on vocabulary acquisition and retention [J]. System, 2019, 81: 14-25.

[218] Lewis M. The lexical approach [M]. Hove, England: Language teaching publications, 1993.

[219] Li F L. The survey and analysis of non-English majors' vocabulary learning [J]. Journal of Huanggang Normal University, 2006, 26: 204-206.

[220] Li J. On the relationship between the breadth and depth and reading comprehension [J]. Foreign language education, 2003, 2: 21-24.

[221] Li X. Vocabulary size, depth of vocabulary knowledge as well as their relationship to English proficiency [J]. Foreign language teaching and research, 2007, 5: 352-359.

[222] Li Y, Li J. Learning on the move: a case study of mobile learning assisted English reading instruction in Chinese tertiary education. 2011 6th International Conference on Computer Science & Education (ICCSE) 978-983[C]. IEEE, 2011.

[223] Lin C C. Learning action verbs with animation [J]. The JALT journal, 2009, 5(3): 23-40.

[224] Lin J J, Lin H. Mobile-assisted ESL/EFL vocabulary learning: a systematic review and meta-analysis [J]. Computer assisted language learning, 2019, 32(8): 878-919.

[225] Liu D. Passing CET4 vocabulary quickly [M]. Xi'an: World Book Inc., 2017.

[226] Liu J Y. Using Facebook for learning writing: EFL students' perceptions and challenges. International Conference on English Teaching and Learning[C]. Taiwan, 2013: 18 – 19.

[227] Liu N, Nation P. Factors affecting guessing vocabulary in context[J]. RELC journal, 1985, 16(1): 33 – 42.

[228] Liu Q Y. A research on the relationship between vocabulary knowledge and second language proficiency among non-English majors[D]. Jiangxi Normal University, 2016.

[229] Liu X. Application of mobile learning based on smartphone in the vocabulary learning of senior high school students[D]. Central China Normal University, 2015.

[230] Liu Y H. Investigating the relationship between vocabulary and academic reading comprehension in CET-4[D]. Guangdong University of Foreign Studies, 2006.

[231] Liu Y L. A study on the vocabulary teaching of college English in China[J]. Journal of Shanxi institute of energy, 2018, 31(4): 95 – 97.

[232] Lu M. Effectiveness of vocabulary learning via mobile phone[J]. Journal of computer assisted learning, 2008, 24(6): 515 – 525.

[233] Luo L L. The study on correlation between the vocabulary knowledge and the result of CET-4[J]. Journal of Hunan Medical University (Social Science), 2009, 11(5): 145 – 148.

[234] Ma D G. Remembering CET-4 vocabulary quickly and skillfully with spark[M]. Shanghai: Shanghai Jiao Tong University Press, 2009.

[235] Ma Q. A contextualized study of EFL learners' vocabulary learning approaches: framework, learner approach and degree of success[J]. Journal of Asia TEFL, 2014, 11(3): 33 – 71.

[236] Ma Q. University L2 learners' voices and experience in making use of dictionary Apps in Mobile Assisted Language Learning (MALL)[M]. International journal of computer-assisted language learning and teaching, 2019.

[237] MacCallum K. Student characteristics and variables that determine mobile

adoption: an initial study. Proceedings of the Universal College of Learning: Teaching and Learning Conference[C]. 2009: 1 – 8.

[238] Mackey A, Gass S M. Second language research: methodology and design [M]. Mahwah, New Jersey: Lawrence ERlbaum Associates, 2005.

[239] MacLeod C M, Gopie N, Hourihan K L, et al. The production effect: delineation of a phenomenon [J]. Journal of experimental psychology: Learning, memory and cognition, 2010, 36(3): 671 – 685.

[240] Makoe M, Shandu T. Developing a mobile app for learning English vocabulary in an open distance learning context [J]. International review of research in open and distributed learning, 2018, 19(4): 208 – 221.

[241] Marello C. Using mobile bilingual dictionaries in an EFL class [J]. Abel/Vettori/Ralli (Eds.), 2014, 63 – 83.

[242] Afshar M A, Mojavezi A. The effect of aural and visual storytelling on vocabulary retention of Iranian EFL learners [J]. English language teaching, 2017, 10 (4): 92 – 99.

[243] Matsuoka W, Hirsh D. Vocabulary learning through reading: Does an ELT course book provide good opportunities? [J] Reading in a foreign language, 2010, 22 (1): 56 – 70.

[244] Mayer R E. Multimedia learning: Are we asking the right questions? [J]. Educational psychologist, 1997, 32(1): 1 – 19.

[245] Mayer R E. The Cambridge handbook of multimedia learning [M]. New York: Cambridge University Press, 2005.

[246] Mayer R E, Fiorella L. Principle for reducing extraneous processing in multimedia learning: Coherence, signaling, redundancy, spatial contiguity, and temporal contiguity principles [M]. 2nd ed. // Mayer R E. The Cambridge handbook of multimedia learning. New York, Cambridge University Press, 2014: 279 – 315.

[247] McBride D M, Dosher A B. A comparison of conscious and automatic memory processes for picture and word stimuli: A process dissociation analysis [J]. Consciousness

and cognition, 2002, 11(3): 423-460.

[248] McCarthy M. A new look at vocabulary in EFL [J]. Applied linguistics, 1994, 5(1): 12-22.

[249] Meara P. The vocabulary knowledge framework [J]. Vocabulary acquisition research group virtual library, 1996, 1-11.

[250] Meara P M, Milton J. X-lex: the Swansea Levels Test [M]. Newbury, UK: Express, 2003.

[251] Merckelbach H, Muris P, Rassin E, et al. Dissociative experiences and interrogative suggestibility in college students [J]. Personality and individual differences, 2000, 29: 1133-1140.

[252] Miangah T M, Nezarat A. Mobile-assisted language learning [J]. International journal of distributed and parallel systems, 2012, 3(1): 309-319.

[253] Miller E K, Cohen J D. An integrative theory of prefrontal cortex function [J]. Annual review of neuroscience, 2001, 24(1): 167-202.

[254] Miller G A. The magical number seven, plus or minus two: some limits on our capacity for processing information [J]. Psychological review, 1956, 63(2): 81-97.

[255] Milton J, Alexiou T. Vocabulary input, vocabulary uptake and approaches to language teaching [J]. The language learning journal, 2012, 40(1): 1-5.

[256] Milton J, Hopkins N. Aural Lex [M]. Swansea, UK: Swansea University, 2005.

[257] Milton J, Meara P. Are the British really bad at learning foreign languages? [J] Language learning journal, 1998, 18(1): 68-76.

[258] Milton J, Wade J, Hopkins N. Aural word recognition and oral competence in a foreign language[M]. // Chacón-Beltrán R, Abello-Contesse C, Torreblanca-López M, and López-Jiménez M. Insights into non-native vocabulary teaching and learning. Multilingual Matters, 2010:83-98.

[259] Min Y K. Vocabulary acquisition: practical strategies for ESL students [J]. Journal of international students, 2013, 3(1), 64-69.

[260] Minichiello V, Aroni R, Timewell E, et al. In-depth interviewing: researching people [M]. Hong Kong: Longman Cheshire Pty Limited, 1990.

[261] Miyake A, Shah P. Models of working memory: mechanisms of active maintenance and executive control [M]. New York, US: Cambridge University Press, 1999.

[262] Mohr G, Engelkamp J, Zimmer H D. Why arts retention improves long-term retention of content [J]. Mind, brain, and education, 1989, 5(2): 89 – 96.

[263] Mollakhan K, Rasouli M, Karbalaei A. The effect of oral corrective feedback on enhancing second language vocabulary learning in Iranian EFL context [J]. European online journal of natural and social sciences, 2013, 2(2): 230 – 239.

[264] Mondria J-A, Wit-de-Boer M. The effects of contextual richness on the guess ability and the retention of words in a foreign language [J]. Applied linguistics, 1991, 12(3): 249 – 267.

[265] Moore K A. Quasi-experimental evaluations. Part 6 in a series on practical evaluation methods. Research-to-results brief [J]. Child Trends, 2008.

[266] Motallebzadeh K, Beh-Afarin R, Daliry S. The effect of short message service on the retention of collocations among Iranian lower intermediate EFL learners [J]. Theory & practice in language studies, 2011, 1(11): 1514 – 1520.

[267] Muhanna W N, Abu-Al-Sha'r A M. University students' attitudes towards cell phone learning environment [J]. International journal of interactive mobile learning, 2009, 3(4): 35 – 40.

[268] Muller-Cajar R, Mukundan R. Triangulation: a new algorithm for inverse kinematics[J]. Proceedings of the image and vision computing, 2007, 181 – 186.

[269] Murre J M, Dros J. Replication and analysis of Ebbinghaus' forgetting curve [J]. PloS one, 2015, 10(7).

[270] McKeown M, Curtis M. The nature of vocabulary acquisition [M]. Hillsdale, NJ: Erlbaum Associates, 1987.

[271] Namaziandost E, Nasri M, Rahimi Esfahani F. et al. The impacts of spaced

and massed distribution instruction on EFL learners' vocabulary learning [J]. Cogent education, 2019, 6(1): 1 – 10.

[272] Nassaji H. Input modality and remembering name-referent associations in vocabulary learning [J]. Canadian journal of applied linguistics, 2004, 7(1): 39 – 55.

[273] Nation P. Beginning to learn foreign vocabulary: a review of the research [J]. RELC Journal, 1982, 13: 14 – 36.

[274] Nation P. Teaching and learning vocabulary [M]. New York: Newbury House, 1990.

[275] Schreuder R, Weltens B. The bilingual lexicon (Vol. 6) [M]. John Benjamins Publishing, 1993.

[276] Nation P. Learning vocabulary in another language [M]. Cambridge: Cambridge University Press, 2001.

[277] Nation P. How large a vocabulary is needed for reading and listening? [J]. Canadian modern language review, 2006, 63 (1): 59 – 82.

[278] Nation P. The four strands [J]. Innovation in language learning and teaching, 2007, 1(1): 2 – 13.

[279] Nation P. Learning vocabulary in another language [M]. 2nd ed. New York: Cambridge University Press, 2013.

[280] Nation P, Beglar D. A vocabulary size test [J]. The language teacher, 2007, 31(7): 9 – 13.

[281] Neisser U. Cognitive psychology (classic edition) [M]. Psychology Press, 2014.

[282] Nguyen L T C, Nation I S P. A bilingual vocabulary size test of English for Vietnamese learners [J]. RELC journal, 2011, 42(1): 86 – 99.

[283] Nikoopour J, Kazemi A. Vocabulary learning through digitized & non-digitized flashcards delivery [J]. Procedia-social and behavioral sciences, 2014, 98: 1366 – 1373.

[284] Nurweni A, Read J. The English vocabulary knowledge of Indonesian university students [J]. English for specific purposes, 1999, 18(2): 161 – 175.

[285] Oberg A, Daniels P. Analysis of the effect a student-centred mobile learning instructional method has on language acquisition [J]. Computer assisted language learning, 2013, 26(2): 177-196.

[286] O'Malley C, Vavoula G, Glew J P, et al. Guidelines for learning, teaching, tutoring in a mobile environment [J]. HAL, 2003, 1-84.

[287] Okunbor D, Retta G. Analysis of a mobile learning pilot study [J]. Math and computer science, 2008.

[288] Olmsted N M, Terry C P. Who's texting in class? A look at behavioral and psychological predictors [J]. Psi Chi journal of psychological research, 2014, 19(4): 183-192.

[289] Ophir E, Nass C, Wagner A D. Cognitive control in media multitaskers [J]. Proceedings of the national academy of sciences of United States of America, 2009, 106(37): 15583-15587.

[290] Ornprapat S, Wiwat W. Using mobile-assisted exercises to support students' vocabulary skill development [J]. Turkish online journal of educational technology, 2015, 14(1): 163-171.

[291] Orozco G. Vocabulary maintenance of seventh grade students with learning disabilities[D]. University of California, Riverside, USA, 2019.

[292] Osaki S, Ochiai N. Electronic dictionary vs. printed dictionary: accessing the appropriate meaning, reading comprehension, and retention. Dictionaries and language learning: How can dictionaries help human and machine learning? Papers submitted to the 3rd ASIALEX Biennial International Conference, Urayasu, The Asian Association for Lexicography (pp. 205-212), 2003.

[293] Ota F. The effectiveness of smartphone and tablet PC apps for Japanese language learning [J]. The IALLT journal of language learning technologies, 2015, 44(2): 64-82.

[294] Ou-Yang F C, Wu W C V. Using mixed-modality vocabulary learning on mobile devices design and evaluation [J]. Journal of educational computing research,

2017, 54(8): 1043-1069.

[295] Oxford R. Language learning strategies: What every teacher should know [M]. Boston, Mass, 1990.

[296] Oxford R L, Scarcella R C. Second language vocabulary learning among adults: state of the art in vocabulary instruction [J]. System, 1994, 22(2): 231-243.

[297] Oz H. Prospective English teachers' ownership and usage of mobile devices as m-learning tools [J]. Procedia-social and behavioral sciences, 2014, 141: 1031-1041.

[298] Ozubko J D, MacLeod C M. The production effect in memory: evidence that distinctiveness underlies the benefit [J]. Journal of experimental psychology: learning, memory and cognition, 2010, 36(6): 1543-1547.

[299] Paas F, Renkel A, Sweller J. Cognitive load theory: instructional implications of the interaction between information structures and cognitive architecture [J]. Instructional science, 2004, 32: 1-8.

[300] Paivio A. Imagery and verbal processes [M]. New York: Holt, Rinehart, and Winston, 1971.

[301] Paivio A. Mental representations: a dual-coding approach [M]. New York: Oxford University Press, 1986.

[302] Paivio A. Mind and its evolution: a dual coding theoretical approach [M]. Mahwah, NJ: Erlbaum, 2007.

[303] Paribakht T S, Wesche M. Reading comprehension and second language development in a comprehension-based ESL program [J]. TESL Canada journal, 1993, 11(1): 9-29.

[304] Coady J, Huckin T. Second language vocabulary acquisition: a rationale for pedagogy [M]. Cambridge: Cambridge University Press, 1997.

[305] Paribakht T S. The influence of first language lexicalization on second language lexical inferencing: a study of Farsi-speaking learners of English as a foreign language [J]. Language learning, 2005, 55(4): 701-748.

[306] Paribakht T, Wesche M. Reading and "incidental" L2 vocabulary

acquisition: an introspective study of lexical referencing [J]. Studies in second language acquisition, 1999, 21(1): 195–224.

[307] Pashler H, Cepeda N J, Wixted J T, et al. When does feedback facilitate learning of words? [J]. Journal of experimental psychology: learning, memory, and cognition, 2005, 31(1): 3–8.

[308] Patton M Q. Qualitative research and evaluation methods [M]. Thousand Oaks, CA: Sage Publications Ltd., 2002.

[309] Pavlik J V. Fueling a third paradigm of education: the pedagogical implications of digital, social and mobile media [J]. Contemporary educational technology, 2015, 6(2): 113–125.

[310] Peters K. M-Learning: positioning educators for a mobile, connected future [J]. International journal of research in open and distance learning, 2007, 8(2): 1–17.

[311] Poláková P, Klímová B. Mobile technology and generation Z in the English language classroom—a preliminary study [J]. Education sciences, 2019, 9(3): 1–11.

[312] Presser S, Couper M P, Lessler J T, et al. Methods for testing and evaluating survey questions [J]. Public opinion quarterly, 2004, 68(1): 109–130.

[313] Preston G, Anderson E, Silva C, et al. Effects of 10 Hz rTMS on the neural efficiency of working memory [J]. Journal of cognitive neuroscience, 2010, 22(3): 447–456.

[314] Punch K F. Introduction to social research: quantitative and qualitative approaches [M]. Thousand Oaks, CA: Sage Publications Ltd., 1998.

[315] Qian D. Assessing the roles of depth and breadth of vocabulary knowledge in reading comprehension [J]. Canadian modern language review, 1999, 56(2): 282–308.

[316] Qian D. Investigating the relationship between vocabulary knowledge and academic reading performance: an assessment perspective [J]. Language learning, 2002, 52(3): 513–536.

[317] Rahman M S. The advantages and disadvantages of using qualitative and quantitative approaches and methods in language "Testing and Assessment" research: a literature review [J]. Journal of education and learning, 2016, 6(1): 102 – 112.

[318] Rajan M K, Kumar S P. Approach and analysis of M-Learning in higher education [J]. International journal of advanced research in computer science, 2014, 5 (1): 160 – 163.

[319] Ramachandran S D, Rahim H A. Meaning recall and retention: the impact of the translation method on elementary level learners' vocabulary learning [J]. Regional language centre journal, 2004, 35(2): 161 – 178.

[320] Ramezanali N. Short and long-term vocabulary learning and retention through multimedia glossing: a mixed methods research [D]. University of Western Ontario, Ontario, Canada, 2017.

[321] Ramezanali N, Faez F. Vocabulary learning and retention through multimedia glossing [J]. Language learning & technology, 2019, 23 (2): 105 – 124.

[322] Read J. The development of a new measure of L2 vocabulary knowledge [J]. Language testing, 1993, 10(3): 355 – 371.

[323] Read J. Validating the word associates format as a measure of depth of vocabulary knowledge [M]. Long Beach, CA: Language Testing Colloquium, 1995.

[324] Kunnan A. Validation in language assessment [M]. Mahwah, NJ: Lawrence Erlbaum, 1998.

[325] Read J. Assessing vocabulary [M]. Cambridge: Cambridge University Press, 2000.

[326] Reimer C K. The effect of retrieval practice on vocabulary learning for children who are deaf or hard of hearing [D]. Washington University, USA, 2019.

[327] Reinders H, Hubbard P. CALL and learner autonomy: affordances and constraints [M]. // Thomas M, Reinders H, Warschauer M. Contemporary computer assisted language learning. London: Continuum Books, 2013: 359 – 375.

[328] Rezaei A, Mai N, Pesaranghader A. The effect of mobile applications on

English vocabulary acquisition [J]. Jurnal Teknologi, 2014, 68(2): 73-83.

[329] Richards C J, Schmidt R. Longman dictionary of language teaching and applied linguistics [M]. New York: Pearson Education Limited, 2002.

[330] Richards J C. The role of vocabulary teaching [J]. TESOL quarterly, 1976, 10(1): 77-89.

[331] Rickard T C, Pan S C. A dual memory theory of the testing effect [J]. Psychonomic bulletin & review, 2018, 25(3): 847-869.

[332] Rinne L, Gregory E, Yarmolinskaya J, et al. Why arts integration improves long-term retention of content? [J]. Mind, brain, and education, 2011, 5(2): 89-96.

[333] Robson C. Real world research: a resource for social scientist and practitioner-researcher [M]. Oxford, UK: Blackwell Publishers, 2002.

[334] Roediger H L, Butler A C. The critical role of retrieval practice in long-term retention [J]. Trends in cognitive sciences, 2010, 15(1): 20-27.

[335] Roediger H L, Karpicke J D. Learning and memory, encyclopedia of social measurement (Vol. 2) [M]. San Diego: Academic Press, 2005.

[336] Rogers J. Learning second language syntax under massed and distributed conditions [J]. TESOL quarterly, 2015, 49(4): 857-866.

[337] Rogers J. The spacing effect and its relevance to second language acquisition [J]. Applied linguistics, 2017, 38(6): 906-911.

[338] Rohrer D. Student instruction should be distributed over long time periods [J]. Educational psychology review, 2015, 27: 635-643.

[339] Rosalia S I. A classroom research study on strategies to promote vocabulary retention in the LOTE classroom [D]. Stony Brook University, New York, USA, 2012.

[340] Rovinelli R J, Hambleton R K. On the use of content specialists in the assessment of criterion-referenced test item validity [J]. Dutch journal for educational research, 1977, 2: 49-60.

[341] Rundus D. Analysis of rehearsal processes in free recall [J]. Journal of

experimental psychology, 1971, 89(1): 63-77.

[342] Rusanganwa J A. Developing a multimedia instrument for technical vocabulary learning: a case of EFL undergraduate physics education [J]. Computer assisted language learning, 2015, 28(2): 97-111.

[343] Sandberg J, Maris M, Geus K. Mobile English learning: An evidence-based study with fifth graders [J]. Computers & education, 2011, 57(1): 1334-1347.

[344] Santos M E C, Taketomi T, Yamamoto G, et al. Augmented reality as multimedia: the case for situated vocabulary learning [J]. Research and practice in technology enhanced learning, 2016, 11(1): 4.

[345] Saran M, Seferoglu G. Supporting foreign language vocabulary learning through multimedia messages via mobile phones [J]. Hacettepe University journal of education, 2010, 38, 252-266.

[346] Saran M, Seferoglu G, Cagiltay K. Mobile assisted language learning: English pronunciation at learners' fingertips [J]. Eurasian journal of educational research, 2009, 34: 97-114.

[347] Schmitt N. Vocabulary learning strategies [M]. // Schmitt N, McCarthy M. Vocabulary: description, acquisition and pedagogy. Cambridge: Cambridge University Press, 1997: 77-85.

[348] Schmitt N. Quantifying word association responses: What is native-like? [J]. System, 1998, 26(3): 389-401.

[349] Schmitt N. Vocabulary in second language teaching [M]. Cambridge: Cambridge University Press, 2000.

[350] Schmitt N. Review article: instructed second language vocabulary learning [J]. Language teaching research, 2008, 12(3): 329-363.

[351] Schmitt N. Researching vocabulary: a vocabulary research manual [M]. Basingstoke: Palgrave Macmillan, 2010.

[352] Schmitt N D, Clapham C. Developing and exploring the behaviour of two new versions of the vocabulary levels test [J]. Language testing, 2001, 18(1): 55-88.

[353] Schuetze U. Spacing techniques in second language vocabulary acquisition: short-term gains vs. long-term memory [J]. Language teaching research, 2015, 19(1): 28–42.

[354] Segaran K, Ali A Z, Hoe T W. Usability and user satisfaction of 3D talking-head mobile assisted language learning (MALL) app for non-native speakers [J]. Procedia-social and behavioral sciences, 2014, 131: 4–10.

[355] Senkfor A J, Petten C V, Kutas M. Enactment versus conceptual encoding: equivalent item memory but different source memory [J]. Cortex, 2007, 44(6): 649–664.

[356] Serrano R, Huang H Y. Learning vocabulary through assisted repeated reading: How much time should there be between repetitions of the same text? [J]. TESOL quarterly, 2018, 52(4), 971–994.

[357] Shahbaz M, Khan R M I. Use of mobile immersion in foreign language teaching to enhance target language vocabulary learning [J]. MIER journal of educational studies, trends and practices, 2017, 7(1): 66–82.

[358] Shao H. A survey of students' vocabulary level at the stage of CET4 in Teachers' University [J]. Foreign language teaching and research, 2002, (6): 421–425.

[359] Shen L, Suwanthep J. E-learning constructive role plays for EFL learners in China's tertiary education [J]. Asian EFL journal, 2011, 49: 1–26.

[360] Shen Y, Wei T. The relative significance of vocabulary breadth and syntactic knowledge in the prediction of reading comprehension test performance [J]. Chinese journal of applied linguistics, 2011, 34(3): 113–126.

[361] Shen Z. The effects of vocabulary knowledge and dictionary use on EFL reading performance [J]. English language teaching, 2013, 6(6): 77–85.

[362] Shi N N. A study on the correlations among ESL learners' breadth of vocabulary knowledge, depth of vocabulary knowledge and oral proficiency [D]. Ocean University of China, Qingdao, China, 2012.

[363] Shillaw J. Using a word list as a focus for vocabulary learning [J]. The language teacher, 1995, 19(2): 9-58.

[364] Silverman D. Doing qualitative research [M]. 3rd ed. London: Sage Publications Ltd., 2010.

[365] Slamecka N J, Graf P. The generation effect: delineation of a phenomenon [J]. Journal of experimental psychology: Human learning and memory, 1978, 4(6): 592-604.

[366] Soleimani E, Ismail K, Mustaffa R. The acceptance of mobile assisted language learning (MALL) among post graduate ESL students in UKM [J]. Procedia-social and behavioral sciences, 2014, 118(1): 457-462.

[367] Somnuek S. A study of automotive engineering students' strategies in coping with vocabulary when reading engineering passages [D]. Thammasat University, Bangkok, Thailand, 2011.

[368] Song Y Y. On the relationship between vocabulary knowledge and reading comprehension [D]. Nanjing Normal university, Nanjing, China, 2014.

[369] Soria S, Gutiérrez-Colón M, Frumuselu A D. Feedback and mobile instant messaging: using WhatsApp as a feedback tool in EFL [J]. International journal of instruction, 2020, 13(1): 797-812.

[370] Sprenger M. How to teach so students remember [M]. 2nd ed. Alexandria, VA: Association for Supervision and Curriculum Development (ASCD), 2018.

[371] Staehr L S. Vocabulary size and the skills of reading, listening and writing [J]. Language learning, 2008, 36(2): 139-152.

[372] Staehr L S. Vocabulary knowledge and advanced listening comprehension in English as a foreign language [J]. Studies in second language acquisition, 2009, 31(4): 577-607.

[373] Steel C. Fitting learning into life: Language students' perspectives on benefits of using mobile apps. In Brown M, Hartnett M, Stewart T(Eds.), Future challenges, sustainable futures. Proceedings ascilite Wellington, 2012: 875-880.

[374] Steel C. Students' perspectives on the benefits of using mobile apps for learning languages [M]. Glasgow: WorldCall, 2013.

[375] Stevick E W. Memory, meaning & method: a view of language teaching[M]. 2nd ed. Boston, MA: Heinle & Heinle Publishers, 1996.

[376] Stockwell G. Vocabulary on the move: investigating an intelligent mobile phone-based vocabulary tutor [J]. Computer assisted language learning, 2007, 20(4): 365 – 383.

[377] Stockwell G. Investigating learner preparedness for and usage patterns of mobile learning [J]. ReCALL, 2008, 20(3): 253 – 270.

[378] Stockwell G. Using mobile phones for vocabulary activities: examining the effect of the platform [J]. Language learning & technology, 2010, 14(2): 95 – 110.

[379] Stockwell G. Tracking learner usage of mobile phones for language learning outside of the classroom[J]. CALICO journal, 2013, 30: 118 – 136.

[380] Stockwell G, Hubbard P. Some emerging principles for mobile-assisted language learning[M]. Monterey, CA: The International Research Foundation for English Language Education, 2013.

[381] Strauss A, Corbin J. Basics of qualitative research techniques [M]. Thousand Oaks, CA: Sage Publications Ltd., 1998.

[382] Sung Y T, Chang K E, Liu T C. The effects of integrating mobile devices with teaching and learning on students' learning performance: A meta-analysis and research synthesis [J]. Computers & education, 2016, 94: 252 – 275.

[383] Sweller J. Implications of cognitive load theory for multimedia learning [M]. // Mayer R E. Cambridge handbook of multimedia learning. New York: Cambridge University Press, 2005: 19 – 30.

[384] Sweller J, Chandler P. Why some material is difficult to learn [J]. Cognition and instruction, 1994, 12(3): 185 – 233.

[385] Sweller J. Working memory, long-term memory and instructional design [J]. Journal of applied research in memory and cognition, 2016, 5: 360 – 367.

[386] Tabatabaei O, Goojani A H. The impact of text-messaging on vocabulary learning of Iranian EFL learners [J]. Cross-cultural communication, 2012, 8(2): 47 – 55.

[387] Taghizadeh M, Porkar P. Tablet, flashcard and SMS and their effects on EFL learners' attitudes and vocabulary knowledge [J]. International journal of English language & translation studies, 2018, 6(1): 105-118.

[388] Tang H J, Yin B L. The study of non-English majors' vocabulary size [J]. Journal of Shangdong University of Technology (Social Sciences.), 2015, 31(3): 76-80.

[389] Tashakkori A, Teddlie C. Mixed methodology: combining qualitative and quantitative approaches [M]. Thousand Oaks, CA: Sage Publications Ltd., 1998.

[390] Tashakkori A, Teddlie C. Handbook of mixed methods in social & behavioral research [M]. Thousand Oaks, CA: Sage Publications Ltd., 2010.

[391] Thalheimer W. How much do people forget? [M] Somerville, MA: Work-Learning Research, Inc.,2010.

[392] Thomas R. Blending qualitative & quantitative research approach to language learning [J]. Englewood Cliffs, HJ: Prentice Hall, 2003.

[393] Thornbury S. How to teach vocabulary? [M]. Harlow: Longman, 2002.

[394] Thornton P, Houser C. Using mobile phones in English education in Japan [J]. Journal of computer assisted learning, 2005, 21(3): 217-228.

[395] Trifanova A, Knapp J, Ponchetti M, et al. Mobile ELDIT: challenges in the transition from an e-learning to an m-learning system. Unitn-eprints Research. University of Trento, 2004: 1-10.

[396] Trofimovich P, Isaacs T. Disentangling accent from comprehensibility [J]. Bilingualism: Language and cognition, 2012, 15(4): 905-916.

[397] Valarmathi K E. Mobile assisted language learning [J]. Journal of technology for ELT, 2011, 2(2), 1-8.

[398] Viberg O, Grönlund A. Mobile assisted language learning: a literature review [C]. World Conference on Mobile and Contextual Learning, Helsinki, 2012.

[399] Viberg O, Grönlund A. Cross-cultural analysis of users' attitudes toward the use of mobile devices in second and foreign language learning in higher education: a case from Sweden and China [J]. Computers & education, 2013, 69: 169-180.

[400] Wammes J D, Meade M E, Fernandes M A. The drawing effect: evidence for

reliable and robust memory if free recall [J]. The quarterly journal of experimental psychology, 2016, 69(9): 1752 –1776.

[401] Wang B T. Designing mobile apps for English vocabulary learning [J]. International journal of information and education technology, 2017, 7(4): 279 –283.

[402] Wang B T, Teng C W, Chen H T. Using iPad to facilitate English vocabulary learning [J]. International journal of information and education technology, 2015, 5(2): 100 –104.

[403] Wang F F. Constructivism-based mobile application for EFL vocabulary learning[D]. Suranaree University of Technology, Nakhon Ratchasima, Thailand, 2015.

[404] Wang H. A study of college students' vocabulary proficiency and vocabulary strategic learning[D]. Shan Xi Normal University, Lin Fen, China, 2010.

[405] Wang Q. EFL incidental vocabulary acquisition and retention: effects of different collaborative output tasks on field independent/dependent learners [J]. Journal of Asia TEFL, 2019, 16(4): 1201 –1218.

[406] Wang S D, Higgins M. Limitations of mobile phone learning [J]. The JALT CALL journal, 2006, 2(1): 3 –14.

[407] Wang T X, Wu M J, Hou X X. Relationship between the breadth and depth of vocabulary and grammatical knowledge and listening comprehension[J]. Technology-enhanced foreign language education, 2011, 142(6): 42 –46.

[408] Wang Y. Study on EFL students' mobile assisted English learning in Guizhou University[D]. Guizhou University, Guiyang, China, 2015.

[409] Wang Y, Christiansen M S. An investigation of Chinese older adults' self-directed English learning experience using mobile apps [J]. International journal of computer-assisted language learning and teaching, 2019, 9(4): 51 –71.

[410] Wang Y C, Hsu L. Shall we go to the MALL? — Students' perceptions of a business English learning app [J]. International journal of information and education technology, 2020, 10(2): 110 –116.

[411] Wang Y H, Shih S K H. Mobile-assisted language learning: effects on EFL vocabulary learning[J]. International journal of mobile communications, 2015, 13(4): 358 –375.

[412] Wang Z Y. An empirical study of the predictability of the vocabulary size test on language proficiency [J]. Foreign language learning theory and practice, 2014(2): 71-75+96.

[413] Wei J C. The impact of explicit vocabulary instruction on L2 advanced Chinese learners' vocabulary retention [D]. University of Pittsburgh, Pittsburgh, USA, 2018.

[414] Wesche M, Paribakht T. Lexical inferencing in a first and second language: cross-linguistic dimensions [M]. Clevedon: Multilingual Matters, 2009.

[415] Wesche M, Paribakht T S. Assessing second language vocabulary knowledge: depth versus breadth [J]. Canadian modern language review, 1996, 53(1): 13-40.

[416] White J, Mills D. Examining attitudes towards and usage of smartphone technology among Japanese university students studying EFL [J]. CALL-EJ, 2014, 15(2): 1-15.

[417] Wiersma W, Jurs S G. Research methods in education: an introduction [M]. 8th ed. Boston: Allyn and Bacon, 2005.

[418] Wilkins D. Linguistics in language teaching [M]. London: Arnold, 1972.

[419] Woodcock B, Middleton A, Nortcliffe A. Considering the smartphone learner: an investigation into student interest in the use of personal technology to enhance their learning [J]. Student engagement and experience journal, 2012, 1(1): 1-15.

[420] Wozniak R H. Introduction to memory: Hermann Ebbinghaus (1885/1913). [M]. Bristol UK: Thoemmes Press. WL, 1999.

[421] Wu H M. An English vocabulary test survey among non-English majors [J]. Higher education forum, 2011 (9): 102-104.

[422] Wu J P. The role of breadth and depth of vocabulary knowledge in English writing[D]. Shaanxi Normal University, Xi'an, China, 2010.

[423] Wu Q. Designing a smartphone app to teach English (L2) vocabulary [J]. Computers & eduction, 2015, 85: 170-179.

[424] Wu W, Wu Y J, Chen C Y, et al. Review of trends from mobile learning studies: A meta-analysis [J]. Computers & education, 2012, 59(2): 817-827.

[425] Yang J. Mobile assisted language learning: review of the recent applications of

emerging mobile technologies [J]. English language teaching, 2013, 6 (7): 19 -25.

[426] Yang Y F. Main problems existing in college English vocabulary teaching and solutions [J]. Education teaching forum, 2018(42): 187 – 188.

[427] Young D J, Oxford R. A gender-related analysis of strategies used to process written input in the native language and a foreign language [J]. Applied language learning, 1997, 8(1): 43 –73.

[428] Younus A D. Investigation of a mobile government: a case study in Iraq[D]. Near East University, Nicosia, Northern Cyprus, 2014.

[429] Yu A Q. Understanding information technology acceptance and effectiveness in college students' English learning in China [D]. University of Nebraska, Nebraska, USA, 2019.

[430] Yu M H. Memorizing CET-4 vocabulary based on their roots and associations [M]. Beijing: Dolphin Publishing House, 2008.

[431] Zahar R, Cobb T, Spada N. Acquiring vocabulary through reading: effects of frequency and contextual richness [J]. Canadian modern language review, 2001, 57 (4): 541 –572.

[432] Zeng Q. The study of non-English majors vocabulary acquisition effects under the multimedia and network environment[D]. Xi'an Polytechnic University, Xi'an, China, 2012.

[433] Zha H L. A Research on the relationship between vocabulary knowledge and listening comprehension among English majors[D]. Jiangxi Normal University, Nanchang, China, 2015.

[434] Zhang H, Song W, Burston J. Reexamining the effectiveness of vocabulary learning via mobile phones [J]. Turkish online journal of educational technology, 2011, 10(3): 203 –214.

[435] Zhang J. Memory process and the function of sleep [J]. Journal of theoretic, 2004, 6(6): 1 –7.

[436] Zhang M Z. An Empirical study on depth of vocabulary knowledge in relation to L2 production in the senior high school [D]. Sanxia University, Yichang, China, 2012.

[437] Zhang X C. A study of non-English majors' vocabulary level and vocabulary learning strategies [D]. Shanghai International Studies University, Shanghai, China, 2008.

[438] Zhang X D. On the relationship between vocabulary knowledge and listening comprehension [J]. Foreign language world, 2011 (2): 36 – 42.

[439] Zhang X B, Qiu T H. On the relationship between vocabulary knowledge and reading comprehension [J]. Foreign language education, 2006 (1): 38 – 42.

[440] Zhen Z. An experimental study on the correlation between vocabulary knowledge and language proficiency [D]. Beijing Language and Culture University, Beijing, China, 2007.

[441] Zheng L L, Xu Y J, Wang H C. An investigation of English vocabulary learning methods among Chinese university students and proposed solutions based on relevant theories [J]. Foreign language learning and teaching, 2015 (8): 143 – 146.

[442] Zimmerman C B. Historical trends in second language vocabulary instruction [M]. //Coady J, Huckin T. Second language vocabulary acquisition. Cambridge: Cambridge University Press, 1997.

[443] Zou B, Li J Y. Exploring mobile apps for English language teaching and learning [C]. Critical CALL-Proceedings of the 2015 EuroCALL Conference, Padova, Italy, 2015: 564 – 568.

APPENDICES

APPENDIX A

Top 80 High-frequency CET-4 Words of the Corpus as Target Words

1. treat	21. illegal	41. casual	61. launch
2. abundant	22. economical	42. staff	62. reluctant
3. transfer	23. alter	43. prohibit	63. chill
4. chew	24. register	44. appeal	64. boast
5. objective	25. ensure	45. tackle	65. chase
6. intend	26. emit	46. reputation	66. switch
7. optional	27. distribute	47. slip	67. contrast
8. despite	28. strategy	48. contact	68. pitch
9. intense	29. influence	49. assignment	69. negotiation
10. expand	30. dim	50. entitle	70. drift
11. local	31. individual	51. illustrate	71. kit
12. acknowledge	32. insert	52. discipline	72. drain
13. behalf	33. discharge	53. characteristic	73. squeeze
14. generous	34. hint	54. criticize	74. collect
15. resolve	35. remark	55. exhaust	75. install
16. automatic	36. efficient	56. assist	76. response
17. species	37. adequate	57. deceive	77. convey
18. involve	38. appropriate	58. overtake	78. commercial
19. estate	39. brand	59. consume	79. imitate
20. conduct	40. overall	60. legal	80. crack

APPENDIX B

The Informed Consent Form for the Experiment Group

You will participate in a research project to explore the effects of using a mobile application on CET-4 vocabulary learning and retention. It will be conducted for a period of 8 weeks in the first semester of academic year 2019—2020. Your role in this study is to learn 80 CET-4 words via a mobile app independently by the five-time week schedule, and keep diaries. Besides, the relevant pre-test, post-test, delayed post-test will be conducted. Also, diaries will be collected weekly and the semi-structured interview will be performed at last. All information that you provide will be kept strictly confidential. I promise not to use your real name during my whole thesis. Once this study is completed, I will summarize my findings, which hopefully are helpful for your vocabulary learning, especially CET-4 vocabulary learning. If you have any questions about this research project, please feel free to contact me at *maxxjxnu@ qq. com*. If you agree to participate in this project, please sign below. Thank you for your cooperation.

Sincerely,

Researcher: Xingxing Ma, a Ph.D candidate in Suranaree University of Technology

Signed Participant: Date:

Signed Researcher: Date:

APPENDIX C

The Informed Consent Form for the Control Group

You will participate in a research project to explore the effects of using a paper-based wordlist on CET-4 vocabulary learning and retention. It will be conducted for a period of 8 weeks in the first semester of academic year 2019—2020. Your role in this study is to learn 80 CET-4 words with the paper-based wordlist independently by the five-time week schedule, and keep diaries. Besides, the relevant pre-test, post-test, delayed post-test will be conducted. Also, diaries will be collected weekly. All information that you provide will be kept strictly confidential. I promise not to use your real name during my whole thesis. Once this study is completed, I will summarize my findings, which hopefully are helpful for your vocabulary learning, especially CET-4 vocabulary learning. If you have any questions about this research project, please feel free to contact me at *maxxjxnu@qq.com*. If you agree to participate in this project, please sign below. Thank you for your cooperation.

Sincerely,

Researcher: Xingxing Ma, a Ph. D candidate in Suranaree University of Technology

Signed Participant: Date:

Signed Researcher: Date:

APPENDIX D

Sample of the First Wordlist for the Control Group

Week 2（**10 words**）

involve /ɪnˈvɑːlv/ v. 包含；需要；牵涉；影响；(使)参加	discharge /dɪsˈtʃɑːdʒ/ v. 解雇；释放；排出；放(电) n. 排出(物)；流出(物)；免职；退伍
abundant /əˈbʌndənt/ adj. 丰盛的；大量的	collect /kəˈlekt/ v. 收集；收藏；聚集；募捐 adj. 由受话人付费的
expand /ɪkˈspænd/ v. 增加；扩大；详述	influence /ˈɪnfluəns/ n. 影响；控制力；（对……）有影响的人（或事物） v. 影响；对……起作用
insert /ɪnˈsɜːt/ v. 插入；嵌入 n. 插入物；插页	prohibit /prəˈhɪbɪt/ v. 禁止；阻止
squeeze /skwiːz/ v. 挤进，塞进；挤压；挤出；削减，压缩 n. 挤，塞；榨出的液体	commercial /kəˈmɜːʃl/ adj. 商业的，贸易的 n. （电台或电视播放的）广告

APPENDIX E

Vocabulary Size Test

An excerpt of ten words in VST (Nation & Beglar, 2007) is presented. The complete test can be reached at http:// www.lextutor.ca/.

Instructions: choose the letter a—d with the closest meaning to the word in bold in the sentence.

1. see: They **saw** it. ( )

   a. cut   b. waited for   c. looked at   d. started

2. time: They have a lot of **time**. ( )

   a. money   b. food   c. hours   d. friends

3. period: It was a difficult **period**. ( )

   a. question   b. time   c. exam   d. book

4. figure: Is this the right **figure**? ( )

   a. answer   b. place   c. time   d. number

5. poor: We are **poor**. ( )

   a. have no money   b. feel happy

   c. are very interested   d. do not like to work hard

6. drive: He **drives** fast. ( )

   a. swims   b. learns   c. throws balls   d. uses a car

7. jump: She tried to **jump**. ( )

   a. lie on top of the water   b. get off the ground suddenly

   c. stop the car at the edge of the road   d. move very fast

8. shoe: Where is your **shoe**? ( )

   a. the person who looks after you   b. the thing you keep your money in

   c. the thing you use for writing   d. the thing you wear on your foot

9. standard: Her **standards** are very high. ( )

   a. the bits at the back under her shoes   b. the marks she gets in school

   c. the money she asks for   d. the levels she reaches in everything

10. basis: This was used as the **basis**. ( )

    a. answer   b. place to take a rest

    c. next step   d. main part

APPENDIX F

Knowledge Scale Test of 80 Words

Choose the most suitable one (I — V) for you to fill in the bracket, and do as told in the bracket if you choose one from III to V. One example is shown how to do it. I. I don't remember having seen the word before. II. I have seen this word before, but I don't know what it means. III. I have seen this word before, and I think it means _____. (synonym or translation) IV. I know this word. It means _____. (synonym or translation) V. I can use this word in a sentence: _____ (make a sentence). If you do this section, please also do Section IV.

1. treat( )	21. illegal( )	41. casual( )	61. launch( )
2. abundant( )	22. economical( )	42. staff( )	62. reluctant( )
3. transfer( )	23. alter( )	43. prohibit( )	63. chill( )
4. chew( )	24. register( )	44. appeal( )	64. boast( )
5. objective( )	25. ensure ( )	45. tackle( )	65. chase( )
6. intend( )	26. emit( )	46. reputation( )	66. switch( )
7. optional( )	27. distribute( )	47. slip( )	67. contrast( )
8. despite( )	28. strategy( )	48. contact( )	68. pitch ( )
9. intense( )	29. influence( )	49. assignment( )	69. negotiation ( )
10. expand( )	30. dim( )	50. entitle( )	70. drift ( )
11. local( )	31. individual ( )	51. illustrate( )	71. kit( )
12. acknowledge( )	32. insert ( )	52. discipline( )	72. drain( )
13. behalf( )	33. discharge ( )	53. characteristic( )	73. squeeze( )
14. generous( )	34. hint ( )	54. criticize ( )	74. collect( )
15. resolve( )	35. remark ( )	55. exhaust( )	75. install( )
16. automatic( )	36. efficient( )	56. assist( )	76. response( )
17. species( )	37. adequate( )	57. deceive( )	77. convey( )

(续表)

18. involve( )	38. appropriate( )	58. overtake( )	78. commercial ( )
19. estate( )	39. brand( )	59. consume( )	79. imitate ( )
20. conduct( )	40. overall( )	60. legal( )	80. crack ( )

APPENDIX G

Checking Item-objective Congruence (IOC) of Draft Questionnaire

Items	Expert A	Expert B	Expert C	Agreement
1. The vocabulary learning app is easy to use.	1	1	1	√
2. Learning vocabulary via the app is convenient, for I can choose place and time to learn new words.	1	0	1	×
3. The app makes vocabulary learning easier for me compared with a wordlist.	1	1	1	√
4. It is a good method to learn vocabulary via the app.	1	1	1	√
5. I like the app more than the method I used.	1	1	0	×
6. The vocabulary learning app motivates me to learn new words.	1	1	1	√
7. The app is useful for me to learn vocabulary.	1	1	1	√
8. The learning sections in the app help me learn vocabulary more effectively.	1	0	0	×
9. The immediate feedback in the app can push me to monitor and adjust my vocabulary learning.	1	1	1	√
10. The retrieval section in the app enables me to review and remember the vocabulary very well.	1	1	1	√
11. The app makes learning vocabulary more convenient outside the classroom.	1	1	1	√
12. I can learn the words easier based on the clues of the images and example sentences in the app.	1	1	1	√

(续表)

Items	Expert A	Expert B	Expert C	Agreement
13. The contexts of the example sentences facilitate words' knowledge in my mind.	0	0	1	×
14. The vocabulary learned via the app is not easily forgotten.	1	1	1	√
15. The context of the example sentences helps me learn how to use the words appropriately.	1	1	1	√
16. In the future, I will continue to use the app to learn vocabulary.	1	1	1	√
Total score	15	13	14	

Notes: (1) "1" for the item is congruent with objective; (2) "0" for the uncertainty of the item; (3) "-1" for the item is not congruent with objective.

Result of IOC:

$$IOC = ÓR/N$$

$$ÓR = 15 + 14 + 13 = 42 \text{ (Scores from experts)}$$

$$N = 3 \text{ (Number of experts)} \quad IOC = 42/3 = 14$$

Number of Items: 16

IOC index: $14/16 = 0.875 > 0.5 = $ valid

APPENDIX H (English Version)

Questionnaire of Students' Perceptions of the App

Using the questionnaire is for collecting information about your perceptions on the app. The questionnaire is not a test sheet with "right" or "wrong" answers. Also, the questionnaire you responded to will only be for this study and treated carefully. Your nice cooperation will be thanked much.

Part 1: Personal Information

Instructions: Please read each of the following items carefully and fill in the blanks or mark (√) the responses which best describe your situation.

1. Gender: ☐ male ☐ female

2. Age: _____ Length of learning English: _____
English scores in NCEE: _____

3. Have you ever used any mobile application to learn English? Yes or no? If yes, what was it? And for which English skills? (listening, speaking, reading, writing and translation)

_____

4. Have you ever used any mobile application to learn English vocabulary? Yes or no? If yes, what was it?

_____

Part 2: Perceptions on Using the App

Instructions: Please read each statement carefully and choose (√) the responses which best describe your perceptions on using the app.

1 = Strongly Disagree; 2 = Disagree; 3 = Not sure; 4 = Agree; 5 = Strongly Agree

Items	Strongly Disagree	Disagree	Not sure	Agree	Strongly Agree
1. The vocabulary learning app is easy to use.	1	2	3	4	5
2. Learning vocabulary via the app is convenient, for I can choose place and time to learn new words.	1	2	3	4	5
3. The app makes vocabulary learning easier for me compared with wordlist.	1	2	3	4	5
4. It is a good method to learn vocabulary via the app.	1	2	3	4	5
5. I prefer the app to traditional wordlist for learning vocabulary.	1	2	3	4	5

(续表)

Items	Strongly Disagree	Disagree	Not sure	Agree	Strongly Agree
6. The vocabulary learning app motivates me to learn new words.	1	2	3	4	5
7. The app is useful for me to learn vocabulary.	1	2	3	4	5
8. The learning sections in the app help me learn vocabulary more effectively.	1	2	3	4	5
9. The immediate feedback in the app can push me to monitor and adjust my vocabulary learning.	1	2	3	4	5
10. The retrieval sections in the app enable me to review and remember the vocabulary well.	1	2	3	4	5
11. The app makes vocabulary learning more convenient outside the classroom.	1	2	3	4	5
12. I can learn the words easier based on the pictures and example sentences in the app.	1	2	3	4	5
13. The example sentences can consolidate words in my mind.	1	2	3	4	5
14. The vocabulary learned via the app is not easily forgotten.	1	2	3	4	5
15. The example sentences help me learn how to use the words appropriately.	1	2	3	4	5
16. In the future, I will continue to use the app to learn vocabulary.	1	2	3	4	5

APPENDIX H（Chinese Version）

一份关于使用四级词汇学习应用软件的问卷调查

这份问卷不是测试,所以你的选择没有对错之分。非常感谢各位同学的配合。

第一部分:个人信息,根据自己的信息打勾或填写

1. 性别:男(　　　),女(　　　)

2. 年龄:_____ 学习英语的年限_____
高考中的英语分数:_____

3. 你以前用过手机应用软件(mobile app)学英语吗？用过或没用过？如果用过,那款应用软件叫什么名字？你用它学过英语的哪项技能呢？（听/说/读/写或是翻译）

_____

4. 你以前使用过学习英语词汇的应用软件吗？有或没有？如果有使用过,请写出软件的名字。

_____

第二部分:使用这款四级词汇学习应用软件后的感觉

仔细阅读每一项陈述,根据自身的使用情况或感受在相应数字上打勾做出选择。

1 = 非常不同意;2 = 不同意;3 = 不太确定;4 = 同意;5 = 非常同意

陈述	非常不同意	不同意	不太确定	同意	非常同意
1. 这款应用软件用起来很简单。	1	2	3	4	5
2. 使用这款应用软件学习词汇很便利,因为我可以选择学习新单词的地点和时间。	1	2	3	4	5
3. 与单词表相比,这款应用软件让我学单词很轻松。	1	2	3	4	5

(续表)

陈述	非常不同意	不同意	不太确定	同意	非常同意
4. 使用这款应用软件学单词是个好方法。	1	2	3	4	5
5. 相比以前词汇表学单词,我更喜欢使用这款应用软件学单词。	1	2	3	4	5
6. 这款软件激发我去学新单词。	1	2	3	4	5
7. 这款应用软件对我学单词很有用。	1	2	3	4	5
8. 这款应用软件里的与单词相关的学习内容能帮我更有效地学习单词。	1	2	3	4	5
9. 这款应用软件里的及时反馈能促使我监控以及调节学习单词的过程。	1	2	3	4	5
10. 这款应用软件上的复习和练习环节能让我有效地复习单词并记住单词。	1	2	3	4	5
11. 在课外,这款应用软件让我学单词更加方便。	1	2	3	4	5
12. 根据应用软件里的图片和例句,我学单词更加容易了。	1	2	3	4	5
13. 这款应用软件里的例句能帮助我在脑海里巩固单词。	1	2	3	4	5
14. 通过这款应用软件学过的单词不容易忘记。	1	2	3	4	5
15. 这款应用软件里的例句能帮我学会如何恰当地使用单词。	1	2	3	4	5
16. 将来我会继续使用这款应用软件学习单词。	1	2	3	4	5

APPENDIX I

Checking IOC of the Interview Questions

Questions	Expert A	Expert B	Expert C	Agreement
1. Do you enjoy learning vocabulary via the app? Yes or no? And why?	1	1	1	√
2. Is the app helpful for your vocabulary learning? Yes or no? And why?	1	1	1	√
3. Is the app interesting to you? Yes or no? And why?	1	1	1	√
4. Comparing the traditional word list-based learning approach with the app-assisted vocabulary learning, which one do you prefer? And why?	1	1	1	√
5. Is it convenient for you to learn vocabulary via the app? Yes or no? And why?	1	1	1	√
6. Do you think that the pictures or example sentences are helpful for you to learn vocabulary? Yes or no? And Why?	1	1	1	√
7. Do you believe that the vocabulary exercises can facilitate your retention of vocabulary? And why?	1	1	1	√
8. Is the feedback provided by the app useful for you to adjust your vocabulary learning? Yes or no? And why?	0	1	0	×
9. What else would you like to say about the app-assisted vocabulary learning in the present study?	1	1	1	√
10. What do you think of the mobile app in general?	1	0	0	×
11. What don't you like about the mobile app?	1	1	1	√
Total score	10	10	9	

Notes: (1) "1" for the item is congruent with the objective; (2) "0" for the uncertainty of the item;

(3) " -1" for an item which is not congruent with the objective

Result of IOC index:

$$IOC = ÓR/ N$$

$$ÓR = 10 + 10 + 9 = 29 \text{ (Scores from experts)}$$

$$N = 3 \text{ (Number of experts)}$$

$$IOC = 29/3 = 9.67$$

Number of Items: 11

IOC index: $9.67/11 = 0.88 > 0.5 =$ valid

APPENDIX J (English Version)

The Interview Questions on Perceptions of the App

1. Do you enjoy learning vocabulary via the app? Yes or no? And why?

2. Is the app helpful for your vocabulary learning? If yes, in what ways? If no, why not?

3. Is the app interesting? If yes, in what ways?

4. Comparing the traditional word list-based learning approach with the app-assisted vocabulary learning, which one do you prefer? And why?

5. Please describe your opinions of the app.

6. Is it convenient for you to learn vocabulary via the app? If yes, in what ways?

7. What do you think of the pictures or example sentences in the app?

8. What do you think of the vocabulary exercises in the app?

9. What do you think of the prompt feedback in the app?

10. What else would you like to say about the app-assisted vocabulary learning in the present study?

11. What do/don't you like about the mobile app? Please describe it.

APPENDIX J（Chinese Version）

关于应用程序认知的访谈问题

1. 你喜欢用四级词汇应用软件学单词吗？喜欢或不喜欢？为什么？
2. 四级词汇应用软件对你学单词有帮助吗？如果有，哪些方面有？如果没有，为什么？
3. 你认为四级词汇应用软件有趣吗？如果是，具体表现在哪些方面？
4. 用四级词汇应用软件学单词与传统的词汇表学单词相比，你更喜欢哪种学单词的方式？为什么？
5. 请描述一下你对四级词汇应用软件的看法。
6. 你用四级词汇应用软件学单词方便吗？如果是，具体表现在哪些方面？
7. 你认为四级词汇应用软件里的图片和例句怎么样？
8. 你认为四级词汇应用软件里的词汇练习怎么样？
9. 你认为四级词汇应用软件里提供的及时反馈怎么样？
10. 关于四级词汇应用软件，你还有什么想说的吗？
11. 关于四级词汇应用软件，有哪些你喜欢或不喜欢的地方？请描述一下。

APPENDIX K

Criterion for Determining a Representative Interview Sample（AMHSA, 2010）

Participants	Minimum Interviews	Participants	Minimum Interviews	Participants	Minimum Interviews
0—9	ALL	86—99	22	339—369	53
10—12	9	100—149	24	370—475	58

(续表)

Participants	Minimum Interviews	Participants	Minimum Interviews	Participants	Minimum Interviews
13—17	11	150—199	26	476—550	65
18—24	13	200—220	30	551—600	70
25—30	15	221—240	35	601—700	80
31—44	17	241—299	37	701—800	86
45—64	19	300—320	42	801—900	90
65—85	21	321—338	47	901—1000	100

APPENDIX L

Pilot Study

1. Participants

According to availability and convenience, two intact classes with 116 non-English major newcomers were selected from Anshun University of China for taking part in this pilot study in the first semester in the 2018 academic year. One class with 56 students was the experiment group, and the other one with 60 students was the control group. The demographic information of the two groups was shown in Table 1 below.

Table 1 **The demographic information of the two groups in the pilot study**

	Number	Average age	Gender	Length of Learning English	English Proficiency	Sig.
Experiment Group	56	19	Male = 26	7—9 years	Mean = 88.68	.351
			Female = 30			
Control Group	60	18	Male = 33	8—9 years	Mean = 91.82	
			Female = 27			

Significant level $p < 0.05$

As seen in Table 1 above, the two groups had similar features in number, age, the proportion of male/female, and the length of English learning. Their English proficiency was from the English scores of the National College Entrance Exam (NCEE). NCEE is held yearly for screening out students for universities all over China, which is well known as being high reliability and validity all the time. With an independent-samples t-test, few differences in English proficiency between them were found for $p = 0.351 > 0.05$.

2. Research Questions

(1) What are the effects of using the app on EFL students' vocabulary learning achievement?

(2) What are the effects of employing the app on EFL students' vocabulary retention?

(3) What are the EFL learners' perceptions of vocabulary learning via the app?

3. Research Instruments

The same instruments used in the pilot study as those in the main study are not repeated because the details of the instruments have been presented in Section 3.3 of Chapter 3. Being slightly different from the questionnaire and interview questions in the main study, the perception questionnaire and the list of interview questions for the pilot study were shown in Appendix M and Appendix N, respectively.

4. Experiment and Data Collection

The pilot study started in September of 2018 academic year. On week 1, the Vocabulary Size Test (Appendix E) and the knowledge scale of 80 target words (Appendix F) were used as pre-tests to examine whether a big difference existed on VST or VKS.

Firstly, with the analysis of independent-samples t-test, as shown in Table 2 below, few differences ($P = 0.788 > 0.05$) in their vocabulary size between two groups were revealed. Next, based on two groups' mean from Table 2, their vocabulary size was about 2,300 words, which were far away from the requirement of 4,500 words for CET-4. This means that they have more CET-4 words to learn in order to pass CET-4. The 80 words in the treatment are the high frequency in CET-4, whose mastery would be beneficial for their passing CET-4. So they were suitable for the experiment.

Table 2 Comparison of the vocabulary size between the two groups

	Group	N	Mean	S.D.	Sig.
Vocabulary size test	EG	56	2335.00	454.539	.788
	CG	60	2375.00	477.960	

EG: Experiment Group; CG: Control Group (Significant level $p < 0.05$)

Furthermore, as shown in Table 3 below, there was no significant difference (P = 0.119 > 0.05) in their knowledge of the target words between the two groups in the pre-test with independent-samples t-test. Besides, according to the means of 80 target words for the two groups in the pre-test (M of EG = 153.11; M of CG = 160.20), they were worth learning for the students, because they were mostly unfamiliar or unknown to the students.

Table 3 **Comparison of the means of the words' knowledge between the two groups**

	Group	**N**	**Mean**	**S. D.**	**Sig.**
Pre-test	EG	56	153.11	26.700	.119
	CG	75	160.20	24.057	

EG: Experiment Group   CG: Control Group (Significant level p < 0.05)

After finding that both groups had similar vocabulary sizes and were almost unfamiliar with the target words above, in week 2, the researcher began to provide the experiment group with a tutorial on how to download and use the mobile app containing the 80 target words (see Section 3.3.2). The control group was offered a paper-based list of the same words (Appendix D) by the researcher. Both of them learned and retained the target words independently outside the classroom in the following four weeks.

In week 6, both groups took the knowledge scale as a post-test. Next, the experiment group filled in the questionnaire (Appendix M). Then, according to AMHSA (2010) (Appendix K), the number of 19 students in the experiment group was decided. The 19 students whose ID numbers were odd (1,3,5,7...ending with 37) were selected as interviewees to answer the interview questions (Appendix N) in the same week. Moreover, the data from the interview was collected with the help of a tape recorder and notes taking. In week 11, two groups took the knowledge scale as a delayed post-test.

5. Results of the Pilot Study

In this section, two parts are included. The first part presents the results obtained from the test. The second part reports the findings from the questionnaire and the semi-structured interview.

(1) Comparison between the Scores from the Pre-tests and Post-tests

Table 4 **Comparison of the two tests' scores between the two groups**

Group	Tests	Mean	S. D.	N	Sig.
EG	Pre-test	153.11	24.057	56	.000
EG	Post-test	289.09	45.893	56	.000
CG	Pre-test	160.20	26.700	60	.000
CG	Post-test	248.44	50.939	60	.000

EG: Experiment Group   CG: Control Group (Significant level $p < 0.05$)

As shown in Table 4 above, with descriptive analysis, the means of the pre-test and post-test for the experiment group and control group were 153.11 and 289.09, respectively. With the paired-samples t-test of the experiment group, a huge difference in the scores above was seen ($p = 0.000 < 0.05$). For the control group, between the score of pre-test and that of post-test, a large difference was disclosed ($p = 0.000 < 0.05$), and the mean of the pre-test differed obviously from that of the post-test (M of pre-test = 160.20; M of post-test = 248.44). The mean of the post-test (M of EG = 289.09; M of CG = 248.44) was higher than that of the pre-test (M of EG = 153.11; M of CG = 160.20). This signified that both groups were enhanced noticeably on target words' knowledge after treatment.

Table 5 **Comparison of the post-test scores between the two groups**

	Group	N	Mean	S. D.	Sig.
Post-test	EG	56	289.09	45.893	.000
Post-test	CG	60	248.44	50.939	.000

EG: Experiment Group   CG: Control Group (Significant level $p < 0.05$)

As seen in Table 5 above, by applying independent-samples t-test of the post-test scores between the two groups, a significant difference was demonstrated ($p = 0.000 < 0.05$), and the mean of EG (M of EG = 289.09) was much larger than that of CG (M of CG = 248.44). It showed that students in the experiment group achieved much more improvement on the words' learning by using the app compared with those from the control group. This illustrated that using the app had a significantly positive effect on improving learners' achievements in vocabulary learning, which was the answer to the first research question.

(2) Comparison of the Scores from the Post-tests and Delayed Post-tests

Table 6 **Comparison between delayed post-tests and post-tests from the two groups**

Group	Tests	Mean	S. D.	N	Sig.
EG	Delayed Post-test	274.59	47.708	56	.104
	Post test	289.09	45.893	56	
CG	Delayed Post-test	202.73	36.926	60	.000
	Post-test	248.44	50.939	60	

EG: Experiment Group   CG: Control Group (Significant level p < 0.05)

As seen in Table 6 above, the means of the delayed post-tests from the two groups were 274.59 and 202.73, respectively, which both decreased compared with those of the post-tests (M of EG = 289.09; M of CG = 248.44). Based on the means of delayed post-tests, the retention of the words for the control group decreased very much, while the retention of the words for the experiment group decreased little.

By paired-samples t-test for the experiment group, there was no significant difference between the delayed post-test and post-test scores because the p-value was 0.104, which was higher than 0.05 (p = 0.104 > 0.05). Nevertheless, with paired-samples t-test for the control group, a significant difference was found between the delayed post-test and post-test scores, because the p-value was lower than 0.05 (p = 0.000 < 0.05).

Table 7 **Comparison of the delayed post-test scores between the two groups**

	Group	N	Mean	S. D.	Sig.
Delayed Post-test	EG	56	274.59	47.708	.000
	CG	60	202.73	36.926	

EG: Experiment Group   CG: Control Group (Significant level p < 0.05)

As demonstrated in Table 7 above, by applying an independent-samples t-test for the delayed post-test scores between the two groups, a large difference was found (p = 0.000 < 0.05). Besides, it could be seen that the mean of the experiment group (M = 274.59) in the delayed post-test was much higher than that of the control group (M = 202.73).

The students' retention of the words from both groups declined after four weeks. However, the students from the experiment group employing the app could remember more words than those from the control group. So the answer to the second research question could be that using the app had a significantly positive effect on helping learners retain more words.

(3) Results from the Student' Questionnaires

Table 8 **Responses from the questionnaire with percentages** (N = 56)

Items	Strongly Disagree	Disagree	Not sure	Agree	Strongly Agree
1. The vocabulary learning app is easy to use.	1.8%	1.8%	3.6%	71.4%	21.4%
2. Learning vocabulary via the app is convenient, for I can choose place and time to learn new words.	0%	0%	10.7%	60.7%	28.6%
3. It is easier for me to learn vocabulary via the app.	1.8%	3.6%	21.4%	55.4%	17.9%
4. It is a good method to learn vocabulary via the app.	0%	7.1%	12.5%	53.6%	26.8%
5. I prefer the app to the traditional wordlist for learning vocabulary.	1.8%	8.9%	19.6%	41.1%	28.6%
6. The vocabulary learning app motivates me to learn new words.	1.8%	1.8%	30.4%	53.6%	12.5%
7. The app is useful for me to learn vocabulary.	0%	3.6%	17.9%	55.4%	23.2%
8. The learning sections in the app help me learn vocabulary more effectively.	0%	3.6%	14.3%	51.8%	30.4%
9. The immediate feedback in the app can push me to monitor and adjust my vocabulary learning.	1.8%	7.1%	10.7%	57.1%	23.2%
10. The retrieval sections in the app enable me to review and remember the vocabulary very well.	0%	3.6%	28.6%	46.4%	21.4%
11. The app makes vocabulary learning more convenient outside the classroom.	0%	1.8%	8.9%	55.4%	33.9%

Items	Strongly Disagree	Disagree	Not sure	Agree	Strongly Agree
12. I can learn the words easier based on the clues of images and example sentences in the app.	0%	3.6%	14.3%	58.9%	23.2%
13. The example sentences in the app can consolidate knowledge of the words.	0%	7.1%	35.7%	41.1%	16.1%
14. The vocabulary learned via the app is not easily forgotten.	1.8%	7.1%	41.1%	41.1%	8.9%
15. The example sentences help me learn how to use the words appropriately.	0%	8.9%	39.3%	42.9%	8.9%
16. In the future, I will continue to use the app to learn vocabulary.	0%	0%	17.9%	53.6%	28.6%

Based on Chang et al. (2012) and Davis (1989), the items of the questionnaire concerning technology-assisted language learning can be summarized into five categories containing continuance intention to use, attitude towards using, perceived ease of use, perceived convenience, and perceived usefulness. So all items from the questionnaire are separated into the five categories. The separation result of the items is shown in Table 9 below.

Table 9 Items of the questionnaire separated into categories

	Perceived convenience	Perceived ease of use	Perceived usefulness	Attitude towards using	Continued intention to use
Items	2, 11	1,3,12	6,7,8,9,10, 13,14,15	4,5	16

Firstly, according to the responses of items 2 and 11 in Table 9 above, the number of the students who perceive the mobile app as convenient to use accounts for 89.3% of total students in the experiment group. Next, from the responses of items 1, 3 and 12, it is found that 82.7% of the students consider the app makes their vocabulary learning easy. Thirdly, in terms of the responses on items 6,7,8,9,10,13,14 and 15, 65.4% of the students refer to the app as being useful for vocabulary learning. Fourthly, based on their responses of items 4 and 5, it is shown that 75.1% of the students hold positive attitudes towards the usage of the app. Finally, 82.2% of the students express their willingness to continuously use the app in the future from the responses of item 16.

(4) Results from the Student' Interviews

Based on Dörnyei (2007), the matic analysis was used to analyze the data from the interviews in the pilot study. In order to form the themes from data, the responses of the interviewees were used as evidence. Each interviewee was numbered according to the time of the order of being interviewed. For instance, St.1 stood for the first student to be interviewed. Through data analysis, four categories were found and then formed into one theme. The theme, categories, and evidence were shown in Table 10 below.

Table 10 **Theme and categories found from the interviews**

Theme: perception	Evidence (interviewees' responses)
Category 1: feel helpful	St.19: "...the three kinds of exercises help me remember the learned words." St.11: "...it only focuses on CET-4 words, so it helps me a lot with the preparation of CET-4." St.8: "the immediate feedback makes me realize shortcoming and pay more attention to the words."
Category 2: feel interesting	St.1: "...the pictures and example sentences are very interesting to arouse my interest in learning words." St.6: "...it is interesting to learn and review vocabulary by the app with flexibility."
Category 3: feel convenient	St.5: "...there is no limitation of time and space for learning words via the app, so it is convenient." St.9: "...as long as the mobile phone is on me, I can use the app to learn vocabulary, so convenient."

(续表)

Theme: perception	Evidence (interviewees' responses)
Category 4: feel no pressure	St. 13: "...when I take the textbook and look at the word list, I feel so stressful for there are lots of words to learn and recite. The app makes me no pressure and happy to learn words." St. 16: "...learning ten words one time via the app brings me fun just like to complete a mission. And the contents are diversified that I can not feel depressed."

According to the interviewees' responses, four categories were formed and a theme could be refined from them. Firstly, as seen in Table 10, students considered the app as being helpful mainly for the contents' design and the target words. Next, the app was perceived as being interesting because of the presentation ways of the words and the app itself. Thirdly, most of the students thought the app as being convenient, because it is much more convenient to carry a mobile phone than to carry a textbook, and they can use it anytime, anywhere to learn words through the app. Fourthly, the students referred to the app as a method to learn vocabulary without pressure, because the diversified contents and the number of words to be learned make them feel fun, especially compared with the traditional long word list for them to learn. Finally, based on the four categories above, one theme, perception of the app, could be refined. To conclude, students had good perceptions of vocabulary learning via the mobile app.

APPENDIX M

Questionnaire of Students' Perceptions for Pilot Study

The purpose of the questionnaire is for understanding your perceptions on using the app. So your responses would not be judged "right" or "wrong". Besides, what you responded is only applied for this study and used cautiously with confidentiality. Many thanks for your nice cooperation.

Part 1: Personal Information

Instructions: Please read each of the following items carefully and fill in the blanks or mark (√) the responses which best describe your situation.

1. Gender: ☐ male ☐ female

2. Age:_____ Length of learning English:_____
English scores in NCEE:_____

3. Have you ever used any mobile application to learn English? Yes or no? If yes, what was it? And for what English skills? (listening, speaking, reading, writing and translation)

_____

4. Have you ever used any mobile application to learn English vocabulary? Yes or no? If yes, what was it?

_____

Part 2: Perceptions on Using the App

Instructions: Please read each statement carefully and choose (√) the responses which best describe your perceptions on using the app.

1 = Strongly Disagree; 2 = Disagree; 3 = Not sure; 4 = Agree; 5 = Strongly Agree

Items	Strongly Disagree	Disagree	Not sure	Agree	Strongly Agree
1. The vocabulary learning app is easy to use.	1	2	3	4	5
2. Learning vocabulary via the app is convenient, for I can choose place and time to learn new words.	1	2	3	4	5
3. It is easier for me to learn vocabulary via the app.	1	2	3	4	5
4. It is a good method to learn vocabulary via the app.	1	2	3	4	5

(续表)

Items	Strongly Disagree	Disagree	Not sure	Agree	Strongly Agree
5. I prefer the app to the traditional wordlist for learning vocabulary.	1	2	3	4	5
6. The vocabulary learning app motivates me to learn new words.	1	2	3	4	5
7. The app is useful for me to learn vocabulary.	1	2	3	4	5
8. The learning sections in the app help me learn vocabulary more effectively.	1	2	3	4	5
9. The immediate feedback in the app can push me to monitor and adjust my vocabulary learning.	1	2	3	4	5
10. The retrieval sections in the app enable me to review and remember the vocabulary very well.	1	2	3	4	5
11. The app makes vocabulary learning more convenient outside the classroom.	1	2	3	4	5
12. I can learn the words easier based on the clues of images and example sentences in the app.	1	2	3	4	5
13. The example sentences in the app can consolidate knowledge of the words.	1	2	3	4	5
14. The vocabulary learned via the app is not easily forgotten.	1	2	3	4	5
15. The example sentences help me learn how to use the words appropriately.	1	2	3	4	5
16. In the future, I will continue to use the app to learn vocabulary.	1	2	3	4	5

APPENDIX N

The Interview Questions for Pilot Study

1. Did you enjoy learning vocabulary via the app? Yes or no? And why?

2. Is the app helpful for your vocabulary learning? If yes, in what ways? If no, why not?

3. Is the app interesting? If yes, in what ways?

4. Comparing the traditional word list-based learning approach with the app-assisted vocabulary learning, which one do you prefer? And why?

5. Is it convenient for you to learn vocabulary via the app? Yes or no? And why?

6. Do you think that the pictures or example sentences are helpful for you to learn vocabulary? Yes or no? And Why?

7. Do you believe that the vocabulary exercises can facilitate your retention of vocabulary? And why?

8. Is the feedback provided by the app useful for you to adjust your vocabulary learning? Yes or no? And why?

9. What else would you like to say about the app-assisted vocabulary learning in the present study?

10. What do/don't you like about the mobile app? Please explain.

APPENDIX O

A Sample Interview Script

Interviewer: Ma Xingxing

Interviewee: St. 1

Date: December 27, 2019

Time: 7:05 p.m.

Place: Classroom No. 1007 at Anshun University of China

Me: Good evening.

St. 1: Good evening, Teacher Ma.

Me: Please take a seat.

St. 1: Thank you.

Me: In the following, I will ask you several questions concerning your perception, or anything related to your words' learning with the mobile app.

St. 1: OK, Teacher Ma, go ahead.

Me: Do you enjoy learning vocabulary via the app?

St. 1: Um...yes, I like using the app to learn vocabulary.

Me: Why?

St. 1: Because there are various and interesting contents in the app, and it is convenient to learn the words via the app.

Me: OK, I see. Do you think the app helpful for your vocabulary learning or not?

St. 1: Yes, it helps a lot. When I cannot read the words, I would listen to the audios many times. I also read after the audios until I feel I could pronounce them correctly. And...

Me: Do you feel the app interesting or not?

St. 1: Yes, I think the app is very interesting.

Me: Then, what aspects make you feel the app interesting?

St. 1: Many interesting pictures and sentences arouse my interest in learning vocabulary.

Me: Comparing the traditional word list-based learning approach with app-assisted vocabulary learning, which one do you prefer?

St. 1: Of course, it is no doubt that I prefer the app to learn vocabulary. The traditional wordlist is boring, and the rote vocabulary learning makes me feel like a repetition machine. However, the app is different. I feel using the app to learn words could practice my listening, speaking, reading, writing skills. Also, it is much lighter to carry a smartphone than a heavy textbook to learn vocabulary…

Me: Can you describe your opinions about the app?

St. 1: Um…as I mentioned, the app is good, helpful, and interesting for me to learn and review words. Also, it mainly focuses on CET-4 vocabulary, so it will be beneficial for making me prepare well for CET-4 next year…

Me: Is it convenient for you to learn vocabulary via the app?

St. 1: Yes, it is quite convenient. Let me take an example. During the military training, all courses stopped, so I think all courses study would be suspended. Nevertheless, the task of CET-4 vocabulary learning is going on thanks to the app, for it is convenient to learn the words at any corner anytime.

Me: What do you think of the pictures or example sentences in the app?

St. 1: I think the pictures are interesting, and make me understand the words quickly. Also the example sentences can make me know how to use the words appropriately. When I took the Target Words Knowledge Test, some pictures could make recall the meanings of the words…

Me: What do you think of the vocabulary exercises in the app?

St. 1: The exercises of the app could strengthen my memory of the words. You know, when I almost forget the meaning or the spelling of the words, doing the exercises can push me to squeeze my memory to recall the meanings or forms of the words. Even I failed to recall the words or made wrong choices about the exercise, I do not worry much. Because the link could make me relearn them in the learning sections, my memory of the words would be consolidated again…

Me: What do you think of the prompt feedback in the app?

St. 1: The prompt feedback is really helpful, for it can tell me whether I am wrong or right on my doing the exercises in time. If my responses are wrong, the link would make me learn the words again in the learning sections of the app. Of course, I will reflect on why I made wrong choices, and hopefully, I would not make similar mistakes again…

Me: What else would you like to say about the app-assisted vocabulary learning in the present study?

St. 1: I think it is useful, easy, and convenient to use the app for learning and reviewing CET-4 words. I like it very much. Besides, we only have to learn 10 words at a time, so we do not feel stressful to learn the words.

Me: What do/don't you like about the mobile app? Please explain.

St. 1: Teacher Ma, can I say so far so good? Of course, if the app contains 4,500 CET-4 words, it would be wonderful to persist in using it to prepare for CET-4 in the future.

Me: Many thanks for your responses and precious time. Thank you again. This pen is a gift as my appreciation for your cooperation. See you around.

St. 1: See you, Teacher Ma.

APPENDIX P

The Representative Diaries Concerning the Categories of Feelings about the App from the Experiment Group

1. Preferable

-in memorizing words

D42W2EG: "...I prefer this app to learn CET-4 words. Hopefully, it can help my English learning in the long run..."

D55W2EG: "...In the process of memorizing words, I feel very easy. Memorizing words with this app is very happy and exciting. I have a deep memory of learned words. Now remembering words is not as painful as before. So I prefer memorizing words via the app..."

D9W9EG: "...After learning the words for eight weeks, I think I have learned a lot. Using this app to learn words does not make me feel tired, and I remember them firmly, so I prefer this app..."

D18W9EG: "...I have been using this application for almost three months. I feel used to it and prefer using it to learn words..."

2. Convenient

-in time and place

D37W3EG: "...During the National Day of China, all paper-based course study *stopped for well all go out for fun. But I can learn words with the app when I am on the way…"*

D39W3EG: "*…as long as the smartphone is on me, I can learn and review words via the app anytime, anywhere…*"

D29W4EG: "*… during the military training, I can use breaking time to recite vocabulary via the app. Also, it is convenient to recite words while I am having meals for saving time…*"

D52W7EG: "*…it is getting colder, but I can still learn vocabulary via the app without leaving my warm bed…*"

3. Effective

-in memory of words

D27W2EG: "*…I feel it is very effective in reciting the words with the app, making me think that reciting words is not so difficult as before, and remembering ten words a week is easy to complete…*"

D31W2EG: "*… Words are memorized repeatedly, which effectively enhances the memorization of the word. Moreover, the memorized words could stay in my mind for a long time. It is an effective app of remembering words, and I gained a lot…*"

D56W3EG: "*…Through one-week learning, I feel that my memory time for words has increased. This vocabulary learning app is very effective…*"

D53W5EG: "*…the effects of learning and reviewing words via the app are becoming better, I will keep working on the app…*"

D8W8EG: "*…The more I use this app, the more I get used to it. Remembering words is getting more robust, and the effects are getting better…*"

4. Reasonable

-in learning ten words at a time

D23W2EG: "*…learning ten words at a time did not cost me much time. Also, after four times' review, the words were kept in my mind and not easily forgotten like wordlist learning…*"

D31W2EG: "*…using the app to learn ten words per time outside the class is reasonable and easy…*"

D34W2EG: "*…Through one week, I became more familiar with the ten words, which left me a more profound impression and understanding of these words. So the number of ten* words one week is good with me..."

D27W9EG: "...the number of ten words is not too much every week, which would not make me feel stressful..."

-in a five-time schedule per week

D25W2EG: "...For the first time, I find that using this app to recite words is very flexible, attractive, which is equipped with words, example sentences, parts of speech, pronunciation, and pictures, leaving a profound impression on me. For the second time, 9 hours later, I meet the ten words again, they look very familiar to me. For the third time, I already have a basic understanding of the words, my eyes were no longer limited to words, but I started to pay attention to its usage. For the fourth time, I feel the ten words are already in my mind and never feel so easier to memorize words. For the fifth time, after reviewing the words again, at this time, I felt the ten words had already blended with me. So this five-time arrangement for learning words via the app is reasonable and excellent..."

D44W3WG: "...reciting the word based on the five-time week plan left a deeper impression on my mind than before. So it is worthwhile learning vocabulary by the five-time week arrangement..."

D38W5EG: "...The teacher gave us the five-time schedule of the app so that we didn't have any pressure to learn words..."

5. Satisfied

-with an increase in vocabulary size

D32W6EG: "...Even if I feel noisy for a day, there is a time when I feel fulfilled and satisfied, that time is my vocabulary learning time with the app. As my vocabulary size increases every day, I will become more and more addicted to it..."

D6W7EG: "...It's another full week, and my vocabulary size increases day by day. I feel very satisfied..."

D20W9EG: "...my vocabulary size is increasing; the sense of accomplishment is getting higher and higher; it is another satisfying week..."

6. Fun

-in the process of learning and remembering words

D10W3EG: "...Learning words via the app becomes interesting, not as dull as before..."

D8W5EG: "...I feel that memorizing words has also become a fun thing, easy and fun..."

D14W8EG: "...In the process of memorizing words, there will be some pictures related to the meaning of the words. This will alleviate the boring of reciting words and add more fun..."

D16W9EG: "...The more I used the app, the more fun I felt..."

7. Easy

-in memorizing words

D41W3EG: "...It took a long time to memorize the words for the first time, but it became easier to remember them for the second time. And after each review by the third, the fourth and the fifth time, I found that the words were easy to remember..."

D29W9EG: "...The pictures of new words appear in the app, which can deepen my understanding of the meanings of the words, so it is easier to remember them..."

D46W9EG: "...It feels easy to memorize a lot of words through the app. The words which once cost me a long time to memorize only need a while to stay in my mind now..."

D48W9EG: "...I start to memorize the words skillfully and feel easier than ever..."

8. Useful

-in the pronunciation of words

D21W2EG: "...the app can teach me how to pronounce the words when I cannot read them..."

D31W3EG: "...using the app to review words could correct my pronunciation..."

D39W3EG: "...I could recognize many words but cannot read them out. So my English is called 'dumb' English. Now with the app, I can pronounce the words correctly..."

-in increasing interest in English

D43W4EG: "...after using the app for three weeks, my interest in English learning is much improved..."

D51W7EG: "...with the increasing number of using the app, I become more interested in learning English..."

-in memorizing words

D7W2EG: "...I think this app is very useful, the words I remember are firm in my mind, and it is not easy to forget. Learning words is not in quantity but in quality and how long I can retain the words..."

D35W2EG: "...After five times of learning, I found that memorizing words is more durable than before, remembering them more deeply and easily associating the form with the meaning of words. Generally speaking, it is a very useful app..."

D38W5EG: "...The process of memorizing words has accelerated again this week. Besides, I think using this app to remember words is very helpful, and it suits me very well..."

-in increasing confidence in English

D25W2EG: "...After using the app, my heart has lighted a raging fire, and my confidence in English comes back..."

D34W2EG: "...I believe that as long as I insist every week, there will be more gains in English words, even my English proficiency..."

D15W5EG: "...Memorizing words via the app is making me feel better, and my vocabulary size is continuously improving, which can also increase my confidence in learning English..."

D27W9EG: "...After eight weeks, I feel that this way of learning words is more scientific. The number of ten words is not too much every week, which would not make me feel stressful and make me retain them more robust. So I become confident in English learning..."

9. Willing to persist

-in learning words via the app

D34W4EG: "... It's said that it takes 21 days to form a good habit. After three weeks, I hope I have already developed a good habit of memorizing words via the app. I hope that I will go further on the way of remembering words..."

D47W4EG: "...Gradually, I developed the habit of memorizing words via the app. Military training makes me very tired, and I am a bit unfocused when learning words in the app. It takes longer time than previous weeks, but the effects are acceptable. If I can persist, I believe I can retain more words, and persistence is a victory..."

D32W6EG: "...Memorizing words is getting more relaxed, and more vocabulary is accumulated. I hope I can persist in learning words via the app..."

D24W8EG: "...After seven weeks' words learning, I have also remembered more words, especially the review over and over again made the words leave a deep impression on me. I will persist in the future..."

10. Difficult

-in sticking to the schedule during military training

D43W4EG: "...Because of military training, the arrangement each day was full. It was challenging to stick to the five-time schedule to learn words..."

W52W4EG: "...During the military training, it was challenging to learn and review words by the time schedule, for we were too tired..."

D32W6EG: "...After studying for a few weeks, I found that the most challenging thing to remember is not the words but to learn the words strictly by the time schedule..."

-in remembering the pronunciations and meanings of all words

D24W6EG: "...but it was difficult to remember the pronunciation and meanings of every word completely..."

D13W9EG: "...sometimes I cannot match the pronunciation of the word with its spelling..."

D45W9EG: "...after using the app for many weeks, it became easy for me to confuse some words with other words..."

-in recalling the words

D42W3EG: "...sometimes my memory of the words becomes blank when I shut down the app..."

D52W7EG: "...I felt I could not recognize the words after seeing them if I switched off the smartphone..."

APPENDIX Q

The Representative Diaries Concerning the Categories of Feelings about the Wordlist Learning from the Control Group

1. Good

-with the number of ten words at a time and the schedule of five times per week

D9W2CG: "... This five-time week plan is very suitable for me. It allows me to memorize words with a plan and do not memorize them blindly like before. It leads to decreased self-control, so this five-time week plan for learning words outside class is beneficial..."

D14W2CG: "...when I first saw the words, I had a strong sense of strangeness. By the third time, I became familiar with the words, and I remembered the words. By the fifth time, I was thoroughly familiar with them. So this five-time schedule was good for us to be familiar with the words..."

D16W3CG: "...It took me half an hour to recite the ten words for the first time, and I thought I remembered them. But I still feel strange when I learn them for the second time. After four times' review, I thought I remembered them. So this five-time week schedule is helpful..."

D25W8CG: "...I have used this method several weeks with learning ten words per time, and it took me more than ten minutes to memorize them each time. Remembering these ten words becomes more and more firmly..."

D57W9CG: "...By comparing the words learning in the past with the current method of learning ten words five times a week, I feel this method easy. Vocabulary learning is not on how much I learn, but how much I can keep them in mind. In the past, I tried my best to learn as many words as I can one time, and I forgot most of them after closing English textbooks and did not review them any longer..."

2. Tedious

-in learning and reviewing words

D40W3CG: "...I was tired of learning words with the wordlist, for it is challenging for me to learn and quick to forget..."

D33W5CG: "...it was annoying and painful for me to spend much time learning the wordlist..."

D13W2CG: "...For the first time, it was fresh for me to see the wordlist. But later, I did not want to see the words on the wordlist again, for it was too painful for me to review them..."

D40W3CG: "...the review process with the wordlist is annoying..."

D23W7CG: "...I felt no passion for using the wordlist to review CET-4 vocabulary..."

3. Weak

-in retaining words

D8W2CG: "...English words have many meanings, which take me much time to recite. It's a torture to me..."

D5W3CG: "...The meanings of words were easy to be confused with others. Hence it was difficult to remember the words. Missing or reversed letters often happened to me when I tried to spell the words..."

D14W3CG: "...The meanings of words are easy to be confused with others, and it is difficult to remember all meanings of the words. Missing or reversed letters often happen to me when I was spelling the words..."

-in efficiency

D51W5CG: "...I found that I learned vocabulary slowly and forgot them quickly. The effectiveness of memorizing words with the wordlist was very low..."

D16W9CG: "...Learning the words is slow, and forgetting them is quick. So the efficiency of wordlist learning is low..."

-in pronouncing words

D10W2CG: "...when reading words, I felt my tongue was not smooth. And the pronunciation of the words was challenging for me, and it was not accurate..."

D14W3CG: "...I cannot pronounce the words when I use the wordlist to learn vocabulary..."

D45W4CG: "...after seeing some words, I know the meanings of them. But I cannot read them, even if I try my best to pronounce them, I feel my pronunciation is weird..."